THE COMPLETE IDIOT'S GUIDE® TO

Investing

D0731160

Fourth Edition
by Edward T. Koch and Debra Johnson

ALPHA
A member of Penguin Group (USA) Inc.

There is no dignity quite so impressive, and no independence quite so important,
as living within your means.
—Calvin Coolidge

ALPHA BOOKS

Published by the Penguin Group

Penguin Group (USA) Inc., 375 Hudson Street, New York, New York 10014, USA

Penguin Group (Canada), 90 Eglinton Avenue East, Suite 700, Toronto, Ontario M4P 2Y3, Canada (a division of Pearson Penguin Canada Inc.)

Penguin Books Ltd., 80 Strand, London WC2R 0RL, England

Penguin Ireland, 25 St. Stephen's Green, Dublin 2, Ireland (a division of Penguin Books Ltd.)

Penguin Group (Australia), 250 Camberwell Road, Camberwell, Victoria 3124, Australia (a division of Pearson Australia Group Pty. Ltd.)

Penguin Books India Pvt. Ltd., 11 Community Centre, Panchsheel Park, New Delhi—110 017, India

Penguin Group (NZ), 67 Apollo Drive, Rosedale, North Shore, Auckland 1311, New Zealand (a division of Pearson New Zealand Ltd.)

Penguin Books (South Africa) (Pty.) Ltd., 24 Sturdee Avenue, Rosebank, Johannesburg 2196, South Africa

Penguin Books Ltd., Registered Offices: 80 Strand, London WC2R 0RL, England

Copyright © 2009 by by Edward T. Koch and Debra Johnson

International Standard Book Number: 978-1-59257-915-0
Library of Congress Catalog Card Number: 2009928405

13   12   11   8   7   6   5   4   3

Interpretation of the printing code: The rightmost number of the first series of numbers is the year of the book's printing; the rightmost number of the second series of numbers is the number of the book's printing. For example, a printing code of 09-1 shows that the first printing occurred in 2009.

Printed in the United States of America

Note: This publication contains the opinions and ideas of its authors. It is intended to provide helpful and informative material on the subject matter covered. It is sold with the understanding that the authors and publisher are not engaged in rendering professional services in the book. If the reader requires personal assistance or advice, a competent professional should be consulted.

The authors and publisher specifically disclaim any responsibility for any liability, loss, or risk, personal or otherwise, which is incurred as a consequence, directly or indirectly, of the use and application of any of the contents of this book.

Most Alpha books are available at special quantity discounts for bulk purchases for sales promotions, premiums, fund-raising, or educational use. Special books, or book excerpts, can also be created to fit specific needs.

For details, write: Special Markets, Alpha Books, 375 Hudson Street, New York, NY 10014.

Publisher: *Marie Butler-Knight*
Editorial Director: *Mike Sanders*
Senior Managing Editor: *Billy Fields*
Senior Acquisitions Editor: *Paul Dinas*
Development Editor: *Julie Bess*
Senior Production Editor: *Janette Lynn*
Copy Editor: *Jennifer Connolly*

Cartoonist: *Steve Barr*
Cover Designer: *Rebecca Harmon*
Book Designer: *Trina Wurst*
Indexer: *Celia McCoy*
Layout: *Ayanna Lacey*
Proofreader: *John Etchison*

Contents at a Glance

Contents

Introduction

If our nation's financial crisis has left you reeling and freaked out, you've come to the right place. First, take a deep breath. Second, don't do anything with your investments until you've read this book. Shedding what investments you may have out of panic is not a wise course of action. Remember the Great Depression? Or Black Monday, the stock market crash of 1987? In both cases, investors who sold their holdings when the market bottomed out suffered horrific losses. They thought they were doing the right thing by "cutting" their losses. In most cases, if they had simply held on to their portfolios, they would have seen the value of their holdings not only fully recover, but multiply into significant wealth over time. Yes, the stock market is volatile, but over the long run, *even with the most severe crashes factored in*, a sturdy, well-diversified portfolio can be expected to return about 8 percent per year. So sit tight.

We all have friends who freak out over the stock market constantly. Guess what? Freaking out doesn't make your investments grow one bit faster. And freaking out can cause you to make very bad decisions.

Watching your investments rise or fall each day can be a very emotional experience, like betting at the racetrack or rooting for your favorite sports team. There's nothing wrong with that, if you can keep a single day or event in perspective. But most of us can't. We allow our decision-making to be influenced by the previous day's wins or losses. Winners become elated (and reckless); losers become depressed (and overly cautious).

This is not the way to approach investing, unless you are investing merely for entertainment. If you are investing to meet financial goals, you must not let investing become your own personal emotional roller coaster—*especially* when times are tough.

Start by becoming an intelligent investor, not a trader. Traders live and die on the gains and losses they experience each day. You are in this for the long haul, so forget about day trading—that's an emotional game. If you need some drama in your life, go to the racetrack; it's a lot cheaper!

To become an intelligent investor, start thinking in 10-year time chunks. Here's the best piece of advice we can give you: don't look at the price of your stocks and/or mutual funds every day. If you're a long-term investor, why do you care what happened yesterday? If you're at a cocktail party and people ask you how your stocks are doing, just say, "I don't know; I'll check at the end of the month." Won't that get their attention! If you build a sturdy portfolio based on the principles in this book, you will stay calm, cool, and collected, no matter what the market does from day to day.

If you are new to investing, you've come to the right place. Despite what you may be feeling, given recent events, investing is the key to making dreams come true. Don't avoid it out of fear. You may have tried to tackle investing before and had a bad experience with a blowhard for a financial advisor or a tedious, confusing book. If you threw up your hands in frustration and said "Forget it!" but can't get rid of the nagging feeling that you're missing out on something very important, don't despair. We wrote this book for you.

This book assumes you know less than nothing about investing, but doesn't patronize you by telling you what to do. Instead, we offer you a step-by-step guide so that you can figure out exactly what investment strategies will work for your situation:

- How much you need to save to put the kids through college *and* retire happily

- How much risk you can take on and still sleep at night

- How to create a balanced portfolio of investments tailored to your financial goals

- How to manage your investments from year to year and still roll with life's changes

Questionnaires, worksheets, dreadful jokes—they're all in here. It's best to start at the beginning and work through to the end, but feel free to skip around until you get comfortable. You'll find everything you need in this book to become someone who can make intelligent, disciplined investing decisions. Here's the gist ….

Part 1, "What Does 'Financial Security' Mean to You?," helps you figure out exactly that, because there's no point in investing without specific goals. You'll also take a risk-tolerance questionnaire and create your own income statement and balance sheet. You'll learn how to answer basic questions such as, "If I want to have $100,000 in five years and I can earn a 10 percent return, how much do I need to invest annually?" We also look at what caused the financial crisis of 2008 and explain the basics behind the government bailout.

Part 2, "Creating a Plan," is based on the premise that you have to know what you've got before you can get any more. Here, you'll take a close look at your job benefits and find out how to trim your taxes, so you can keep more of what you earn. We'll also work on reducing spending and getting a grip on debt.

Part 3, "Investing 101," is a primer in the basics. Everything you ever wanted to know but felt too stupid to ask, from what they're really up to on Wall Street to how to pick a mutual fund.

Part 4, "Rolling with Life's Changes," confronts the inevitable upheavals many investment books ignore. Sure, you can steadily sock away dollars in your investment plan when life is smooth, but what about when you get married, get divorced, have kids, buy a house, or change jobs? This part contains event-specific advice so that no matter what life throws at you, your investments keep growing.

Part 5, "Advanced Investing Strategies," is for readers who want to explore more complicated, alternative investments. It's also a source of answers for questions you may have when you hear words like "option" or "futures contract" bandied about.

In addition, you get a comprehensive glossary with clear, straightforward definitions of investment terms and an appendix with some recommendations for further reading and financial exploration.

One caveat: although we have made every effort to confirm our data, accidents do happen. Equally important to keep in mind is that tax laws are under constant revision, reinterpretation, and so on. As a result, please double-check with the appropriate sources (e.g., the IRS or your accountant) before taking any course of action.

Extras

If you're more a scanner than a reader, you'll appreciate our sidebars. These explain confusing jargon, help you avoid expensive mistakes, and offer super inside strategies. Look for the following boxes:

Fiscal Facts

These little boxes contain just-for-fun facts about the financial world. Great for cocktail party chatter.

def•i•ni•tion

Yes, investing has its own language, but it's not hard to learn. Peek in this box for clear, succinct explanations of any italicized terms.

Crash Alert

When dealing with money, mistakes can be costly. This box alerts you to tax issues, legal snarls, and scams, so you can steer clear.

Super Strategies

These boxes outline super-smart investing strategies you can apply right away to improve your finances. Hint: some of these strategies appear only in the box, not in the text, so don't pass 'em up!

Acknowledgments

First off, Ed would like to recognize the efforts of his writing partner, Deb Johnson. Her wry wit, quick response time, and easygoing manner made the seemingly impossible most definitely doable over nearly a decade of collaboration. Who said you can't have a great bi-coastal partnership?

Ed would also like to thank the immediate members of his family. To his daughter Emily and his son John, who fill him with pride. And to his three grandchildren: Henry, Oliver, and Ella, the newest apples of "Booba's" eye. And to Ed's late wife, Joan, who died on April 14, 2003, in a tragic car accident. Although he cannot thank her today, Ed wishes to fondly remember her patience and understanding during deadlines for the first two editions of this book. Thanks also to Skip and Elaine Howland, surrogate family members, best friends, co-workers, and major supporters for over 40 years.

And to former associate and long-time friend José Santillan, currently Head of Investments, Harris Private Bank, and his associates Dan Gerding and Sarah Stew. Couldn't have done this fourth edition without you guys.

And last, but not least, a special thanks to Donna Buys, whose love and support were (successfully) put to the test during "crunch time" for this edition.

Trademarks

All terms mentioned in this book that are known to be or are suspected of being trademarks or service marks have been appropriately capitalized. Alpha Books and Penguin Group (USA) Inc. cannot attest to the accuracy of this information. Use of a term in this book should not be regarded as affecting the validity of any trademark or service mark.

Part 1

What Does "Financial Security" Mean to You?

Investing is really very simple—it's about putting your money to work for you over time. The longer your money is parked in an investment, the more time it has to grow … and grow … and grow!

But what are you growing it for? Before you choose investments, you need to identify your investment objectives. Are you saving to buy a home? To put kids through school? For retirement? Or all three? How much time do you have to reach those goals?

Next, you need to figure out how much risk you're willing to take with your hard-earned cash to try to meet those objectives. Finally, you need to take a look at what you've already got—and what you owe.

There's no point in putting yourself into some cookie-cutter investment plan. To invest really well, you must know yourself really well. In this part, we're going to explore the dark cave that is your financial psyche.

Bubbles and Bailouts: Understanding the Financial Crisis

In This Chapter

- Understanding the financial crisis of 2008
- Avoiding bubbles and investing mania
- How the government contributed to the crisis
- Banking on the bailout

The financial panic of 2008 left most of us asking one question: What happened? The short answer is that the housing bubble burst.

The Old-School Mortgage

Those old enough to remember *Father Knows Best* may also recall how difficult it was to obtain a mortgage back in those days. First, you had to save up a down payment, typically 20 percent of the property's purchase price.

Then it was time to gather up all the family financials and head to the big meeting at the local bank. The mortgage banker wanted to make absolutely sure that your family could afford the monthly P & I (principal and interest). It couldn't be more than 30 to 35 percent of the family income. This was very important to the bank because this locked-in, fixed-rate, 20- or 30-year mortgage was going to stay on the bank's books until maturity. That banker was going to make you jump through hoops before handing over a mortgage, because his career was on the line.

Fast forward to 2007, when a marginally employed person in a "hot" real estate market like Hoboken or San Diego could march into a bank with no down payment and come out with a $400,000 mortgage to buy a swanky condo. When did mortgage bankers, for decades an extraordinarily cautious bunch, become so free and easy with their loans?

New Mortgage Products Set the Stage for the Housing Bubble

The shift began with the realization by bankers around the 1980s that the average homeowner no longer sticks around to pay off a 20- to 30-year mortgage. We are a mobile society now and people change jobs and locations, on average, every five years. Soon, a new mortgage product called the *ARM* (adjustable-rate mortgage) appeared.

Other newfangled mortgage products followed, such as the IO mortgage (interest-only payments for e.g. five years), and the negative mortgage, which sets payments so low that the mortgage principal actually increases.

The change in mortgages partially explains the subsequent rise in home prices: low or no down payments and low interest payments (for the first few years, anyhow) meant more applicants than ever before qualified for mortgages. Soon, the demand for homes was increasing faster than the supply. Remember Economics 101? When demand outpaces supply, prices rise.

def•i•ni•tion

An **ARM** offers a low or "teaser" interest rate for one, three, or five years that rises (considerably) after the teaser term has expired. It is perfect for the short-term homeowner, but dangerous for anyone else.

As real estate kept appreciating, more people wanted in on the game, and a housing bubble began to develop. Remember the dot.com bubble of the 1990s? Many of those exciting "can't fail" Internet-based companies turned into lousy investments by late 2000. After the bubble burst, and the prices of many dot.com stocks sank, burned investors noticed that prices of homes had not fallen nearly as much as the stock market did at that time. Real estate began to look like a more solid investment. The thinking went like this: "Gosh, I can get the same appreciation in home prices, on average, that I can get from stock prices, and with much less volatility or risk. Plus, I can live in my asset or rent it out for additional income while awaiting further home price appreciation." What's not to like about that?

Enter the Flippers

Now new players entered the real-estate market: those who were purchasing homes not purely as residences, but as investments. "Flippers" emerged—people who would buy a new condo on opening day, for example, and "flip" it a few weeks or months later, pocketing a quick and easy $10,000 to $50,000 from the sale. The increase in demand from flippers aided truly dramatic price increases in such areas as Coastal Florida, Las Vegas, San Diego, New York City, and the Bay Area.

The stage was set for a housing bubble. What really blew air into it was the demise of the old-school banker and his old-school mortgage. Increasingly, the local bank was no longer the repository of the mortgage: it was moved to a third party, who packaged it, along with many other home mortgages, into a marketable security that could be traded on Wall Street. Banks and mortgage companies now made their money on closing costs, and the more closings, the more money to be made.

Inevitably, greed led to carelessness. Bankers no longer had time to check W-2s and 1040s. Even if a risky buyer foreclosed on a mortgage, real-estate "always" appreciated, so the bank could just take ownership of the property and sell it for a profit. And what about the new homeowners? Did they understand ARMs and IOs? Did anyone explain to them just how high their mortgage payment could rise in the near future? Perhaps not.

The Bubble Bursts

What popped the housing bubble? An uptick in unemployment, media coverage of sub-prime loans, foreclosures, and a wave of new construction plus rentals converting to condos (which increased supply, driving down real-estate prices). Homeowners were left holding mortgages that cost more than the real estate was worth. Meanwhile, banks were taking huge losses as they foreclosed on properties that (surprise!) they couldn't turn around and sell for a profit anymore.

Some banks failed and the rest seized up, afraid or unable to lend money at all. The resultant credit freeze knocked the stock market for a series of loops, decimating retirement accounts and scaring investors. Has this situation bottomed out yet? Not as of this writing, despite political efforts to intervene. When will we see the bottom? Best guess: second half of 2009 or 2010.

If you are a homeowner caught up in this, there is not much we can do to help you, other than to encourage you to negotiate with your mortgage holder. We can, however, help you to avoid the next financial bubble or mania (and believe us, there will be another one in our lifetimes!).

Dodging Financial Bubbles

For most individuals, the most devastating risk to their financial health is not the poor performers in their stock portfolio, but rather being caught up in a financial bubble. Here are some suggestions so that the next bubble won't leave you "bereft, bothered, and bewildered."

- Read *Devil Take the Hindmost*, by Edward Chancellor (Farrar, Straus and Giroux, 1999). This is a very readable narrative of financial bubbles/manias dating back to the Middle Ages. You'll soon see clearly the warning signs of a financial bubble or mania. Once you are sensitive to these warning signs, you are well on your way to avoiding the next fiasco.

- During bubbles, participants only want to talk about how much money they are making. There is no discussion of risk, just reward. Never acquire an asset without first assessing not only the upside potential, but also its downside risk. Beware of these expressions: "It's going up like a rocket," or "It's like shooting fish in a barrel," or "You can always sell it at a higher price." They are bubble markers.

Fiscal Facts _____

Strange as it may seem, a great mind does not guarantee financial success. Sir Isaac Newton bought shares in the British South Sea Company, (a bubble, if there ever was one!), and sold them at a substantial profit in 1720. The shares continued to rise, much to his consternation. He repurchased shares, at what turned out to be at or very close to the top, and was financially wiped out.

Once an asset starts to rise at an accelerating rate, it's human nature to want to hop on board for the ride. This desire is aided and abetted by friends, neighbors, and relatives, who are all too willing to let you know how much of a "killing" they have made. That's greed talking, or, to quote former Federal Reserve Chairman Alan Greenspan, "irrational exuberance."

Crash Alert _____

> Don't mistake irrational exuberance for investing. Participating in a financial bubble is not investing, it's speculating. Any time there is the potential for high reward, risk is high as well. There is no exception to that rule.

How the Government Contributed to the Financial Crisis

We can't blame the entire financial crisis of 2008 on bankers. The federal government contributed to it, also. First, it did away with the Glass-Steagall Act, which was devised to keep investment banking separate from commercial banking. Glass-Steagall was originally enacted after the Stock Market Crash of 1929 and resulted in, for example, the creation of Morgan Stanley (out of J.P. Morgan), and First Boston (out of First National Bank of Boston).

More recently, commercial banks (the folks who make the mortgages for the family home and run the ATMs) had been hounding Washington to allow them to also act like investment banks (the folks who buy and sell stocks and bonds). Late in the Clinton Administration the banks finally got their wish. The subsequent trouble was caused not so much by granting commercial banks investment banking powers, but rather by a lack of supervision and oversight.

def•i•ni•tion _____

> In simplest terms, commercial banks can take in deposits and make loans; investment banks can buy and sell stocks and bonds and create securities. Commercial banks make money on the spread (between what they pay for deposits and what they charge for loans). Investment banks make money by charging fees or commissions.

Historically, commercial banks have been supervised by the Office of the Comptroller of the Currency (OCC), just as savings institutions were tracked by The Office of Thrift Supervision (OTS). In contrast, investment banking oversight is limited to the Securities and Exchange Commission (SEC). This alphabet soup of supervision and regulation worked fine while commercial and investment banks were separate entities. Now that they were in bed together, busily packaging mortgages to be sold as investment securities, the separate regulators couldn't keep track of what was really going on.

Another factor in the 2008 crash was a seemingly harmless little regulation, the Community Reinvestment Act (CRA), which hit the books in 1977. The CRA required commercial banks to make loans in inner-city neighborhoods where they gathered deposits. Problem: most inner-city dwellers didn't qualify for loans. Mortgages are loans, but the vast majority of lower-income, inner-city citizens couldn't come up with the scratch for the down payment.

The banks were stumped, which is why it was tough to find a commercial bank in a poor neighborhood.

As a crescendo arose out of Washington, D.C., calling for increased home ownership for lower-income citizens, Wall Street devised a new investment product: the mortgage-backed security.

The lender could make the mortgage without *any* down payment, and with a low "teaser" rate, and immediately turn around and sell it to a mortgage bank. The mortgage bank, in turn, would mix the mortgage in with numerous other mortgages, and sell the bundle to an investment bank. The investment bank would slice and dice the product into securities that could be traded in the financial markets. Where was the regulatory oversight? There was none. The alphabet soup of agencies weren't on top of this new business. All was left to the credit-rating agencies, which apparently lacked the requisite skilled personnel to do the job.

For a short time, everybody was happy. Low-income and speculative borrowers were getting sub-prime mortgages to ride the real estate bubble express. Banks could make mortgage loans in poor neighborhoods and meet their CRA quotas. Mortgage banks packaged the mortgages and sold them to investment banks for a profit. The investment banks sold mortgage-backed securities for a profit to pensions, banks, and other institutions for their portfolios.

This happy picture cracked when home prices started to fall at the same time that rates on many existing mortgages were "reset" to interest rates 50 to 100 percent higher than the initial "teaser" rate. Many new homeowners were caught in a trap:

their monthly mortgage payments doubled, but when they went to the bank to renegotiate, they discovered that the mortgage was higher than the value of the home, making refinancing not an option. If you can't refinance your mortgage balance at a lower rate, and you can't afford the new higher rate, what do you do? Foreclosure, sadly, was the only option for many homeowners.

When mortgage holders stop paying their mortgages, banks run low on funds and are reluctant to make more loans. Remember *It's a Wonderful Life?* In the movie, Uncle Billy misplaces an $8,000 deposit for his Building & Loan (Bailey Brothers), and the evil Mr. Potter scoops up the money and circulates the rumor that Bailey Brothers has insufficient cash to meet withdrawals. The next scene shows the long line of customers demanding the return of their savings. When they finally took action, this is what the Treasury and the Federal Reserve were trying desperately to avoid.

Bailout Basics

Several years after the dot.com bubble burst, Wall Street changed for the better. In the wake of the Worldcom and Enron accounting scandals, the regulatory environment was significantly strengthened.

Now that the housing bubble has burst, we can expect new regulations, as well as the $700 billion bailout or Troubled Asset Relief Program (TARP). At this point, TARP is still a "moving train." Initially the plan was for TARP to allow cash-strapped banks to exchange up to $700 billion of their toxic mortgage paper for cash and for this process to be supervised by professional money managers hired by the Treasury. In November 2008, however, the Treasury decided instead to inject cash directly into the institutions. As of April 2009, almost $500 billion in TARP funds had been handed out to troubled insurers and banks—about $110 billion was left.

The $700 billion bailout is not just for Wall Street. If a bank participating in the bailout exchanges some of its mortgage-backed securities for cash, the government will demand an equity participation in the bank. If the government receives, for example, 10 percent of the bank's stock, and the stock rises 50 percent over the next three years, that profit is returned to taxpayers.

Meanwhile, the Federal Deposit Insurance Corp. (FDIC) increased the insured limit on bank deposits from $100,000 to $250,000, through the end of 2009 only. Insured deposits from individuals have, historically, been the cheapest source of funds for commercial bank lending. Not only will this add to bank liquidity, but it reinforces the safety of bank deposits in the minds of individuals. Barring this, individuals will "run" their assets out of banks either to their mattress or to U.S. Treasury bills. People do crazy things when fear prevails.

Here are some details regarding some changes to the tax code:

◆ The alternative minimum tax will be increased from $33,750 to $46,200 (for individual filers), and from $45,000 to $69,950 (for joint filers). This is for 2008 *only*, and is less generous than previous one-year patches.

◆ Write-offs for state and local sales taxes, as well as IRA contributions to charity have been extended.

◆ The Hope Scholarship (the tax credit that applies to the first two years of post-secondary education) has been increased from $1,500 to $3,000. Similarly, the Lifetime Learning Credit was increased from $2,000 to a max of $4,000.

◆ The tuition deduction ($2,000 to $4,000) was extended to the end of 2009. To qualify, your adjusted gross income must be no more than $65,000 ($130,000 for a joint return).

◆ You can receive tax credits starting at $2,000 per unit for solar appliances, wind-mills, or geothermal heat pumps.

◆ Plug-in vehicles that recharge the battery from your home can receive tax breaks ranging from $2,500 to $7,500.

Not satisfied by the alphabet soup known as TARP, the Federal Reserve and The U.S. Treasury Department have unleashed another program. Known as TALF (Term Asset-Backed Securities Loan Facility), it is designed to defrost the frozen markets for consumer financing, such as auto loans and credit card debt. This debt, in turn, represents the "backing" for so-called Asset-Backed Securities. From more than $1 trillion several years ago, ABS is probably running at less than $50 billion on an annualized basis at the present time. This is a key program, and may well exceed, eventually, the $700 billion TARP.

A financial crisis demands immediate action and all parties responsible should experience some degree of pain. We expect to see some commercial banks "eat" some of the loss, as BankAmerica agreed to do. Nor should defaulting homeowners be let completely off the hook. Ignorance or sales pressure are not excuses for breaking a legally binding contract. Finally, the federal government has to implement proper rules and procedures for overseeing and regulating the commercial/investment bank-ing behemoths. The powers that be have not addressed the issue that got us into this mess; namely the "mortgage mania." This all started with loose mortgage credit standards and banks selling off what turned out to be toxic mortgage paper to Wall Street, who, in turn, marketed the resultant package to investors (including other Wall Street firms). This country, right or wrong, runs on credit. Anything or anyone who threatens credit availability threatens the economic well-being of the nation. And that's where we are right now.

To investors, we say don't *ever* purchase an investment, including but not limited to mortgage-backed securities, without thoroughly understanding what you are purchasing. The investing principles you will learn in this book will help you build a sturdy, disciplined portfolio that can weather any storm. If you apply them and avoid financial bubbles and manias, you will be able to achieve your goals. With luck, we will all emerge from this horrific crisis wiser investors.

The Least You Need to Know

- Financial bubbles do emerge; the wise investor doesn't get caught up in them.

- Changes in government regulations that allowed commercial and investment banks to go into business together, as well as pressure on banks to make mortgages to low-income, first-time homeowners, contributed to a housing bubble or "mortgage mania."

- The government bailout will enable beleaguered banks to sell tainted assets to the government for cash in exchange for bank stock.

- Don't ever buy an investment that you don't thoroughly understand.

Put Your Money to Work for You

In This Chapter

- Investing is putting your money to work for you
- Compounding interest can build your wealth
- Using time as a money-making asset
- Forming the 10 percent habit
- The relationship between time, risk, and your sanity
- How interest rates and inflation affect investors

Putting Money to Work Is the Essence of Investing

When John D. Rockefeller was a teen during the mid-1800s, he lent $50 to a neighboring farmer. A year later, the farmer paid him back the $50 plus $3.50 interest on the loan. The week before, Rockefeller had earned a measly $1.12 after 30 hours of backbreaking work hoeing potatoes for another neighbor. "From that time on," Rockefeller wrote in his autobiography, *Random Reminiscences*, "I was determined to make money work for me."

Putting your money to work for you is the essence of investing—and anyone can learn to do it well. Think for a moment about what you envision a successful investor to look like. Maybe you picture someone in a power suit, up at the crack of dawn checking stock quotes in *The Wall Street Journal* before he or she has even had coffee. A real mover and shaker. Well, toss that picture right out of your head and take a walk over to the closest mirror. See that good-lookin' person looking back at you? That's what a successful investor looks like. It's anybody. It certainly could be you.

"But where am I going to get the money I need to start investing?" you may be thinking. That's simple: any dollar you aren't using to pay bills is money you can invest. Luckily, you have a lot more investment options than young Rockefeller did. On the other hand, separating the wheat from the chaff is going to be a little more complicated for you than it was for our boy on the farm. Before you start threshing your investment opportunities, you'll need to lay a little groundwork.

Fiscal Facts

The word *millionaire* is believed to have first come into use in Paris around 1720. A number of French noblemen invested in shares of The Mississippi Company and became fabulously (temporarily) wealthy. They were called "millionaires." The Mississippi Company was a contemporary of the equally and initially profitable South Sea Company ... and both bubbles burst!

The Miracle of Compounding

Albert Einstein, Nobel Prize winner and father of the theory of relativity, once remarked that compound interest was the most powerful force in the universe. Al knew that every time you invest a dollar, it generates interest. After a while, you earn interest on your interest. In a few years, a virtuous cycle is born, resulting in you sipping drinks on a beach in Tahiti. In this chapter, you'll learn to master the math of compounding, improving both your financial health and your ability to impress your less fiscally savvy friends!

How Compounding Makes the Difference

Compounding is affected by two variables:

◆ The amount you invest: It's a simple premise. The more money you invest, the greater the eventual value of your portfolio. Investing an extra $50 per month can increase your wealth by hundreds of thousands of dollars given enough time.

◆ The rate of return you earn: You may not think there is a significant difference between a 10 percent and a 12 percent return. Over the long run, however, a difference of one or two percentage points can result in breathtaking disparities.

For example, two 20-year-olds, Jocelyn and Ashly, invest $5,000 each year until they reach retirement at age 65. The first earns a 10 percent return, the second 12 percent. In the end, Jocelyn will retire with $3.6 million. Ashly, on the other hand, will retire with $6.8 million, or nearly twice as much!

def•i•ni•tion

Interest is payment you receive for lending someone your money. Interest is also the fee you pay when you borrow money.

To see how compounding works its magic, compare these three examples:

1. Fred earns 5 percent per year on his investment of $100,000. He spends that 5 percent on meals at gourmet restaurants. What does Fred have after 10 years? Love handles, some nice memories, and $100,000.

2. Mary earns 5 percent per year on her investment of $100,000 and puts her *interest* income in a shoe box. What does Mary have after 10 years? Well, first, here's a quick lesson on percentages for those of us who spaced out during math class!

Percent means *out of 100*. Five percent, therefore, means 5 out of 100. A dollar comprises 100 pennies, so 5 percent of a dollar is 5 pennies. Five out of one hundred is written as 5 percent.

When you divide 5 by 100, you get .05. This is another way to express any percentage—simply move the decimal point two places to the left.

◆ 5 percent is also .05

◆ 10 percent is also .10

◆ 39.6 percent is also .396

Expressing 5 percent as a decimal makes it super easy to figure out what Mary earned on her $100,000 in one year. Just whip out your handy calculator and multiply $100,000 by .05.

$100,000 × .05 = $5,000

Mary earned $5,000 per year on her investment for 10 years, so she earned $50,000 total in interest. Add that to her initial $100,000 investment, and Mary ended up with $150,000 in 10 years.

Super Strategies

You can save yourself a math step when calculating compound interest. Simply multiply the investment amount by one plus the interest percentage. If the interest on an investment is 10 percent, for example, first convert the percentage to a decimal. Ten percent becomes .10. Then add 1 to .10, which gives you 1.10. Now, multiply your investment by 1.10. If your investment is $50,000, for example:

$50,000 × 1.10 = $55,000

You'll have a total investment of $55,000 after the first year of compounding.

---

def•i•ni•tion

Compound interest is the money you earn on interest you earned in a previous period. Compound interest enables your money to grow exponentially (okay, a lot!).

3. Helen also earned 5 percent per year on an initial investment of $100,000, but she had the good sense to reinvest the interest that she earned each year. The first year, Helen's investment earned $5,000, so she started the second year with $105,000. The second year she earned $5,250 ($105,000 × .05 = $5,250). She started the third year with $105,000 + $5,250, or $110,250. After 10 years of earning interest on her interest (i.e., *compound interest*), Helen has a whopping $162,890!

An Easy Way to Figure Compound Interest

I'll bet you're already thinking, "Well, that Helen was smart, but I really don't want to do 10 tedious calculations to figure out how much my money will earn in 10 years of compounding." This, my friend, is why the Almighty invented charts.

The Future Value of Money chart below shows you how much one dollar will be worth over a certain time period if it is compounded at a given interest rate. In Helen's case, she let $100,000 compound at 5 percent over 10 years. Run your finger down the left side of the chart under "Years" until you find "10." Okay, now move your finger across that row until you're under "5%." There's your answer. Every dollar Helen invests will become $1.6289 dollars in 10 years compounded at 5 percent. If she invests $100,000 dollars, she'll earn $162,890. Use this chart to stoke your financial fantasies.

The Future Value of Money (Amount of $1 at Compound Interest)

Rate Years	1%	2%	3%	4%	5%	6%	7%	8%	9%	10%	11%	12%
1	1.0100	1.0200	1.0300	1.0400	1.0500	1.0600	1.0700	1.0800	1.0900	1.1000	1.1100	1.1200
2	1.0201	1.0404	1.0609	1.0816	1.1025	1.1236	1.1449	1.1664	1.1881	1.2100	1.2321	1.2544
3	1.0303	1.0612	1.0927	1.1249	1.1576	1.1910	1.2250	1.2597	1.2950	1.3310	1.3676	1.4049
4	1.0406	1.0824	1.1255	1.1699	1.2155	1.2625	1.3108	1.3605	1.4116	1.4641	1.5181	1.5735
5	1.0510	1.1041	1.1593	1.2167	1.2763(1)	1.3382	1.4026	1.4693	1.5386	1.6105	1.6851	1.7623
6	1.0615	1.1262	1.1941	1.2653	1.3401	1.4185	1.5007	1.5869	1.6771	1.7716	1.8704	1.9738
7	1.0721	1.1487	1.2299(2)	1.3159	1.4071	1.5036	1.6058	1.7138	1.8280	1.9487	2.0762	2.2107
8	1.0829	1.1717	1.2668	1.3686	1.4775	1.5938	1.7182	1.8509	1.9926	2.1436	2.3045	2.4760
9	1.0937	1.1951	1.3048	1.4233	1.5513	1.6895	1.8385	1.9990	2.1719	2.3579	2.5580	2.7731
10	1.1046	1.2190	1.3439	1.4802	1.6289	1.7908	1.9671	2.1589	2.3674	2.5937	2.8394	3.1058
11	1.1157	1.2434	1.3842	1.5395	1.7103	1.8983	2.1048	2.3316	2.5804	2.8531	3.1518	3.4785
12	1.1268	1.2682	1.4258	1.6010	1.7959	2.0122	2.2522	2.5182	2.8127	3.1384	3.4984	3.8960
13	1.1381	1.2936	1.4685	1.6651	1.8856	2.1329	2.4098	2.7196	3.0658	3.4523	3.8833	4.3635
14	1.1495	1.3195	1.5126	1.7317	1.9799	2.2609	2.5785	2.9372	3.3417	3.7975	4.3104	4.8871
15	1.1610	1.3459	1.5580	1.8009	2.0789	2.3965	2.7590	3.1722	3.6425	4.1772	4.7846	5.4736
16	1.1726	1.3728	1.6047	1.8730	2.1829	2.5403	2.9522	3.4259	3.9703	4.5950	5.3109	6.1304
17	1.1843	1.4002	1.6528	1.9479	2.2920	2.6928	3.1588	3.7000	4.3276	5.0545	5.8951	6.8660
18	1.1961	1.4282	1.7024	2.0258	2.4066	2.8543	3.3799	3.9960	4.7171	5.5599	6.5435	7.6900
19	1.2081	1.4568	1.7535	2.1068	2.5269	3.0256	3.6165	4.3157	5.1416	6.1159	7.2633	8.6127

continues

The Future Value of Money (Amount of $1 at Compound Interest)
(continued)

Rate Years	1%	2%	3%	4%	5%	6%	7%	8%	9%	10%	11%	12%
20	1.2202	1.4859	1.8061	2.1911	2.6533	3.2071	3.8697	4.6609	5.6044	6.7275	8.0623	9.6463
21	1.2324	1.5157	1.8603	2.2788	2.7860	3.3995	4.1405	5.0338	6.1088	7.4002	8.9491	10.8038
22	1.2447	1.5460	1.9161	2.3699	2.9252	3.6035	4.4304	5.4365	6.6586	8.1403	9.9335	12.1002
23	1.2572	1.5769	1.9736	2.4647	3.0715	3.8197	4.7405	5.8714	7.2579	8.9543	11.0262	13.5523
24	1.2697	1.6084	2.0328	2.5633	3.2251	4.0489	5.0723	6.3412	7.9111	9.8497	12.2391	15.1785
25	1.2824	1.6406	2.0938	2.6658	3.3863	4.2918	5.4274	6.8484	8.6231	10.8346	13.5854	16.9999
26	1.2952	1.6734	2.1566	2.7725	3.5557	4.5494	5.8073	7.3963	9.3991	11.9181	15.0798	19.0399
27	1.3082	1.7069	2.2213	2.8834	3.7334	4.8223	6.2138	7.9880	10.2450	13.1099	16.7385	21.3247
28	1.3213	1.7410	2.2879	2.9987	3.9201	5.1117	6.6488	8.6271	11.1670	14.4209	18.5798	23.8837
29	1.3345	1.7758	2.3565	3.1186	4.1161	5.4184	7.1142	9.3172	12.1721	15.8630	20.6235	26.7497
30	1.3478	1.8113	2.4272	3.2434	4.3219	5.7435	7.6122	10.0626	13.2676	17.4493	22.8921	29.9597
31	1.3613	1.8476	2.5001	3.3731	4.5380	6.0881	8.1451	10.8676	14.4616	19.1942	25.4103	33.5549
32	1.3749	1.8845	2.5751	3.5080	4.7649	6.4533	8.7152	11.7370	15.7632	21.1136	28.2054	37.5815
33	1.3887	1.9222	2.6523	3.6484	5.0032	6.8405	9.3253	12.6759	17.1819	23.2250	31.3080	42.0912
34	1.4026	1.9607	2.7319	3.7943	5.2533	7.2510	9.9781	13.6900	18.7283	25.5475	34.7519	47.1422
35	1.4166	1.9999	2.8138	3.9461	5.5160	7.6860	10.6765	14.7852	20.4138	28.1022	38.5746	52.7993
36	1.4308	2.0399	2.8983	4.1039	5.7918	8.1472	11.4238	15.9680	22.2510	30.9125	42.8178	59.1352
37	1.4451	2.0807	2.9852	4.2681	6.0814	8.6360	12.2235	17.2454	24.2536	34.0037	47.5277	66.2314
38	1.4595	2.1223	3.0748	4.4388	6.3854	9.1542	13.0791	18.6251	26.4365	37.4041	52.7558	74.1792
39	1.4741	2.1647	3.1670	4.6163	6.7047	9.7034	13.9947	20.1151	28.8157	41.1445	58.5589	83.0807
40	1.4888	2.2080	3.2620	4.8010	7.0399	10.2856	14.9743	21.7243	31.4092	45.2589	65.0004	93.0503

(1) To find the future value, take a given rate, go down column to correct year; multiply this by your actual number; e.g., $28,000 growing at 5% for 5 years: $28,000 × 1.2763 = $35,736.40.

(2) Can also be used for inflation impact; e.g., what does $5,000 have to grow to in 7 years to offset 3% inflation? $5,000 × 1.2299 = $6,149.37

The "Blow-Your-Mind-by-Adding-Time" Chart

I'll bet you've already guessed that the longer your money compounds, the richer you'll get. Letting time work for you is the key to growing your green. The earlier you start investing, the better off you'll be. In fact, the difference between someone who starts investing at age 22 and someone who waits until age 28 is really dramatic, as illustrated here:

♦ Person A invests $2,000 a year for six years at 12 percent, starting at age 22. Person A's total investment is $12,000.

♦ Person B spends her first six years out of college blowing her salary on facials and designer suits. But then she settles down and invests $2,000 a year for the next 35 years at 12 percent. Her total investment is $70,000.

Now, here's the "blow-your-mind-by-adding-time" moment. If you read standing up, you might want to sit down. Get this—at age 62, Person A, who only invested $12,000, has earned $959,793. Person B, who invested $70,000, has earned $966,926. Person A earned nearly as much as Person B even though she invested $58,000 less! Ah, but Person A started early ….

What's the moral of the story? All together now, kids: Start early. Let time work for you!

The 10 Percent Habit

In the likelihood that you're over the age of 22, don't despair. (Between you and me, how many 22-year-olds do you know who are investing in anything but having fun?) If you are in your early 20s, though, I hope you're feeling fired up enough to start investing—if only so you can spend your 30s feeling smug. There's a great psychological advantage to starting early. It's easier to get into the investing habit when you're unencumbered by kids. You may be sharing an apartment and making a fairly low income, but you don't have to send anyone to college and you're certainly not staring down the barrel of retirement.

No matter what your age, the sooner you get in the habit of investing 10 percent of every paycheck, the more time your investment plan will have to work. Why 10 percent? It's not a big chunk, but it's not insignificant either. Most people can find ways to cut their spending by 10 percent pretty easily (we'll get into cutting expenses in Chapter 6).

Fiscal Facts _____

An easy way to figure out how long it will take an investment to double is to use the "Rule of 72." Take any fixed annual interest rate, and divide it into 72 (the average life span nowadays). The result will be the number of years it will take your investment to double. If you expect to earn 6 percent, for example, divide 6 into 72. Your investment will double in 12 years!

Bear in mind that this formula is based on the assumption that the interest rate never changes.

Become an Educated Investor, Not Just a Consumer

Today, there are a lot of educated consumers, but not many educated investors. The stock market's unusually strong performance during the 1990s was splashed across the covers of financial magazines, convincing individual investors to "come on in, the water's fine!" All the raving about how spectacularly the stock market performed created a new class of investing consumers who jumped into the market feet first.

def•i•ni•tion _____

A rule of thumb is that information is considered **material** if it would have changed reported net income or shareholders' equity by 5-plus percent, or if disclosure would have caused a reasonable investor to increase or decrease his or her holdings.

These are the same investors who panicked and dumped their stock holdings—collectively losing billions—when the market went south in 2002 due to revelations that some important and heretofore respectable corporations were cooking the books and withholding *material* information. Truth is, the stream of accounting scandals was a direct result of the unbridled exuberance of the market during the 1990s, when the stock of many Internet-based companies (the shiny new "dot.coms") took off like rockets despite the fact that many of these businesses were unprofitable.

Time, Risk, and Your Sanity

Now, back to time. When talking about investing, time is simply how long you can let your investment program work. Time affects your investment decisions in two ways:

1. The more time you have, the longer your investment has to compound.

2. The more time you have, the more risk you can handle.

Risk is defined as the potential for permanent loss of *capital*. One of the biggest influences upon the amount of risk involved in any investment is the amount of time you are financially and emotionally able to hold an investment. Let's take a look at how this time and risk relationship works in the stock market.

A *stock* is simply a share of ownership in a corporation. A stockholder literally owns a piece of a company. When you buy AT&T stock, for example, you become one of many owners of AT&T. This, in turn, entitles you to a share of AT&T's profits (or losses!). That share is paid to stockholders as a dividend. Just like an interest payment, you can reinvest a *dividend* or spend it.

def•i•ni•tion

In the business world, **capital** refers to assets (cash, stocks, bonds, machinery, inventory, etc.) that generate income.

When you own **stock**, you own a fraction of the company that issued it. Like any owner, you are entitled to a share of the company's profit or loss.

Corporations issue stock to raise money to finance everything from the building of factories to the creation of new divisions or products. This is called *equity* financing, because equity means ownership, and a corporation that sells stock to raise money is selling ownership. Money raised for business purposes is called *capital*.

def•i•ni•tion

When you own stock, you own a piece of the company that issued it. Like any owner, you are entitled to a share of the company's profits. The share is paid to stockholders as a **dividend**. You are also vulnerable to the company's losses. Corporations issue stock to raise capital, which is a fancy word for money used for business purposes. Raising capital this way is called **equity** financing. Equity means ownership.

History has proven there is no better way to increase your wealth over the long-term than by owning businesses. The ride, however, can be rather bumpy. Here's a real, extreme example from the stock market of the interrelationship between time, risk, and your sanity.

Assume it is the end of October 1987 and you are heavily invested in stocks. You've witnessed the following sickening drops in the stock market:

◆ In one day, October 19, 1987, the Dow Jones Industrial Average fell 22.61 percent.

♦ Within 10 days, the market had fallen 34 percent.

♦ By the end of October, the market was down 21.5 percent.

 Crash Alert _____

> The single most important thing you can do for yourself as an investor is to develop a long-term horizon. This will inoculate you against persuasive pitches to buy the latest hot investment and prevent you from selling based on bits of news and rumors. "Just how long is long term?" you ask. Think 10 years or more.

If your time frame was only a few months, you were one unhappy camper. Putting your family's Christmas money into the stock market in September would have been a lousy idea because you didn't have time to recover from the crash.

But what if you were in the *stock market* for the long haul? Let's expand the time frame. Let's see how well you would have done over the last 10 years. Take a look at the following chart to see how investing 10 years in the stock market stacks up against investing 10 years in Treasury bonds and Treasury bills. FYI: the *S&P 500* is a group of 500 stocks that a Wall Street rating company called Standard & Poor's tracks to get a picture of the stock market. Treasury bonds (T-bonds) and Treasury bills (T-bills) are very safe (i.e., low-risk) investments that are backed by the U.S. government.

def•i•ni•tion _____

> Stocks are bought and sold on the **stock market**. The stock market doesn't exist as a physical place—stocks are traded at various stock exchanges, such as the New York Stock Exchange or the American Stock Exchange. The *Dow Jones Industrial Average* (DJIA) is an average of 30 well-known companies, such as AT&T or McDonald's, chosen by the editors of *The Wall Street Journal* to represent trends in the stock market.
>
> The **S&P 500** is a list of 500 stocks selected by the folks at Standard and Poor's for size, industry, and liquidity. This list, known as an index, is used on Wall Street as a broad measure of stock performance.

Given a decent time frame, though, stocks have historically performed quite well. Here's the data going back to 1926, when the forerunner to the *Standard & Poor's 500*, the Standard & Poor's 90, was first tabulated:

Compound Annual Return 1926—2007	
Standard & Poor's 500 Stock Index	+10.4%
Long-Term Government Bonds Index	+ 5.5%
U.S. Treasury Bills Index	+ 3.7%
Inflation (Consumer Price Index)	+ 3.0%

(Source: Ibbotson Stocks, Bonds, Bills and Inflation R 2008 Classic Edition Yearbook. © 2008 Morningstar. All Rights Reserved. Used with permission. Copies of the Yearbook may be acquired directly from Morningstar. For more information, please visit global.morningstar.com/SBBIYrBks.)

As you can see, the total return for stocks over the past 81 years was nearly twice that of risk-free government bonds and three times the inflation rate. Stocks are clearly worth the risk if you can afford to hold them for 10 years or longer.

Even with the negative return of 12 percent in 2001, stocks still did substantially better than bonds and bills over the 10-year period. And that's the secret to successful investing: holding stocks and/or stock mutual funds for at least 10 years.

Every investing goal will have a different time frame based upon your personal goals. You might want to buy your first house in five years, for example, in which case your savings would need to be in investments that don't fluctuate significantly. Perhaps you just got married, and, although there might not be a child on the scene for a couple of years, you want to begin a 20-year savings plan for his or her college education. Under these circumstances, your investment choices are much broader.

In general, the less time you have to achieve your goal, the less risk you can take with your principal.

The Fed's Balancing Act: Dampening Inflation Without Dumping on Us

With the financial crisis of 2008, you heard a lot about the Federal Reserve. That's our country's central bank, and it monitors the activity of all banks in the nation. The Fed is charged with only one task, but it's a doozy. The Full Employment Act of 1946 and the Humphrey-Hawkins Act demand that the Fed keep the economy stoked so people can find jobs, yet also control inflation. This is an almost impossible task—like squeezing a balloon at one end without the other end blowing up with air.

Inflation is an overall increase in prices. Inflation tends to occur when, as economists love to say, "too much money is chasing too few goods." If everyone in the country has a job and is earning plenty of money to spend, a situation may arise where companies are not able to make enough products to satisfy the demand for them.

If you own a factory that makes stereos and your stereos are flying off the shelves, you will want to make more to satisfy the demand. Only problem is, with full employment, you can't find any workers to hire. So you can't make more stereos. "Well," you think, "all those flush consumers really want to buy my stereos, so I could definitely make some money here. I can't find anyone to help me make more stereos, but I'll bet if I raise the price, people will pay it." This is how full employment can fan the fires of inflation.

The Problem with Inflation

The problem with inflation is that once it takes off, it can outpace wages and lower living standards. If you can buy a bag of groceries in August for $60 and by December the same groceries cost you $75 but your salary hasn't budged, you're going to have to start eating less or going to fewer movies or playing fewer rounds of miniature golf on the weekend. Now that's no fun!

When the Fed sees evidence of inflation building up, it takes the one action it can, which is to raise interest rates. If you're one of those folks rushing out to throw a new stereo on your credit card and your credit card company informs you that your rate has gone up from 12.5 percent to 14.5 percent, you may give that purchase a second thought. When the Fed raises interest rates, spending calms down a bit and inflation is dampened. Conversely, when a recession hits, as it did in late 2008, the Fed cuts rates to try to encourage people to spend.

How does the Fed raise rates? Well, every bank in the country is required to keep at least 20 percent of its customers' deposits in its vault overnight. But sometimes a bank runs short at the end of the day and has to borrow money from another bank. The rate that banks charge each other for these short-term loans is called the *federal funds rate.*

The Fed doesn't set the funds rate directly but can affect it by adding or draining the cash reserves to or from the bank system.

In the same way that too much money chasing too few goods causes inflation, if the Fed drains reserves from the system, banks have fewer dollars on hand to lend each other overnight. Since they have less to lend, there will be pressure on the funds rate to rise.

The Fed can also directly control interest rates by raising and lowering the *discount rate*. This is the rate at which banks borrow from the Fed.

def•i•ni•tion

The Fed manipulates the interest rates we pay for auto loans, mortgages, and the like in two main ways. It raises or lowers the **discount rate,** which banks must pay when they borrow from the Fed. If the banks have to pay more, they'll turn around and charge you more. The Fed can also indirectly affect the **funds rate** that banks charge each other by adding or draining cash from the banking system.

Now, the one thing you can count on is that when it costs a bank more money to borrow money, it'll turn around and charge you more money to borrow. So when the funds rate or the discount rate rises, every other interest rate in the country starts to climb. Suddenly, it costs you more money to buy that stereo or a new house. You slow down your spending. Factories slow down their hiring. The economy begins to contract.

Conversely, when interest rates fall, it encourages borrowing, expansion, spending, and hiring. When the Fed thinks inflation is under control but jobs are scarce, it encourages the economy to grow by adding reserves to the banking system. This increases the cash available for banks to lend each other, and the funds rate comes down. Interest rates start to decline—people start buying again and companies start expanding and hiring. The economy begins to expand.

What Do Interest Rates Have to Do with Stocks and Bonds? Glad You Asked!

What does all this have to do with stocks and bonds? Plenty! You've already learned that stocks are a form of equity financing—corporations sell ownership in the form of stock to raise capital. Well, bonds are simply a different instrument corporations use to raise capital. A *bond* is a form of debt financing.

When you buy a bond, you are *lending* money to a corporation for a specified length of time, not buying ownership. In return, the company promises to pay back the value of the bond at *maturity* with interest. We'll get into this in more detail later,

def•i•ni•tion

A **bond** is an IOU that a corporation or government issues when it wants to borrow money for more than 10 years. The issuer agrees to pay back the bond holder at a specified *maturity* date, with interest.

but for now all you need to know is that if you buy a $100 bond today, when the bond matures in, for example, five years, you will get that $100 back, plus interest. Nothing more, nothing less.

But what if inflation has risen so much during those five years that your $100 only buys $80 worth of groceries? Bonds don't protect investors from inflation at all. That's why when investors hear economic news that makes them worry about inflation, they tend to become more interested in stocks. Inflation can really degrade the value of a bond. Stock prices, on the other hand—just like all other prices in the economy—tend to rise over time, so if you are worried about inflation, you'll find stocks more attractive than bonds because they offer some protection from the corrosive effect of inflation.

Both the stock and bond markets react to changes in interest rates, which in turn affects expectations about inflation—which in turn affects investors' decisions. If you understand that, you're on your way to becoming an educated investor.

The Least You Need to Know

- The first line of defense against financial disaster is a portfolio tailored to your individual needs and objectives.

- The first step toward financial security is to make it a habit to save 10 percent of everything you earn.

- When you buy stock, you become an owner of a business. You share that owner-ship with everyone else who owns stock in the company, and you share in the profits (and losses).

- Riskier investments, such as stocks, can make you a lot of money, but only if you have time to ride out the ups and downs.

- The later you start investing, the less risk you can afford to take.

Chapter 3

How Do You Really Feel About Risk?

In This Chapter

◆ How much risk is too much for you?

◆ How to calculate simple return on investment

◆ Understanding the relationship between risk and return

◆ Getting a grip on your own risk tolerance

◆ Evaluating your unique time frame

Jumped out of any airplanes lately? Or are you the type who white-knuckled it and sucked down three drinks during your last commercial flight?

Whether we perceive a given situation as exciting or terrifying has to do with our tolerance for risk. Many of us like to kid ourselves about how much risk we're willing to accept. We dream of jumping out of a plane or skiing top-speed down a steep slope, but when we find ourselves at the door of that plane or the top of that slope, we wish we had our feet firmly planted on terra firma.

You can chicken out of skydiving or skiing with only your pride to salvage, but if you make investments that require more risk tolerance than you have, you'll be a miserable, sleep-deprived wreck. So the first step before you invest in anything is to analyze and get comfortable with your risk tolerance. The investing world is no place for false bravado.

What Is Return?

In investing, risk is defined as the possibility of permanent loss or impairment of capital. When you invest in something, you decide to do so because you expect to receive more money in the future than you invested today. The difference between the amount you put in and the total amount you receive at the end of the investment period is your *return*. You're going to learn how to calculate return in several ways in Chapter 22. For now, let's cover the basics.

Return on investment (ROI) is also called rate of return. It's typically expressed as a percentage of the original investment. Let's say your little brother asks to borrow $500 to buy an old car that he intends to fix up and resell. When he sells the car for $1,000, he gives you back your $500 and splits the $500 profit with you. You get $500 plus $250, or $750. Because $250 is half of $500, for every dollar you invested, you earned 50¢. Your ROI is 50 percent.

def•i•ni•tion

Return is the amount you earn from an investment over a given period of time. Generally, higher returns require the investor to assume greater risk.

Return on investment (ROI), also called rate of return, is expressed as a percentage of your original investment.

What You Made, What You Paid

Here's a formula you can use to calculate the return on any investment:

1. The total you receive at the end of the investment period is your end-of-period wealth (A).

2. Your original investment is called your beginning-of-period wealth (B).

3. If you subtract your beginning-of-period wealth (B) from your end-of-period wealth, you'll get your *return*: A – B.

Now that you've figured out your return, you can easily calculate your ROI. Use the following formula to figure out your return as a percentage of your original investment (B).

$$\frac{[A - B]}{B} \times 100 = ROI$$

Fiscal Facts _____

When the word *on* shows up in a business term, it means "divided by." So return *on* investment really means return *divided by* investment.

Applying the formula to the preceding example, you get:

$$\frac{[\$750 - \$500]}{\$500} \times \$100 = \frac{\$250}{\$500} \times 100 = .50 \times 100 = 50\%$$

An easy way to remember this formula is the following:

What you made (e.g., $250) divided (÷) by what you paid (e.g., $500), times (×) 100.

Fear of Heights: The Higher the Return, the Greater the Risk

When you lent your brother the money to buy that car, you took the risk that a number of things could have gone wrong:

◆ He might not have been able to sell the car.

◆ The car might have been stolen or vandalized before he sold it.

◆ He could have sold it for a disappointing return.

Before lending him the money, you calculated your expected ROI in your head—even if you didn't know that's what you were doing!—and found it sufficient payback for the risk you were accepting. If your brother lives in a neighborhood where cars are stolen every night, maybe you would have decided not to risk your $500. Then again, if he swore to you that he could resell the car for $1,500, making your return $500 instead of $250, maybe you'd have gone for it anyway. After all, a 100 percent return on investment is a pretty sweet deal.

This concept is one of the basic rules of investing: generally speaking, the higher the rate of return, the greater the risk. Only you can determine how much risk you want to take.

Crash Alert _____

Now that you understand the relationship between risk and return, you'll never be fooled by investments that promise a high return with little or no risk of losing your money. If someone is offering you a high return on your investment, it's because the investment is high risk. There's no such thing as a low-risk investment that generates high returns.

The rate of return from investing in a small business, for example, can be very high. But roughly one out of every seven small businesses fails, so the risk of losing your investment is very high as well. In contrast, the return banks offer on savings accounts is typically very low—3 or 4 percent. But the risk that you will lose your money if you put it in a savings account is also very low.

The Tools of the Trade

To control risk, investment professionals use several tactics, which you can apply yourself to your own *portfolio* of investments.

def•i•ni•tion _____

Your **portfolio** is the mix of assets in which you have invested. A portfolio contains investment instruments that you've selected to achieve your financial goals, such as common stocks, bonds, Treasury bills, etc.

Before we discuss these tactics, let's look at a basic tenet of investment theory: standard deviation. Don't panic. No need to fear scary flashbacks of the math section of the SAT. It's just a mathematical term that helps to frame the likelihood (or, in quantitative terms, probability) of a given number recurring.

Standard Deviation and a Podunk Potato

Freddie has played third base for the Podunk Potatoes for the past 12 years. His batting average each year has been:

(1) .290	(5) .390	(9) .330
(2) .380	(6) .320	(10) .340
(3) .300	(7) .270	(11) .350
(4) .310	(8) .370	(12) .370

What will he bat in his thirteenth year? Let's look at his average. To calculate the average of any group of figures, simply add them together and divide by the number of figures—12, in this case.

Freddie's average is .335. But maybe in years two and five, Freddie got lucky and his batting average was boosted by a slew of easy pitches. And let's say he was bothered by injuries in years one and seven, when his scores were particularly unattractive. These aren't normal situations, so why don't we just throw out those four years? This is similar to what figure skating and gymnastics judges do when scoring a routine—they throw out the highest and lowest scores.

This is also what financial analysts do when they are trying to find a pattern in a bunch of numbers. They disregard the very highest and the very lowest numbers. Analysts usually dump about a third of the numbers they are given, which is what we're doing in this case by getting rid of 4 out of 12 of Freddie's batting averages.

If we get rid of years one, two, five, and seven, Freddie's lowest score turns out to be the .300 he batted in year three. His highest score becomes the .370 he batted in year 12. The difference between those two years, or the spread, is:

.370 − .300 = .07

So we could think of Freddie as someone who tends to bat between .300 and .370. If we divide that .07 difference in half, we could say that Freddie bats his average of .335 plus or minus .035. That "plus or minus .035" is called the first level standard deviation. It gives you a pretty clear picture of Freddie's potential future performance. His batting average in a given year can deviate up or down from the overall average by .035.

Fiscal Facts _____

A huge amount of wealth is invested in the stock market. It is estimated that of the $33 trillion in worldwide capitalization, 50 percent, or $16.5 trillion, is capitalized in the United States. (Source: Ibbotson Associates, Inc. Stocks, Bonds, Bills and Inflation © 2004 Yearbook.)

Deviant Behavior

We can follow the same procedure with the stock market by looking at the annual returns as far back as we want to go. Let's assume that for a single year, the stock market returned 12 percent with a standard deviation of plus or minus 15. This would mean that stocks returned between +27 percent (12 + 15) and −3 percent (12 − 15) that year.

That same year, bonds returned 5 percent and money market instruments returned 3 percent. Well, if the stock you were holding was at the low end of the stock market return, you would've actually lost –3 percent and probably would've been happier with your money parked in bonds or even in a savings account.

What's interesting, though, is that when we look at stock market returns over a 20-year period, the standard deviation really comes down from ±15 to closer to ±3. This means stock investors who stay in the market for 20 years could expect returns of 12 percent +/-3. The low would be 12 percent minus 3, or 9 percent. The high would be 12 percent plus 3, or 15 percent. This means that, for investors with a 20-year time horizon, stocks have historically performed very well. Also, for each and every 20-year period, stocks have returned more than bonds. Over time the returns from stocks smooth out and the deviation drops.

Basically, the longer you hold a high-risk investment like stock, the smaller the standard deviation will become. Over time all the fluctuations matter less and less. What matters is how the investment performs over the long run, not the short term. Historically, stocks have been very volatile over short periods, but have performed very well over 10 to 20 year horizons.

Therefore, we can say that the standard deviation (risk) of the highest-risk/ highest-return investment declines as the time frame increases. This is a key concept in investment theory and, for your purposes, asset allocation, which we discuss in Chapter 21.

How does this all apply to you? Once you understand how time, risk, and return interact, you can begin to think about how to allocate your investment assets. Simply put, if your time frame is short, you shouldn't own much common stock. If you have a long time frame, you should have a substantial portion of your assets allocated to stock, because over time the ups and downs in the stock market—as represented by the standard deviation—tend to neutralize each other.

The Three Broad Investment Classes

There are basically three broad classes of investments from which you can choose when you build your portfolio:

1. Common Stocks

2. Bonds

3. Money Market Instruments

As you learned in Chapter 1, *common stocks* represent shares of ownership in a company. Corporations sell ownership in the form of stock to raise capital. This is called equity financing.

def•i•ni•tion

When a corporation issues stock, it is essentially selling pieces of ownership (called "equity") in the company. When you buy a share of GM common stock, you become an owner of General Motors. You are now entitled to a share of the company's profits, which are paid to stockholders as dividends. Most stock is simply **common stock,** but some is preferred. The owners of *preferred stock* get their dividends first.

As an owner, you are entitled to the fruits of the company's success: higher cash dividends and, ultimately (and hopefully), a higher stock price. On the other hand, you are vulnerable to the costs of failure: a reduction in (or even elimination of) the cash dividend and a lower (perhaps substantially lower) stock price.

Bonds, you'll recall from Chapter 1, are a form of debt financing. When you buy a bond you are lending money for a specified length of time.

Money market instruments pay rates that vary from day to day, week to week, or month to month. They are very *liquid*. This means they can be converted to cash easily and quickly. A savings account or a money market fund can be cashed in any day for the same price you paid. Treasury bills can be sold within 24 hours. To liquidate a bond (or stock), on the other hand, might take some time because you have to find someone to buy it. The purpose of money market instruments is to provide instant (or close-to-instant) liquidity in your portfolio.

def•i•ni•tion

An investment is considered **liquid** if it can be converted into cash quickly and easily. Money market instruments offer liquidity because they can be converted to cash right away, generally within 24 hours, whereas some types of investments penalize you for liquidating them before a certain time, such as a retirement IRA.

Stocks are riskier investments than money market instruments or bonds, but because they are riskier, they generate higher returns.

Variety Is the Spice of Life

What's life without a little diversity? Well, in the world of investing, diversity can mean the difference between taking off or crashing and burning. *Diversification* is another method investment pros use to increase your portfolio's ability to handle greater risk—and thereby earn greater returns.

The more stocks you add to your portfolio, the closer your long terms will be to the market average of a benchmark such as the S&P 500. The reason for increasing your number of stock holdings is to help minimize event risk. This is the risk that one event could really damage the value of a stock you own.

In 1997, while the S&P 500 was up 33 percent, McDonald's stock rose only 6 percent. Why? Well, the Arch Deluxe didn't exactly fly off the grill, if you recall. There was also some media flap about the quality of your average McDonald's meal. So if you had all your money in McDonald's stock, you were probably too queasy to eat a dozen Arch Deluxes for the sake of saving your investment. On the other hand, in the first six months of 1998, the S&P was up almost 18 percent, but McDonald's stock price skyrocketed 50 percent. Why? McDonald's went on a campaign to solve its problems—dumping the loser burger and running some popular specials, like its Beanie Baby giveaway. Now here's what's really interesting—over that year and half, the returns for the S&P 500 and for McDonald's stock are very close. The S&P 500 didn't perform as spectacularly as McDonald's did in the first six months of 1998, but neither did it drop as dizzyingly in 1997. This is the value of diversification—over time it may dampen the highs, but it cushions the lows. We'll discuss ways to diversify in Chapter 21.

Quiz Thyself to Know Thyself: Risk Tolerance Quiz

The key to successful investing is to determine how much risk you can handle, taking into consideration:

- Your future obligations, such as children, a mortgage, or a business.

- Your liquidity constraints. If you don't have health insurance and you break your leg, for example, you'll need cash to cover the medical bills.

- Your growth requirements, such as the standard of living you want to maintain when you retire. Social Security probably won't do it for you, so you'll need some investments that really grow, such as stocks.

♦ Your investment objectives (which we'll delve into in the next chapter).

♦ Your investment philosophy; in other words, how willing are you to take risk?

But how do you know whether you can ride out the bumps and take the lumps that long-term investors in high-risk, high-return investments like stocks have to tolerate? How do you know your *risk tolerance* level? To complete the quiz, make a checkmark next to the statement that best describes your feelings. To score the quiz, simply add up the numbers next to your checkmarks. Then look up your score on our handy Risk Chart.

def•i•ni•tion _____

Risk tolerance is how much risk an investor is willing to assume in order to increase the level of potential reward.

A. ____1) I'd be willing to do without some of the potential to earn more money on my investments in order to receive some minimal assured rate of return.

____2) I'm much more concerned with getting solid, consistent results on my investments than superior investment returns.

____3) Hey, you've got to be in it to win it! I can accept fluctuating year-by-year returns in order to achieve higher total returns in the long run.

B. ____1) Although I may not get as much income right now on my investment, I'm interested in preserving what capital I have and don't want to see the market value of my securities decrease. When it comes to my future, I like to play it safe.

____2) When it comes to my investments, show me the money: current income is more important than capital preservation.

____3) Sure, I'm interested in preserving my capital, but I can take some decrease of market value to increase the income I'm earning on my investments right now.

C. ____1) Even looking at dice gives me the willies! I am definitely not much of a gambler. I'm more concerned in preserving the value of my current assets than in investing in riskier securities that have the potential to increase in value later on.

_____2) Growth of my assets in the future is as important to me as preserving the value of my current assets.

_____3) I am more concerned with providing greater future growth than playing it safe now and preserving my current assets.

D.   _____1) Keeping risk very low is more important for me than taking a chance in order to achieve superior investment returns.

_____2) Hey, there's chance in everything. Some market risk is inevitable in order to get the growth I deem necessary from my investments.

_____3) The final result is more important than how I got there. If I have to risk a bad year to meet my goal, that's okay.

E.   _____1) I feel I can make a fairly accurate prediction of what my future liabilities will be.

_____2) Well, I may not have a crystal ball, but I think I can accurately predict some of my future liabilities. Other possible liabilities are subject to rough estimates.

_____3) Do I look like a fortune teller? I am relatively uncertain about what my future liabilities will be.

F.   _____1) I don't like to put my eggs in one (or two) baskets. I believe in keeping my investment portfolio well diversified.

_____2) I don't like complications. I think it's best to keep the investment process simple. I use one or two types of investments with which I am comfortable. That's all I need.

_____3) You don't get to be a billionaire by playing it safe. The final result is more important than how it was derived. Diversification is not a major issue for me.

G.   _____1) The blue chip (high-quality) stocks of solid, mature companies give me the perfect combination of income and stability. I don't need to have superlative growth on my investments to be satisfied.

_____2) Blue chip companies are great, but I don't necessarily need to be that conservative with my investments. The stocks of solid companies in growing businesses will give very good results with a level of risk I can tolerate.

_____3) Entrepreneurship is where it's at. Small companies' stocks may be more volatile, but I prefer them because they reward me with the highest long-term rates of return.

Fiscal Facts _____

Interestingly enough, the term _blue chip_ was coined in nineteenth-century poker games. The blue chip is the one with the highest value.

H. Given the choice of the following three investments identical in every other respect, I would choose:

_____1) Investment 1: 100 percent chance of a 5 percent rate of return per year over the next five years.

_____2) Investment 2: 75 percent chance of a 10 percent rate of return per year, 25 percent chance of a 4 percent rate of return per year over the next five years.

_____3) Investment 3: 50 percent chance of a 20 percent rate of return per year, 50 percent chance of a 0 percent rate of return per year over the next five years.

I. Use the following graph to answer the following question.

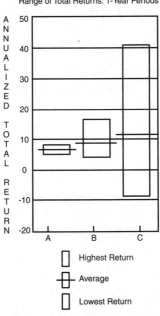

Range of Total Returns: 1-Year Periods

Assuming the expected rate of inflation over the next year is 4 percent, which investment option would you choose for a one-year time horizon?

_____ 1) Investment A would be the most appropriate of the three alternatives for my needs.

_____ 2) Investment B would be the most appropriate of the three alternatives for my needs.

_____ 3) Investment C would be the most appropriate of the three alternatives for my needs.

Calculate Your Score:

Your Risk Tolerance Rating

POINT TOTAL	RISK LEVEL		
	Low	*Medium*	*High*
9–14	X		
15–21		X	
22–27			X

Got the Time? Take the Time Horizon Quiz

Are we done? Can you go to sleep now? Not quite. We haven't addressed time frame.

Each of us has our own attitude toward time, and before you invest a dime, you need to determine yours. Believe it or not, though, almost everybody is a short-term, medium-term, and long-term investor simultaneously. How so? You might be saving for retirement, investing to send your kids to college, *and* saving for a vacation all at once. Each of these savings plans has its own time horizon; that is, each has a limit as to how much time is needed to reach the intended goal. How do you figure out what this time horizon is? Well, sometimes you may find that your investment priorities conflict. The manner in which you most consistently opt to resolve those conflicts indicates your true investment time horizon. Take the following quiz and check your results on the scale. Again, simply add up the numbers next to each question and find where you fall on the Time Frame Chart:

A. Considering time to be the most important factor distinguishing the three investments shown on the following page:

_____ 1) Investment A would be most appropriate for my needs.

_____ 2) Investment B would be most appropriate for my needs.

_____ 3) Investment C would be most appropriate for my needs.

B. _____1) It is most important to grow assets in an investment fund in the next one to two years.

_____ 2) It is most important to grow assets in an investment fund in the next five years.

_____ 3) It is most important to grow assets in an investment fund in the next 10 years or longer.

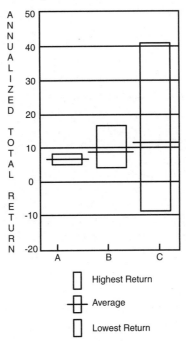

C. _____ 1) I'm not one to jump to conclusions. I don't feel it's necessary to make decisions based on individual quarterly rates of return. However, four consecutive disappointing *quarters* may cause me to rethink my investment strategy.

_____ 2) I do not make decisions based on one year of investment returns. However, two consecutive disappointing years or a disappointing five-year period may weaken my confidence in my current investment strategy.

_____ 3) I know that good things are worth waiting for. Ten years is my preferred barometer for measuring investment results.

D. _____ 1) My concerns lie in the here and now. I am most interested in maintaining my current financial position.

_____ 2) I've done fairly well over the past five years. Why not continue in that progress over the next five years?

_____ 3) Time is on my side. My financial position has barely started to reach its potential. I look forward to rapid growth.

E. _____ 1) Safety first, I always say. If I can get high yields from bonds, I will forgo the future potential for gains in stocks.

_____ 2) I don't need to totally play it safe, but I would be willing to accept lower levels of growth over a period of five years in order to hold on to consistent annual returns.

_____ 3) You've got to take the bad with the good. I'm willing to accept one year with a negative rate of return (for example, between –5 percent and –10 percent) in order to provide greater total returns over a period between 5 and 10 years.

def•i•ni•tion

In the investment world, the year is divided into three-month **quarters**. Companies are required to report their financial performance to stockholders every quarter. The _quarterly rate of return_ is the return on investment for one quarter, as opposed to _annual return_, which is an investment's return over one year. Companies and mutual funds report results both quarterly and annually.

F. Given a choice between receiving $100,000 this year or $300,000 10 years from today:

_____ 1) I would accept $100,000 this year.

_____ 2) I consider both offers to be equally attractive.

_____ 3) I would accept $300,000 10 years from today.

Check Your Score:

Your Time Horizon Score

POINT TOTAL	TIME FRAME		
	Short *(0–2 yrs.)*	*Intermediate* *(2–10 yrs.)*	*Long* *(over 10 yrs.)*
6–9	X		
10–13		X	
14–18			X

If you had any difficulty getting through these quizzes, don't panic. You're just going with your gut reaction right now. In fact, for those who are intimidated, we recommend that you return to them after you've read a few more chapters and feel a little more confident. Once you've completed these quizzes and found yourself on the tables, you should have a much clearer picture of your time frame and how you really feel about risk. Now your personal investment philosophy is shaping up.

The Least You Need to Know

- ◆ Return is the amount you expect to earn from an investment.

- ◆ The higher the promised return on an investment, the greater the risk that you will be disappointed in the investment's performance.

- ◆ To reduce risk, you can increase both the time you give your investments to perform and the diversification of your portfolio.

- ◆ There are three broad investment classes: stocks, bonds, and money market instruments.

- ◆ Money market instruments offer greater liquidity than stocks and bonds. In other words, they can be more easily and quickly changed into cash.

Selecting Your Investing Objectives and Style

- Getting your investment objectives straight right now
- How to build your emergency fund
- Where to keep your rainy-day cash
- How best to juggle your present and future investment objectives—without dropping any balls
- What does comfortable retirement mean?
- Pros and cons of retiring early

Remember Aesop's fable of the "Ant and the Grasshopper"? The grasshopper mocks the hard-working ant for wasting a beautiful summer afternoon toiling away storing food for the winter. Of course, the warm summer rays give way to colder northern winds. As the grasshopper gets stuck out in the cold with nothing, nada, zip to eat, the ant is happily feeding his face in his warm anthill.

The moral of the story is that if you don't prepare now, you're going to be one sorry grasshopper later. But does this mean you can't have any fun? Of course not. It just means that if you want to have *any* fun in the future, you'd better get your investment objectives straight now. For instance, most people don't think about retirement planning for the simple reason that they've got plenty of other really important things to think about and plan for, like getting married, buying a house, or sending the kids (whether you have them now or are planning to soon) to college. How do you juggle your multiple financial goals and pressures and still save for a comfortable retirement? Read on!

Just-in-Case Cash

Most investors either never get around to establishing a plan for retirement, or if they do they deviate from it. Think of your financial plan as a stroll down a beautiful trail in the woods. If you stay on the path, you'll eventually reach your destination, but if you chase every butterfly or every storm sends you running for shelter, you'll get lost and may never find your way back to your path.

Hospitalizations, funerals, weddings, auto or home repairs, gifts, taxes, etc., don't show up programmed on a calendar. They occur with little or no advance warning, and you either have funds set aside to cover them or you go into debt. And going into debt, both financially and psychologically can take the fun out of a happy event or make a sad one even sadder.

Your umbrella for those times when life drenches you with unexpected expenses is your emergency fund. This should be roughly 10 percent of your annual income or $10,000, whichever is greater. Some experts recommend keeping half your annual salary in an emergency fund, but that's a bit extreme. If you're making $50,000 a year or less, it's awfully hard to save $25,000. These days—what with low down payments available on homes and easy car financing—few emergencies require $25,000, as long as you have health insurance. Ten percent or $10,000 should cover you for most of life's financial emergencies. This is the single most important thing you can do to secure your financial future; an emergency fund ensures that you never have to touch your investments.

> **Super Strategies**
>
> Don't forget the 10 percent rule: Put aside 10 percent of every paycheck and you'll be able to painlessly create your emergency fund.

Mattresses Are for Sleeping, Not Stashing

It's important to save money for emergencies—but it's equally vital that you have immediate access to that money when a serious situation does arise. Keeping your cash under the mattress is *not* the best place, even if it is immediately accessible! So, what investments are available that combine liquidity and safety for amounts under $100,000? (We assume you are not John D. Rockefeller.) You have four options for *liquid investments:*

1. Treasury Bills
2. Certificates of Deposit
3. Savings Accounts
4. Money Market Funds

All these investments are called cash equivalents, because they can be quickly and easily turned into cash.

def•i•ni•tion

Liquid investments are those which can be turned into cash within 24 hours. Treasury bills, CDs, savings accounts, and money market funds are all *cash equivalents* that are highly liquid.

Treasury Bills

You can park your emergency fund in *Treasury bills* (a.k.a. *T-bills*) and earn a nice return on your money while you enjoy the security of knowing that your funds are now a direct obligation of the U.S. government. This means that, if necessary, the Treasury will turn on the printing press to make sure you receive your principal. Treasury bills are sold at a discount that reflects their yield, or interest. A $10,000 six-month T-bill, for example, might be sold for $9,750. You buy the bill for $9,750 and six months later you get $10,000.

def•i•ni•tion

Treasury bills, or **T-bills,** are essentially IOUs from the U.S. government. They are available in three-month, six-month, and one-year maturities and are used by the U.S. Treasury Department to finance the national debt and day-to-day government cash flow crunches. They are fully guaranteed by the government and can be sold within 24 hours.

To figure out the *yield*, simply apply our old pal, the ROI (return on investment) formula:

$$\$10,000 - \$9,750 \div \$9,750 \times 100 = 2.564\%$$

That's the return for six months; the annual return would be 2.564 percent times two, or 5.1282 percent.

def•i•ni•tion

The **yield** on a Treasury bill is its return on investment; it's a way of expressing as a percentage the difference between the discount price and the value at maturity of the bill. You place an order to buy Treasury securities at auctions and actually pay for them on the settlement date.

Bills are sold by the Treasury at sales called "auctions." They are usually available in 4-week, 13-week, 26-week, or 1-year maturities. The minimum purchase is $1,000. Auction purchases for 13- and 26-week T-bills are typically held every Monday and settled on Thursday. The settlement date is the day you must actually pay for your bill purchase. Sales proceeds are available on a next-day basis.

Crash Alert

Although you can always cash Treasury Bills within 24 hours, if you sell before the maturity, you may receive less than the maturity value, and perhaps even less than the amount you invested!

The U.S. government sells Treasury bills through the Treasury Direct Program or via banks or brokers, usually for a service fee. If you buy directly from the Treasury, you can do so in person, by mail, by phone (1-800-722-2678), or via the Internet at www. publicdebt.treas.gov/sec/secinvsr.htm. You'll need to provide a signature to open your account if you want to purchase by phone or via the Internet.

Certificates of Deposit

"CDs" are issued by banks or thrifts (another term for savings and loans), with the first $100,000 insured by the federal government. Terms typically are for a fixed maturity ranging from 3 months to 10 years. If you need your funds before maturity, you will pay a penalty that may run as high as three months of interest for CDs maturing within one year, and six months of interest for CDs maturing after a year. The minimum purchase required is $1,000, but any dollar sum above $1,000 is acceptable ($1,100.21, for example).

When using CDs you have to stay on top of your maturity dates or the bank will automatically roll it over for another period. Prior to maturity, the financial institution will usually inform you in writing of the upcoming maturity date and give you three options:

1. Collect the proceeds.

2. Roll over the sum due.

3. Change the amount or the maturity.

Crash Alert _____

If you cash in a CD early, you will be penalized. For example, the typical six-month $1,000 CD might incur a penalty of around $12 if you cashed it at three months. If the CD was paying 4 percent interest, you would have expected a return of $40 for a year or $20 for six months, so that $12 penalty sucks up more than half of what you'd hoped to have earned.

Usually the CD is rolled over into a new CD of like maturity if you do nothing. If you invest in CDs, just be aware that banks love to automatically roll them over when they mature. If you don't tell your bank prior to maturity that you want to collect the proceeds of your six-month CD, for example, the bank will automatically lock you into another six months, and you won't be able to withdraw your money before then without paying a penalty. And the penalties for early withdrawal can be pretty stiff.

Savings Accounts

Savings accounts offer one advantage over T-bills and CDs—same day deposit and withdrawal. With T-bills and CDs it takes 24 hours to get at your emergency fund. Like CDs, saving accounts are insured by the federal government up to $100,000. Rates typically run 1 to 2 percent below other money market fund rates. Interest checking accounts pay even less (e.g., 1–2 percent) but are very convenient.

Money Market Funds

Money market funds (MMFs) are mutual funds that invest only in safe, short-term money market instruments, such as Treasury securities, CDs, or short-term debt (called commercial paper) issued by credit-worthy corporations.

Shares in a *money market fund* are bought and sold on a daily basis and are priced at $1 each. Although these funds are not insured or guaranteed, no money market fund wants to "break the buck" or admit to being unable to pay your $1 per share price if you want to cash in your shares. In those few instances where an asset was in question, the fund stepped in to insure the $1 price.

Fiscal Facts _____

The Federal Deposit Insurance Corporation (FDIC) was created in 1933 to furnish insurance protection for depositors in the event that their bank fails. Savings and checking accounts, and certificates of deposit are all protected up to $250,000 through 2013 by the FDIC.

def•i•ni•tion

Money market funds are mutual funds that invest in safe, short-term investments like Treasury securities or CDs. Some also invest in commercial paper, which is short-term debt issued by corporations to raise cash. Some MMFs lend the securities in their funds to broker-dealers in order to earn more interest. These securities are called repos.

If you want greater assurance, limit your choice to money market funds that only buy Treasury or other government securities, without *repos*. Repos are securities the fund lends to broker-dealers who pledge assets to cover the loan equal to typically 102 percent of the sum borrowed. Much as a bank earns interest by lending out your deposits as loans, the MMF earns interest on these repos.

The other catch with repos is that you can't deduct all the interest on your state tax return. The interest earned by the repos is taxable.

The Wall Street Journal lists approximately 880 taxable money market funds and approximately 350 tax-free funds. The *Journal* also lists the average maturity of the assets in each fund. Look in *The Wall Street Journal* on Thursdays under Money Market Mutual Funds in the Money & Investing Section. Your local newspaper also probably lists MMFs.

 Crash Alert

If you have mutual funds, don't use them for emergencies. Many folks get so excited about investing that they run out and purchase mutual funds before setting up emergency funds. But if your adventurous significant other wrenches his or her back while skydiving in Zimbabwe and you suddenly need a $2,000 airplane ticket and don't have an emergency fund, you'll have to sell your mutual fund. That's a taxable act, bud, so not only will you trash your investment program, you'll pay the Feds for the privilege.

For a minimum balance, your money market fund may provide you with a free checking account. Checks usually have to be for at least $250. If you have a brokerage account, your broker may offer you a limited choice of MMFs. You may also open an account directly with some money market funds, such as The Vanguard Group (flagship. vanguard.com/VGApp/hnw/PersonalHome), for example. Some people really like the convenience of opening a brokerage account with their local bank and transferring funds between the brokerage account and their checking account. Before you take this route, investigate the fees, if any, your bank will charge for transfers and other services.

Eenie, Meenie, Minie, Mo

Let's take a moment to evaluate these four options, as they pertain to your emergency fund:

	Pros	Cons
Savings Account	insured, liquid	low rates
CD	insured, competitive	fixed rates and maturity, penalty if redeemed before maturity
Money Market Account	liquid, competitive rates	not insured
Treasury Bills	liquid, competitive rates	can lose some principal if sold before maturity, min. purchase required

Before deciding where to keep your emergency fund, think, above all, about what's most convenient for you:

♦ How easy or inconvenient is it for you to get to your bank?

♦ Does it offer all the services you desire, such as Treasury securities, savings bonds, CDs, automatic teller machines (ATMs), brokerage services, etc.?

♦ How do the interest-earning rates on liquid accounts at your bank compare to others? Can you earn more somewhere else? Is it convenient?

♦ Would you prefer to let a bank reinvest (roll over) your CDs rather than have to call or see your broker when T-bills mature?

How Can I Bring Home the Bacon, Fry It Up in a Pan, and Have Some Left Over?

You want cash for a rainy day. You want to chill out on a warm beach when you hit 65 because, hell, you deserve it. But what about all the in-between stuff? You want a nice house. You want smart, well-educated kids. Maybe you even have dreams of becoming your own boss one of these days. These aren't such lofty goals—but achieving them will require some careful planning. We're going to go into greater detail about these topics later on, but for now, let's take a quick look at these near-future investment objectives.

And Baby Makes How Much?

New parents dote on their kids, live and breathe for their kids, usually; at least until the little darlings hit surly adolescence and start applying Goth makeup. That's perfectly fine and how it should be, but be careful that your children don't become butterflies that delight you but lure you off your financial path into dark and spooky woods.

When you have children, it's natural to want to plan to send them to the finest schools in the land and to save for their education first and foremost. At the risk of heresy, though, let's agree that your retirement needs must take precedence over your children's education. Remember, first, that their admission to the college of their (or your) choice is driven as much by their secondary school achievements as by the size of your checkbook. In addition, there are many more options available to fund a college education—such as loans, grants, gifts from relatives, scholarships, work/study programs, and summer jobs—than there are for retirement. And if you *really* want to secure a happy future for your children, don't saddle them with destitute elderly parents. Risking your financial security to ensure your child's college education does not make sense. (The same advice applies to grandparents who are involved in financing their grandchildren's educations.)

> **Super Strategies**
>
> A good habit to establish early in your family's beginnings is to dump all cash gifts for the children from relatives and friends into their educational funds.

Also remember that you will have devoted much love and support to bringing them to the point where they are eligible for college. Let them help you share the next step by contributing money from summer or part-time jobs to their college funds. Their own contributions might make their college experience more meaningful to them, grumble as they may. As Dear Abby (Abigail Van Buren) once counseled: "If you want your children to turn out well, spend twice as much time with them and half as much money."

Having said all that, of course you should save for your children's education. But first establish your emergency fund. By the time you've done this, you should have established a pretty steady habit of saving 10 percent of your salary for investment purposes. From this sum, target 20 percent for educational purposes from the time of the birth of your first child until the graduation from college of your last child. So for every $10 of your salary you save, invest $2 in education and put $8 toward retirement.

> **Crash Alert** _____
>
> The biggest financial planning error new parents make is to put saving for their children's education ahead of saving for their own retirement. It's much wiser to put your own financial security first. A great rule of thumb is to divide the 10 percent of your salary you should be saving for the future so that 2 percent of it goes to college funds and 8 percent goes toward your retirement.

This time frame means that if you're going to work for 40 years, for about half of those years you can save 10 percent exclusively for retirement. The remaining 20 years you will probably be splitting the 10 percent 20/80 between education and retirement. We'll take a close look at the best places to put your education dollars in Chapter 16.

Oh, Give Me a Roof

Another big expenditure you may face, besides retirement and college, might be the down payment on a home. But if you think of this expense properly, it needn't throw you off your path to retirement savings.

First off, think of a home as shelter, not as an investment—no matter how many ex-baseball pitchers you've heard extolling second mortgages on TV. A home down payment, ideally, would come from the $10,000-plus in emergency savings you've already set aside. We'll get into home ownership in greater detail in Chapter 15.

Who's the Boss? You!

Are entrepreneurial dreams occupying your unconscious nocturnal activity? You may think you need to use every ounce of capital you have to start your own small business. Before you go cracking open the piggy bank, though, remember this: it is akin to buying shares in a business, and you might be tempted to rationalize the use of equity dollars from your retirement plan for this purpose. Bear in mind our discussion in Chapter 2 about diversification, though. Do you really want to sink your retirement dollars into one business—even if it is your own? Would you feel comfortable buying only Sears & Roebuck stock for your portfolio? Undiversified equities are high risk and you would be mortgaging your retirement by resorting to this approach—not to mention the unpleasant fact that many business start-ups fail. In fact, most successful entrepreneurs have had several failed businesses under their belts before hitting one out of the park. As Henry Ford said, "Failure is a chance to begin again more intelligently."

How Gold Do You Want Your Golden Years to Be?

If planning for retirement is the farthest thing from your mind, you're not alone. According to the *1998 Retirement Confidence Survey* conducted by The Employee Benefit Research Institute, only 45 percent of all workers have figured out how much they'll need to retire—up from 32 percent the prior year. What's more:

◆ Half of all baby boomers born between 1946 and 1953 haven't given it a thought, reports The Institute's Paul Yakoboski (Source: *Pensions & Investments Magazine*, Arleen Jacobius, June 29, 1998).

◆ Among boomers born between 1954 and 1964, 47 percent are investigating their retirement savings needs this year, up from 32 percent last year.

◆ Only 33 percent of Generation X-ers have looked into retirement, up a mere 3 percent since 1997.

And for some weird reason, the percentage of smug individuals who say they are "very confident about retirement" has remained flat at 20 to 25 percent for the last six years. (Who are those people, anyway?) This means that three quarters of us have either blocked the entire disconcerting business out of our minds or toss and turn enough at night to wrinkle our wrinkle-free sheets.

Unless you want to spend your twilight years pushing a shopping cart around town looking for recyclables, you must add retirement into your overall investment-objective picture. Your logical next step in planning your financial future is to figure out how much money you need to put aside so you can not only retire, but retire comfortably.

What does this mean, exactly? Just this: a comfortable retirement is the manner in which you will maintain your present standard of living without heading off to the salt mines 40-plus hours a week. Presently, you probably don't often have to do without or scrimp; you have the means to eat well and entertain when you wish. When you retire, you'll have roughly the same expenses, with four possible exceptions.

The good news is there are four categories of expenses in which you will probably save money once you retire:

1. **Car expense.** If you have two cars now and one is primarily used for commuting, you might be able to get by with one after retirement. This'll mean significant savings on car payments, insurance, gas, and maintenance.

2. **Home expense.** If you have a four-bedroom colonial, you might consider moving to a smaller house or condo when the kids leave the nest. This would free up capital and reduce monthly payments and taxes.

3. **Clothing expense.** Not going to work means not having to wear a different snazzy suit or dress every day; Bermuda shorts and Converse hi-tops are a lot cheaper.

4. **Taxes.** Income tax will come down as your income declines; property taxes can be reduced if you sell a large home.

Because these expenses are likely to be reduced once you retire, and because the dollars you're saving now for retirement will become dollars you can consume, a good rule of thumb is to expect that you'll require an annual retirement income of 50 to 70 percent of your present salary. The range accounts for a mortgaged home versus one owned free and clear. So, for example, if you live comfortably now on $60,000 a year and you expect to pay off your home by the time you retire, you need to save a pool of money that will generate 50 percent of $60,000, or $30,000, per year for your retirement.

Now the question is do you spend down that pool of money you have accumulated by age 65, or do you leave it to your heirs? It's probably wiser to assume that you'll spend it to zero by, say, age 85. If you include your savings as part of your retirement support (and face the gruesome fact of your own actuarial mortality!), you'll have to save far less to reach your goal. It's very important when planning your financial security to set realistic, reachable goals. If you establish a goal that requires too much scrimping and saving, you'll eventually shrug your shoulders and say, "Well, whatever happens, happens." Better to set a goal you recognize as doable. Start now, save consistently, get reasonable rates of return, and you'll have that pool of money when you retire.

In Chapter 5 we'll figure out exactly how much you will need to save in order to retire comfortably.

The Least You Need to Know

- Before you invest in anything, set up an emergency fund, so you never have to dip into your investments to cover unexpected expenses.

- Keep your emergency fund in a liquid account or investment you can cash within 24 hours.

- The amount of income you'll need to retire is about 50 to 70 percent of what you need now to live comfortably.

- For every 10 percent of your salary you save to invest, put 2 percent toward your children's education and 8 percent toward retirement.

5

What Do You Have Right Now—and What Will You Need to Retire?

In This Chapter

- ◆ Creating a personal balance sheet
- ◆ Creating a personal income statement
- ◆ Real-life examples of personal financial statement
- ◆ Calculating what it will take to fund your dreams
- ◆ Major life mistakes to avoid

Believe it or not, over 80 percent of the 77 million baby boomers (those born between 1946 and 1964) think they're going to keep working at least part-time after age 65, according to a survey published in *AARP Bulletin*. Of these boomers who intend to stay in the harness, 52 percent claim they're going to do it for fun, while 13 percent cop to fearing that they'll need to work into their dotage just to keep up payments on the Beamer.

When you consider that only 12 percent of people over 65 hold jobs today, you have to wonder whether the boomers who say they intend to work as seniors are deluding themselves out of fear that they won't be able to fund decent retirements. In fact, as long as you start reasonably early, it's not that difficult to fund retirement. Assuming an 8 percent return, the following savings are required to accumulate $100,000 by age 65.

- At age 25: $7.14/week

- At age 35: $16.32/week

- At age 45: $40.40/week

- At age 55: $127.61/week

As you can see, the person who waits until age 55 to start saving for retirement will have to save almost eight times as much per week as the person who starts at 35. So if your head has been in the sand, pull it out and let's take a look at what you have—right now—and what it'll take to make your dreams of a great retirement come true.

So What Will Social Security Do for Me, Anyway?

Half of the baby boomers surveyed said they had no faith that Social Security would be there for them when they retire. But the fact is, *Social Security* is one of our most revered social programs, and no young congressional firebrand is going to be able to dismantle it anytime soon. At least not with fearsome senior groups like the Gray Panthers ready to storm the Capitol with Uzis in hand. No politician wants to have anything to do with abolishing Social Security.

Look at your paycheck. See the section marked *FICA*? That's how much you pay each week into the Social Security system, which pays out Social Security and *Medicare* benefits. If you are employed, your employer pays an amount equal to 7.65 percent of your income to Social Security. The other 7.65 percent comes out of your paycheck, for a total of 15.3 percent of your income each year, up to a salary of $102,000. After that, only Medicare is deducted, which is 1.45 percent of your salary.

def•i•ni•tion

Social Security is a system managed by the federal government that provides money to people who are retired or are not able to work due to disability.

FICA stands for the Federal Insurance Contributions Act.

Medicare is included under Social Security. This is a national health program that pays certain medical and hospital expenses for elderly and disabled people. The Social Security system is funded by employees, employers, and the government.

The Social Security Administration can tell you what your Social Security benefits will be based on when you retire. Call them at 1-800-772-1213 or visit their website at www.ssa.gov to obtain Form SSA-7004, the Request for Social Security Statement (formerly known as the Request for Earnings and Benefits Estimate Statement). You will receive your Statement by mail. The left page shows how much you have contributed to Social Security and to Medicare for every single year you've been employed. On the right page are your estimated Social Security benefits. This shows how much you can expect to receive each year from Social Security:

- If you retire at age 62 (reduced benefit)

- If you retire at full-retirement age, e.g., 65

- If you work until age 70

Check to see if there are any mistakes. If, for example, you know you earned about $30,000 in 1999 and your Social Security Statement shows $0 for that year, call the Social Security Administration and go through your statement carefully with someone. It's a good idea to get this statement updated every five years.

Fiscal Facts

To estimate what Social Security will pay you during your leisurely retirement years, call 1-800-772-1213 or visit the Social Security website at www. ssa.gov. You'll need to fill out Form SSA-7004. Social Security will send you your very own Social Security Statement. Check it carefully for bureaucratic boo-boos.

Time to Pester Human Resources

Now let's figure out what, if anything, you've built up in retirement benefits at your job. Stop by your employer's personnel or human resources department and ask them to calculate your retirement benefits for you. (They probably won't be thrilled, but hey, this is your future we're talking about here.)

Do this only if your employer offers a *defined benefit* or *pension plan*, or *DB*. A DB is simply an employer-financed retirement plan that promises to pay you a certain sum annually at retirement, with the sum dependent upon when you retire, how long you worked, and how much you received in salary. (If your employer doesn't have a DB, you can skip the rest of this section.)

Ask your HR representative two questions:

1. "What would my annual benefits be (if any) at age 65 if I left the firm tomorrow?" If you haven't put in the minimum time (e.g., five years), tell them to assume that you have. Having put in the minimum time is called *vesting*, or *being vested*.

2. "What would my annual benefits be at 65 if I continued to work here until 65?" Have human resources either use your present salary or assume a 3 percent annual raise.

def•i•ni•tion

A **pension** is simply a regular payment made to you (or your family, if you've passed away) by your employer that reflects how much you earned and how many years you worked at your job.

A **defined benefit plan,** or **DB,** is an employer-financed retirement plan that will pay you an annual sum upon retirement. Pensions typically require you to have worked for the employer at least five years before you are considered *vested*, or eligible, for the pension.

Generally, the second number is going to be bigger than the first number. For our purposes in this chapter, use the smaller number. If you've had several jobs where you've earned retirement benefits, go back to each of the human resources departments and repeat the above procedure. You may get snarled at, but that's a small price to pay to get a grip on your finances.

Help, I'm Self-Employed!

If you are self-employed, you make (or should be making!) quarterly estimated tax payments. Included in these tax payments is a federal self-employment tax that covers Social Security and Medicare.

When you work for an employer, your employer is required to contribute a sum equal to 7.65 percent of your income into the Social Security system. The other half is deducted from your paycheck. Self-employed people pay the whole amount, which is presently 15.3 percent of income, themselves. On the plus side, self-employed people get to deduct half of this self-employment tax from their income tax. If you're running your own business, you must pay self-employment tax if you earn more than $400 per year after expenses, even if you have another job. (Oddly, you also must pay self-employment tax if you performed services for a church as an employee and received income of $108.28. Who comes up with this stuff?!)

If you are fully or partially self-employed, check in with Social Security to find out how your retirement benefits are shaping up.

Creating Your Own Fabulous Pension Plan

Whether you work for yourself part-time or full-time, you are entitled to create a pension for yourself, since an employer isn't creating one for you. You can choose from special Individual Retirement Accounts (IRAs) for self-employed people, or a Keogh Plan. An IRA is basically a shell that protects any investment you put underneath it from taxation. It's the government's way of encouraging us to save for retirement.

If you own a small business, you can create pensions for yourself and your employees. This is also a great way to reduce your income tax, as contributions to self-employment retirement plans are deductible up to a point. We'll get into this in more detail later in the book, but you have four options:

- **Keogh Plan.** These are primarily for small-business owners who need to set up retirement plans for themselves and employees. Keoghs require a lot of paperwork, so you'll probably need professional help. There are two types of Keogh plans: the profit-sharing and the money-purchase plan. You must make the same percentage contribution to a money-purchase plan each year, whether you have profits or not. The contribution to a profit-sharing plan can change each year. The two types of Keogh Plans are defined contribution (i.e., profit sharing) plans, and defined benefit (i.e., pension) plans. The maximum tax-deductible contribution to a *defined contribution plan* is the lesser of $44,000 or 100 percent of compensation. The maximum tax-deductible contribution to a defined benefit plan may not exceed the lesser of 100 percent of the participant's average compensation for the highest three consecutive tax years as an active participant or $220,000. Not complicated at all! (We jest.)

def•i•ni•tion

A **defined contribution plan** is a retirement plan that allows *you* to define how much is contributed to it. You tell the company how much to take from your check and put into your retirement plan.

- **SIMPLE-IRA.** SIMPLE stands for Savings Incentive Match Plan for Employees. This seems to be taking the place of the SEP IRAs. An employer can match up to 3 percent of your total compensation. The contribution limit was raised to $11,500 for 2009.

◆ **Owner-only 401(k).** The Uni-K Plan (from Pioneer in Boston) will let you max out contributions in 2009 at $49,000 ($54,500 if you're over 50).

A Super-Easy Way to Figure Out How Much You Need to Save

Now that you know how much will be coming in from Social Security and any retirement plans, you're ready to figure out how much you need to save and invest each year to retire, using the worksheet below. This worksheet gives you two options. One assumes that you'll own your house by retirement, so you'll only need 50 percent of your current annual income. The other assumes that you may still be paying a mortgage and will need 70 percent of your current annual income.

1. Present Annual Salary $_____ $_____

2. Times Percent at Age 65 _____.50_____.70

3. Gross Amount Required _____

4. Less Social Security[1] _____

5. Less Pension (if any)[2] _____

6. Less Existing Savings and Investment Income[3] _____

7. Equals Add'tl Income Required _____

1 Get this number from the Personal and Benefit Estimate Statement sent to you by Social Security.

2 Get this number from your employer's personnel office. If you have worked there fewer than five years, request that they use five years in the calculation. Do the same with all previous employers. Enter the total on Line 5.

3 Do not use your savings account balances here; what you want is the current annual income that savings and all other investments are generating annually. An easy way out is to simply multiply your total balances by .04 and use that sum for Line 6.

Your total in Line 7 is how much additional income you will need each year of retirement to supplement what you will be receiving from Social Security and any existing pension. Your goal now is to save and invest a pool of money that will generate that additional income.

Let's say, for example, that you are a 35-year-old making $30,000, and your worksheet looks like this:

1. Present Annual Salary	$30,000	$30,000
2. Times Percent at Age 65	.50	.70
3. Gross Amount Required	$15,000	$21,000
4. Less: Social Security[1]	$7,000	$7,000
5. Less: Pension (if any)[2]	$5,000	$5,000
6. Less: Existing Savings & Investment Income[3]	$0	$0
7. Equals: Add'tl Income Required	$3,000	$9,000

You need at least $15,000 per year of retirement income, and your Social Security ($7,000) and pension benefits ($5,000) add up to $12,000. That means when you retire, you'll be $3,000 short per year. Uh-oh.

Let's say you had $37,500 in investments that generated 8 percent income. You would get an extra $3,000 per year from those investments. That's exactly what you need. But you don't have $37,500 in investments, do you? So you have to grow it by saving over the next 30 years.

Let's say you invest these savings at 8 percent, and assume inflation is going to eat 4 percent per year. How much should you invest each year? Well, we can multiply $37,500 by 1.04 (4% = .04; $100 that earns 4% = $104, or $100 × 1.04) each year for 30 years or just sneak a peek at our old friend the Future Value of Money Chart. Either way, we'll find out that $37,500 today will have to grow to $121,627 by age 65 for you to avoid having your savings eroded by inflation. Remember, a dollar tomorrow won't buy as much as a dollar does today, but you want to be able to maintain your standard of living. You need to include inflation, therefore, when you calculate how much money you'll need to retire happily. If $37,500 a year would be enough for you today, you'll need $121,627 in 30 years to buy the same stuff.

So how much will you have to invest each year, assuming it will grow at 8 percent per year, in order to reach $121,627 by age 65? Well, we can do a whole bunch of calculations or we can look on the "Annual Savings Required" table that follows. (Note: This table assumes you are earning 8 percent per year on your investments.) Look down the "Residual Needs" column until you get to $3,000, which is the annual amount you're looking to cover during retirement. Now, if you're 35, you have 30 years until retirement, so look under the "30" column across from $3,000 and there's your answer: you'll need to save $1,074 a year to create a pool that will generate $3,000 a year once you retire.

Annual Savings Required

Residual Needs[6]	Years to Retirement							
	40	**35**	**30**	**25**	**20**	**15**	**10**	**5**
$2,000	463	573	716	912	1,197	1,658	2,555	5,185
3,000	659	859	1,074	1,367	1,796	2,487	3,832	7,777
4,000	927	1,145	1,431	1,823	2,394	3,316	5,109	10,369
5,000	1,158	1,431	1,789	2,279	2,993	4,145	6,386	12,962
6,000	1,391	1,717	2,148	2,732	3,593	4,974	7,663	15,553
7,000	1,623	2,003	2,506	3,187	4,192	5,803	8,940	18,145
8,000	1,855	2,289	2,864	3,642	4,791	6,632	10,217	20,737
9,000	2,087	2,575	3,222	4,097	5,390	7,461	11,494	23,329
10,000	2,319	2,861	3,580	4,552	5,989	8,290	12,771	25,921
11,000	2,551	3,147	3,938	5,007	6,588	9,119	14,048	28,513
12,000	2,783	3,433	4,296	5,462	7,187	9,948	15,325	31,105
13,000	3,015	3,719	4,654	5,917	7,786	10,777	16,602	33,697
14,000	3,247	4,005	5,012	6,372	8,385	11,606	17,879	36,289
15,000	3,479	4,291	5,370	6,827	8,984	12,435	19,156	38,881
16,000	3,711	4,577	5,728	7,282	9,583	13,264	20,433	41,473
17,000	3,943	4,863	6,086	7,737	10,182	14,093	21,710	44,065
18,000	4,175	5,149	6,444	8,192	10,871	14,922	22,987	46,657
19,000	4,407	5,435	6,802	8,647	11,380	15,751	24,264	49,249
20,000	4,639	5,721	7,160	9,102	11,979	16,580	25,541	51,841
21,000	4,871	6,007	7,518	9,557	12,578	17,409	26,818	54,433

Residual Needs[6]	Years to Retirement							
	40	*35*	*30*	*25*	*20*	*15*	*10*	*5*
22,000	5,103	6,293	7,876	10,012	13,177	18,238	28,095	57,025
23,000	5,335	6,579	8,234	10,467	13,776	19,067	29,372	59,617
24,000	5,567	6,865	8,592	10,922	14,375	19,896	30,649	62,209
25,000	5,799	7,151	8,950	11,377	14,974	20,725	31,926	64,801
26,000	6,031	7,437	9,308	11,832	15,573	21,554	33,203	67,393
27,000	6,263	7,723	9,666	12,287	16,172	22,383	34,480	69,985
28,000	6,495	8,009	10,024	12,742	16,771	23,212	35,757	72,577
29,000	6,727	8,295	10,382	13,197	17,370	24,041	37,034	75,169
30,000	6,959	8,581	10,740	13,652	17,969	24,870	38,311	77,761
31,000	7,191	8,867	11,098	14,107	18,568	25,699	39,588	80,353
32,000	7,423	9,153	11,456	14,562	19,167	26,528	40,865	82,945
33,000	7,655	9,439	11,814	15,017	19,766	27,357	42,142	85,537
34,000	7,887	9,725	12,172	15,472	20,365	28,186	43,419	88,129
35,000	8,119	10,011	12,530	15,927	20,964	29,015	44,696	90,721
36,000	8,351	10,297	12,888	16,382	21,563	29,844	45,973	93,313
37,000	8,583	10,583	13,246	16,837	22,162	30,673	47,250	95,905
38,000	8,815	10,869	13,604	17,292	22,761	31,502	48,527	98,497
39,000	9,047	11,155	13,962	17,747	23,360	32,331	49,804	101,089
40,000	9,279	11,441	14,320	18,202	23,959	33,160	51,081	103,681
42,000	9,743	12,013	15,036	19,112	25,157	34,818	53,635	108,865
44,000	10,207	12,585	15,752	20,022	26,355	36,476	56,189	114,049
46,000	10,671	13,157	16,468	20,932	27,553	38,134	58,743	119,233
48,000	11,135	13,729	17,481	21,842	28,751	39,792	61,297	124,417
50,000	11,599	14,301	17,900	22,752	29,949	41,450	63,851	129,601
52,000	12,063	14,873	18,616	23,662	31,147	43,108	66,405	134,785

continues

Annual Savings Required   (contineud)

Residual Needs[6]	Years to Retirement							
	40	35	30	25	20	15	10	5
54,000	12,527	15,445	19,332	24,572	32,345	44,766	68,959	139,969
56,000	12,991	16,017	20,048	25,482	33,543	46,424	71,513	145,153
58,000	13,445	16,589	20,764	26,392	34,741	48,082	74,067	150,337
60,000	13,919	17,161	21,480	27,302	35,939	49,740	76,621	155,521
62,000	14,383	17,733	22,196	28,212	37,137	51,398	79,175	160,705
64,000	14,847	18,305	22,912	29,122	38,335	53,056	81,729	165,889

[6]*From Line 7 on Annual Savings Required Form*

This works out to about $83 per month. That's not a whole lot, when you think about it. Of course, this is what you'll need to meet your *minimum* requirements for retirement. If you want to really be secure and comfortable, you may want to save enough to generate the $9,000 in additional income you'll need if you follow the far right side of your worksheet. If you look on the table under $9,000 and 30 years, it says you'll have to save $3,222 per year.

Use the 401(k) Plan, Stan

So how do you save this much? Well, if your employer offers a groovy matching *401(k)* or *403(b)* pension plan, it's a great start. Many companies offer plans where for every $1 you contribute, the company will put in 50¢ (or 25¢ or 75¢, depending on the company—companies aren't *required* to contribute anything). That's free moolah for you. If you are lucky enough to be in this situation, contribute the maximum of pre-tax earnings—usually around 6 percent of your annual gross income.

def•i•ni•tion

Many corporations offer **401(k)** plans to their employees. Under this type of retirement savings plan, employees who are eligible are allowed to choose how much of their pay is to be deducted for investment purposes. They also decide how the dollars are to be invested. The **403(b)** is a version of the 401(k) used by public employers, such as schools, hospitals, and other nonprofit organizations.

As of 2009, all employees regardless of age who have a 401(k) may contribute up to $16,500. If you reach age 50 by December 31, 2009, then you can contribute an additional $5,500, for a total contribution of $22,000. Now, if your employer contributes half of that, or 3 percent, that's 9 percent (which is really close to the 10 percent we recommend you invest, anyway). Just increase your deductions to 7 percent by continuing to have that 6 percent taken out of your pre-tax earnings and ask the personnel department if it can arrange for you to invest another 1 percent of your after-tax earnings in your company's plan.

You're painlessly on your way to establishing the 10 percent habit—and you don't even have to contribute all of it yourself. Just remember that the 10 percent rule applies as your salary increases, giving you a growing pool of assets that benefit from the magic of compounding interest each and every year.

Use your employer's plan first, if offered. There are tax advantages in that you may be able to shelter up to 15 percent of pre-tax earnings in an employer's plan depending on your salary and other restrictions. That's pretty cool—it means some of your hard-earned money escapes the clutches of the IRS by going straight into your tax-sheltered retirement plan. In addition, there are usually partial company matching dollar contributions.

Get an IRA!

Of course, you can also shelter money for your retirement in an IRA. As of 2009, all individuals, regardless of age, can put up to $5,000 annually into a traditional IRA. If you are over 50, you are allowed to contribute up to $6,000. Again, this is the government's way of encouraging you to get on the stick.

You can contribute to a regular IRA or a Roth IRA. The Roth IRA is named after Senator William V. Roth, Jr., then-chairman of the Senate Finance Committee, and a result of the Taxpayer Relief Act of 1997. The Roth IRA provides no deduction for contributions, but if you meet certain requirements, *all earnings are tax-free* when you or your beneficiary withdraw them. The rules governing these tax-free distributions are pretty complicated, but basically they come down to this: once you've kept your money in your Roth IRA for five years, if you are buying a home for the first time, you can take money out of your Roth IRA without paying taxes on it.

Trust Us, You Really Don't Want to Wait

Now let's look at an annual savings worksheet for someone age 50 earning $50,000. She'll need 50 to 70 percent of her annual salary for retirement, or $25,000 to $35,000. Social Security and retirement benefits will be greater than those for our 35-year-old, but not dollar-for-dollar, because there is a cap on annual Social Security benefits.

Let's assume that her combined benefits are $18,000. She needs to self-fund at least $7,000 per year. Assuming a return on investment of 8 percent, she'll need a pool of $87,500 to generate $7,000 per year in retirement income. Assuming 4 percent inflation, she'll actually need $157,583 ($87,500 × 1.04 for 15 years).

So how much does she need to invest at an 8 percent return per year to reach $157,583 in 15 years? More than $5,000 per year, or $417 per month. Argh! That's a hefty chunk—five times the annual investment needs of our 35-year-old. Plus, age 50 is a time when you are usually deep into college expenses for the kiddies and can least afford to put aside retirement dollars. Yet put them aside she must.

But My Circumstances Will Change... Won't They?

Of course, we all pray for raises, promotions, lottery winnings, and the like to lift us out of our present standard of living. How do you account for higher income over time when figuring out your retirement savings needs? By using a *fixed percent*, not a fixed dollar sum, of salary for retirement planning.

Back to our example of you as a 35-year-old putting aside 3 percent of $30,000. If you get a 3.5 percent raise every year, by age 50, your salary will be about $50,000. You wouldn't need to change a thing about your investment strategy. In fact, if you get a 3.5 percent raise every year and continue to invest a steady 3 percent per year of your salary (and earn 8 percent on it per year), you'll have accumulated $34,792 by age 50 and $154,354 by age 65. Trust us, we did the math! That's pretty close to what we calculated as the pool you'll need to generate as additional required retirement income.

You still need to redo your annual savings worksheet periodically, though, to see if a higher or lower percent is warranted. The best time to do this is every year on your birthday. This is also the time to have Social Security and pension benefits recalculated. You may need to start saving more, but never set aside less than the percent of salary with which you started.

Crash Alert _____

Whatever you do, don't wait to start investing for retirement. Every 10 years the amount you'll have to put aside goes up drastically. A 50-year-old will have to invest roughly *seven times* the amount a 35-year-old will invest to get the same results. Plus, remember that the older you get, the less risk you can afford to take by holding stocks. This means you have to turn to investments that don't earn as much as stocks usually do—slowing down the growth of your retirement pool further.

Stagger Your Debt

In *Hamlet*, Shakespeare wrote: "Neither a borrower nor a lender be." These are wise words to heed these days, as we are strongly encouraged by advertising and tempting credit card offers to live debt-heavy lives.
But if you're earning 8 percent on your investments and paying 18 percent in credit card and other debt, you're never going to get ahead.

The two biggest debts you are likely to take on are the following:

Fiscal Facts _____

Many early American homes have a knob on the top of the banister that leads to the second floor, which signified that the home was owned free and clear. Some early Americans even hollowed out the banister and inserted the paid-off mortgage!

1. College loans for you or your children

2. Your home mortgage

Try to avoid incurring both at the same time. A great rule of thumb is this: Pay off your student loans before assuming a mortgage, and pay off your mortgage before incurring children's educational loans. The good thing about both education and home mortgage loans is they are used to finance assets that will probably increase in value over time. An education will ideally increase earning capacity and a home should appreciate over the years. Try timing your indebtedness something like this:

Age 21	Take out student loans
Age 30	Pay off student loans
Age 30	Buy a home
Age 45	Pay off mortgage
Age 45	Take out loans for first child's college education

Crash Alert _____

Avoid taking on loans to finance assets that lose value over time, such as home furnishings, clothing, and cars.

Of course, this is idealistic for most people, but it's a good idea to at least start thinking this way!

Your Personal Balance Sheet: A Snapshot of Your Finances

Before we can begin selecting individual accounts and investments (which you learn about in the remainder of the book), we have to figure out where you are right now—at this very moment. It may not be pleasant. It may even be a little terrifying. But it's important that you face reality; otherwise, you can't begin to craft a plan to achieve your dreams.

To accomplish this task, you are going to prepare two personal financial statements—a *balance sheet* and an *income statement*.

Your Personal Balance Sheet: A Snapshot of Your Finances

Let's start with the balance sheet. A balance sheet shows your assets, liabilities, and *net worth*. Your net worth is the difference between your assets (what you own) and your liabilities (what you owe). It's a snapshot of your finances at a specific moment in time.

def•i•ni•tion

A **balance sheet** is like a photograph of your finances at a given moment in time. It shows what you own (your assets) and what you owe (your liabilities).

Your **net worth** is the difference between assets and liabilities. Net worth can be positive (if assets are greater than liabilities) or negative (if liabilities are greater than assets). An **income statement,** in contrast, shows the flow of money through your life. It allows you to compare your income with your expenses.

To create a personal balance sheet for you or your family, fill out the following worksheet. Make a habit of doing this once a year so you can compare your progress.

John and Suzie Q. Personal Balance Sheet as of 00/00/00

Assets	Liabilities
Cash _____	Credit Card Debt _____
Checking Account Balance _____	Student Loans _____
Savings Account Balance _____	Other Personal Loans _____
Individual Investments _____	Home Mortgage _____
Profit Sharing (401[k], 403[b], etc.)_____	Car Loan _____
Home (estimated value) _____	Other Debt _____
Car (estimated value) _____	
Collectibles (antiques, stamps, etc.) _____	
Furnishings (estimated value) _____	
Total Assets _____	**Total Liabilities** _____

Note that on the asset side, we have left out two potential retirement benefits that some financial advisors would include: Social Security and earned pension benefits. You may add them in if you are close (five years or less) to retirement, but otherwise exclude them because:

◆ They cannot be converted to cash if necessary.

◆ They don't technically belong to you right now. In some cases, a former employer may offer to meet your earned pension sum by offering a lump-sum payment, prompting you to transfer the sum to a rollover IRA and include it under the profit-sharing line.

Your first goal is to get your assets to exceed your liabilities. Your ongoing goal is to continually widen that spread so that you maximize your net worth. There are two ways to do this:

◆ Increase the total return on your assets.

This can be accomplished by either earning more money or cutting expenses. This will result in a higher net income on your income statement, which we discuss later, and, as a result, more assets on your balance sheet.

The key to true financial independence is in maximizing *income-producing* assets. If you purchase furniture for your new home, for example, you still have the same amount of assets—you just transferred your capital from cash to a loveseat—but the cash has now been taken out of the compounding process. You saw in Chapter 2 the dramatic effect time can have on even the smallest amounts. For that reason, $1 invested in stocks, bonds, mutual funds, and other income-producing assets is more valuable than $1 in hard goods (for you purists out there, we must mention that this ceases to be true in periods of high inflation).

◆ Decrease the cost of your liabilities.

When you reduce the interest rate you pay on your debt, you not only increase your net worth by the amount of interest expense saved, but also by the profit generated from those funds if invested.

To illustrate: you have a $100,000 loan that matures in 10 years with a current interest rate of 8 percent. You refinance at 5 percent. You invest the $3,000 you save annually. The investment generates returns of 8 percent per annum for the next 10 years. Using the future value of an annuity formula, you see that you will be $43,460 richer—$30,000 resulting from reduced interest expense and $13,460 from the profit of investing that capital. Following is the equation for figuring this out:

$100,000 × 8 percent old interest expense = $8,000
$100,000 × 5 percent net interest expense = $5,000
Annual Interest Savings = $3,000

Get a Grip with a Personal Income Statement

A great deal of financial planning is just getting a clear view of your situation. Before you can get a handle on your spending, you'll need to tally up your expenses and compare them to your income. If your expenses are 90 percent or less of your income, great! If they are equal to or are greater than your income, well, now you know there is a problem and can take remedial action.

For most people, getting a truly accurate picture of your expenditures is eye-opening. Consider the following: A 22-year-old recent college graduate stops by Starbucks on the way to work to purchase a drink and a muffin, spending $5 each morning. That works out to around $1,300 per year. If this young professional skipped the morning routine, ate at home, and instead opted to invest that money in the stock market each year, earning a 12 percent long-term rate of return, she would have $1,405,407 when she retired at age 65. She will have given up 11,180 cups of coffee and the same number of muffins, but her retirement will be much fatter.

For some of you, skipping the gourmet coffee isn't an option. That is where individual choice comes into the picture. Armed with this data, you can ask yourself the question, "Is giving up my morning coffee and muffin worth $1.4 million by retirement?" There is no right or wrong answer—that is the art of living.

"But isn't the point of being rich so that I don't *have* to control my consumption?" you ask. Au contraire! In his bestselling book *The Millionaire Mind*, Dr. Thomas Stanley revealed that the average American millionaire, despite having a median net worth of $4.3 million and annual income of $436K, has never spent more than $41,000 for an automobile or $340K for a home; a stark contrast to the popular image most people have of the wealthy.

By tracking your costs through a personal income statement that clearly delineates your income and expenses, you become aware of expenditures—such as gourmet coffee—and the ultimate economic cost to you and your family. Unlike the balance sheet, which is a snapshot of your assets and liabilities at a specific point in time, the income statement covers a range of dates—January 1 to December 31, for example. If you prepare an income statement once a month, you can really get a grip on how much money is coming in and how it's being spent. Before you fill out the following worksheet, you might want to make 20 or so copies of it. Fill out one using yearly figures and use the others to create an income statement each month.

John and Suzie Q. Personal Income Statement
12 Months Ending 00/00/00

Income	Expenses
Salary _____	FICA, etc. _____
Gifts to You/Yours _____	Federal Taxes _____
Income from Savings[1] _____	State Taxes _____
Alimony Received _____	Life Ins. Premiums _____
	Rental/Mortgage Payments _____
	Real Estate Tax[2] _____

continues

John and Suzie Q. Personal Income Statement
12 Months Ending 00/00/00   (continued)

Income	Expenses
	Food _____
	Clothing _____
	Alimony Paid _____
	Medical/Dental _____
	Entertainment _____
	Gifts Given _____
	Auto Payments _____

Income	Expenses
	Student Loan Payments _____
	Credit Card Payments3 _____
	Other Loan Payments _____
	Auto Related (gas, service, etc.) _____
	Home Repairs _____
	Furnishings _____
	Vacation _____
	Utilities (gas, electric, phone) _____
	Education Related _____
	Other _____
Total Income _____	**Total Expenses** _____

(1) Limited to savings for car, etc.

(2) If not included in mortgage payment

(3) Deduct sums covered elsewhere (e.g., clothing, etc.)

There are a few things you can do immediately to increase the income side without affecting your current lifestyle:

- ◆ Divert any raises you get at work toward your investments.

- ◆ Make sure your savings are with the bank that offers the highest interest rate in your area.

- ◆ Be sure to put any cash gifts into your savings/investing accounts. This is "found" money for you. And you might hint to family members that you would prefer cash to gifts going forward.

A Happy Couple on the Right Track

If you've had a little trouble filling out your personal financial statements, here's an example. Let's call this couple Jim and Jane. They are both 33 years old, have one 3-year-old child, and own their condo. Jim is a private school teacher and Jane works part-time at a retail firm. Credit cards are paid off in full each month.

Balance Sheet – Jim and Jane: July 15, 2008

Assets			Liabilities	
Savings		$20,000	Student Loans	0
Investments			Other Personal Loans	0
Bill (403b)	$12,000			
Pension	$5,600			
Mary (401k)	$600			
Child	$5,000			
Roth IRA	$2,000	$25,200		
Home		$240,000	Mortgage	$99,000
Auto		$5,400	Auto Loans	0
Total		$290,000	**Total**	**$99,000**
Net Worth:	**$191,600**			

Income Statement – Jim and Jane: July 15, 2008

Income			Expenses	
Salary:	Jim	$37,000	Mortgage	$8,184
	Jane	$11,000 $48,000	Real Estate Tax	$1,416
Investment Income		$800	FICA	$702
Gifts (cash)		$1,000	Medicare	$684
			Federal Tax	$6,004
			State Tax	$2,950
			Medical Plan	$1,344
			Pension	$2,064
			Gifts	$1,000

Income			Expenses	
			Auto Repair	$1,000
			Credit Cards	$200
			Home Insurance	$783
			Auto Insurance	$510
			Phone	$672
			Electric & Gas	$1,192
			Food	$5,200
			Clothing	$6,500
			Home Repairs	$2,000
			Entertainment	$2,600
			Vacation	$1,000
			Balance Savings/ Investments	$3,795
Total		**$49,800**	**Total**	**$49,800**

Incidentally, Jim and Jane are still young enough to be able to keep all their investments in stock, and therefore can take advantage of the high returns available.

Looking good!

Your Typical Young Guy Living Hand to Mouth

Here is another example. Fred is also a teacher, but he's 30 and single. You can see how the unpaid balance on credit cards hinders his opportunities for savings and investment.

Fred's Balance Sheet as of 7/08

Assets		Liabilities	
Checking	0	Car Loan	$1,000
Retirement Plan	$7,088	Student Loans	$17,400
Car	$2,000		
		Credit Cards	$8,325
Total	$9,088		$26,725
Net Worth: –$17,637			

Income Statement as of 7/08 (Monthly)

Income		Expenses	
Salary	$2,517	Federal Tax	$275
Other	$147	State Tax	$170
Gifts	$90	FICA	$165
		Medicare	$39
		Workers Comp	$2
		Union Dues	$51
		Retirement Plan	$160
		Student Loans	$367

continues

Income Statement as of 7/08 (Monthly) (continued)

Income	Expenses	
	Credit Cards	$350
	Rent	$515
	Auto Insurance	$70
	Auto Club	$5
	Gas	$50
	Telephone	$40
	Electricity	$50
Income	**Expenses**	
	Cable	$45
	Water & Sewer	$12
	Food	$170
	Entertainment	$120
Income	**Expenses**	
	Other	$20
	Auto Loan	$58
	To Savings	$0
$2,754		$2,734

Super Strategies

When developing an emergency cash fund, your objective should always be capital preservation. This means money should be kept in the most liquid and marketable investments possible—things like money market funds or Treasury bills. Why? It's not likely that you'll be able to postpone surgery to match up with a Treasury note to mature so you can get your principal back!

Fred has a negative net worth and lives hand to mouth on a month-to-month basis. The credit cards are his big handicap not only because he is making such large payments, but because the interest rates are high enough that it will take him decades to pay off the balance at his current pace. Paying off this debt should be Fred's highest priority (you'll learn how to decide whether to invest or pay off your debt in Chapter 7).

Fiscal Facts

For a variety of reasons, many financial pundits believe the stock market returns going forward will be significantly lower than they have been over the past two decades. In the interest of conservatism, you may want to limit your estimate for long-term growth to 10 percent (versus a current average of 12 percent). This will build in a margin of safety and protect you from coming up short in the end.

Fred's first student loan will be paid off in November (saving him $164 per month). Unfortunately, payments on the other loan increase to $318 per month, so his net savings will be $89 per month.

Fred's very first goal must be to build up an emergency savings balance. Any of life's blips would put him deeper in debt (auto repairs, etc.).

His second goal must be to work off the remaining student loan. Although the interest rate (8 percent) is reasonable, the size of the debt is going to prevent him from getting ahead. But the good thing about looking unflinchingly at your finances like this is it forces you to face your problems—and every problem has a solution. In Fred's case, for example, he might consider taking a part-time job for one or two years to knock off that loan. He could take a roommate to lower his rent.

Fred's situation is typical of recent college graduates. They need to catch a break, get a promotion and/or raise, inherit some cash, or all of the above in order to cross over into financial security. Let's hope all three happen to Fred so he can shore up his foundation, which is the focus of our book's next part.

The Least You Need to Know

- You can request a statement from Social Security that will show exactly how much per month you can expect to receive from Social Security upon retirement.

- Ask your personnel department to figure out how much you stand to receive from your company retirement plan.

◆ You can start financing your own retirement plan to make up the difference between what Social Security and your employer's plan will give you and what you will need.

◆ The sooner you start saving for retirement, the less you'll need to save.

◆ Figure out what percentage of your salary you need to save to meet your goals and stick to it.

◆ Try to stagger college loans and your home mortgage so they don't all hit you at once.

◆ Create a personal balance sheet and income statement at least once a year—on your birthday.

Part **2**

Creating a Plan

We have a personal question: What's the interest rate on your maxed-out credit card? Eighteen percent? Youch! So what if your investments are earning 12 percent if you're paying 18 percent to those sharks? Kinda defeats the purpose, wouldn't you say?

Well, you're in luck! This section is about wiping out debt, improving your credit score, purchasing a house, funding your own (or a child's) education, and planning for retirement—all the things you need to establish a firm financial foundation.

6

Retirement Plans 101

In This Chapter

- ◆ Defined benefit versus defined contribution plans
- ◆ 401(k) loans
- ◆ The differences between a traditional and Roth IRA
- ◆ Avoiding the 10 percent early withdrawal fee on nonqualified IRA distributions

How many of you reading this book have invested in an employer-sponsored retirement plan? Can we see a show of hands? Okay, not bad. Now for the real question: How many of you, upon leaving a job and receiving a lump-sum payment out of your retirement account, invested it in your new employer's plan? How many of you spent it?

That's what we thought. Well, if you spent it, you're not alone. At least a third of the people who receive lump-sum payments of their retirement savings when they change jobs fail to roll the money over into other tax-deferred accounts. And approximately one third of employees who qualify for 401(k) plans don't bother to contribute to them at all.

If you haven't yet contributed, it's probably because you don't really know what employer-sponsored retirement plans are and what they can do for you. And you've been too busy to really pay attention to the whole deal anyway. Well, since you've taken the time to crack open this book, let us make it easy for you. In this chapter, let's take a look from the ground up at the kinds of retirement plans that employers offer and the role these plans should play in your investment strategy.

If You Aren't Planning for Retirement Yet, You're Not Alone

If planning for retirement is the furthest thing from your mind, you're not alone. According to a survey conducted by The Employee Benefit Research Institute, only 42 percent of all workers have figured out how much they'll need to retire. What's more:

- Twenty percent of those who say they are very confident about retirement preparation are not currently saving for retirement, 52 percent do not have an IRA opened with money saved outside of an employer's retirement plan, and 37 percent have not done a retirement needs calculation.

- More than half (52 percent) report that the total value of their savings and investments, excluding the value of their primary residence, is less than $25,000.

- Fifty-five percent of folks feel like they are a "little" or "a lot" behind schedule in funding their retirement while only 7 percent feel like they are "a little" or "a lot" ahead of schedule.

Defined Benefit Plans

Millions of people in this country contribute to retirement accounts sponsored by their employers. There are several types of plans, but they all work on the same basic principle: you don't have to pay taxes on the money you put in your retirement plan until you start taking it out to support yourself during retirement. And no tax is due while it grows. That's why these are called tax-deferred plans.

A corporation is under no legal obligation to set up a 401(k) plan for its employees— it's a perk, part of your total package of employee benefits.

In the past, most retirement plans offered by employers were defined benefit plans. The employer promised you a specific pension upon retirement (in other words, the "benefit" was defined) and invested money with insurance companies or bank trust departments in order to be able to provide that benefit.

The most popular form is a good, old-fashioned pension. Because defined benefit plans are more expensive to run than defined contribution plans—which we'll talk about later in the chapter—many companies have moved away from them.

Most defined benefit plans have four characteristics:

♦ A vesting schedule requiring that you work a minimum number of hours per year—1,000, for example. This eliminates part-timers.

♦ A minimum number of years must be vested before qualifying for the pension; five years is common. This is to discourage job hoppers. The total of vested years you've accumulated is called "credited service."

Fiscal Facts _____

Just in case some of you have forgotten how to convert a mixed fraction to a decimal, here's the trick: multiply the denominator (the bottom number of the fraction) by the whole number. Add the resulting number to the numerator (the top number of the fraction). Now, divide the denominator by the new numerator. For example, for the mixed fraction $1\frac{2}{3}$:

3 (the denominator) × 1 (the whole number) = 3;

3 + 2 (the numerator) = 5, giving you a new fraction of $\frac{5}{3}$;

5 ÷ 3 = 1.66

♦ The value of the pension increases as you put more years in at the company.

♦ The value of the pension is weighted so that the last few years generate a disproportional chunk of the ultimate benefit you will receive. This is to encourage you to stay at this company until you retire. You maximize your pension by staying put.

How the Amount of Your Monthly Pension Is Determined

In the end, the amount of your pension is based on a formula that takes all these factors into consideration. For example, Ralph's Dog Biscuit Company figures out its employees' monthly retirement benefit based on the following convoluted formula:

♦ Take 2 percent of final average monthly pay.

♦ Multiply it by number of vested years (credited service) up to a maximum of 35 years.

♦ Subtract $1\frac{2}{3}$ percent of Social Security benefit and then multiply the resulting number by credited service up to a maximum of 30 years.

♦ Finally, subtract the latter from the former.

♦ This equals the monthly benefit at age 65.

Whew!

Let's look at an example. Assume loyal Ralph's Dog Biscuit Company employee Lindsay Jackson will be 65 on January 1, 2009, and will have 20 years of fully vested, credited service at that time. Let's say her Social Security benefit is $1,007 a month. Let's also assume that her final average pay is $2,500 a month ($30,000 a year). Now we can apply the formula.

Figure out 2 percent of $2,500 (final average monthly pay), and multiply it by 20 (total vested years of slaving away).

2 percent = .02

2,500 × .02 = 50.00

50.00 × 20 = $1,000

Then, take 1⅔ percent of $1,007 (the S.S. benefit), and multiply that by 20 (those hard-earned years again): 1⅔ percent expressed as a decimal is 1.66. Finally, subtract that number from the number above.

1,007 × 1.66 = $16.72

16.72 × 20 = $334.40

1,000 – 334.40 = $665.60

Monthly Benefit = $665.60

Ms. Jackson will receive a monthly pension of $665.60, as well as $1,007 per month from Social Security. Her total monthly retirement income, unless she has other investments, will be $1,672.60.

Fiscal Facts _____

Safeguards to prevent pension plans from defaulting on paying retirement benefits to employees were an important reason for the passage of the Employee Retirement Income Security Act of 1974 (ERISA). ERISA also codified 401(k) and 403(b) plans and prohibited employers from conducting certain transactions with retirement plan dollars.

A Whole Lotta Lumps or Just One: The Lump-Sum Option

Pensions are a promise or guarantee from your employer to you to pay a certain sum at a certain age until death. As you learned in Chapter 2, a regular payment over time like this is called an *annuity*. In some cases, you may be given a choice between the monthly pension payment and receiving the entire pension upon retirement as a lump sum.

How can you tell if the lump sum is better than the monthly payment? Well, first it depends on how involved you want to be. Some people are simply intimidated by large sums of money and are grateful to get a monthly check from their former employer. But you could shop the lump sum to several reputable insurers for their annuity rates and then compare. Many insurers "write" annuities and may offer you a better deal (i.e., higher monthly payment) for your lump sum than your employer's plan does. You can also use your broker or friendly banker to help in the process. However, you will not be given all the time in the world to decide which plan is best for you, so be aware that you need to give this some thought before the day of your retirement party.

If Your Employer Drops the Ball

Note that a defined benefit plan like a pension is a promise to pay on the part of the employer. The employer, or plan sponsor, is totally responsible for providing pension payments to retired employees (traditional profit-sharing plans, on the other hand, only tie the employer's contribution to the plan to the level of profitability of the corporation: no profit, no contribution).

The employer is supposed to be making annual contributions to the company's retirement fund and investing this money wisely. If the company goes broke or anything else happens to its ability to pay the benefits promised to retirees, responsibility for the pension is turned over to a federal agency called the Pension Benefit Guaranty Corp. (PBGC). Probably not who you expected to be handling your future, but at least it's a backup plan.

Defined Contribution Plans

Defined contribution plans, unlike defined benefit plans, limit the employer's role and responsibility. Employees decide ("define") how much they are going to contribute to their retirement account and then choose individual investments from a menu of options provided to them. There are no promises or guarantees; ultimately, your economic well-being depends upon the total amount contributed and the performance of the investments chosen.

401(k) and 403(b) Plans

The most popular defined contribution plans are the 401(k) and the 403(b). These accounts, codified by the Employee Retirement Income Security Act of 1974 (ERISA) provide an attractive way for the average worker to save for their retirement.

- 401(k) plans are for employees of private-sector companies.

- 403(b) plans are for employees of nonprofits, such as public schools, philanthropic foundations, and hospitals.

- Eligible state or local government employees have so-called Section 457 plans ("457s"). Named for Section 457 in the IRS Code, they are set up similar to a 401(k).

Tens of millions of employees in this country contribute to 401(k) and 403(b) plans, mainly because many employers add 25¢ or 50¢ or even more to every dollar an employee puts into his or her plan. If your employer contributes to your 401(k) plan like this, there's one simple rule for you to follow: Fund it to the max! This is *free money* you're getting here—and how rare is that?

Benefits of 401(k) and 403(b) Plans

There are several benefits to defined contribution plans. Chief among these are:

- **Tax-Deferred Growth.** Capital gains, dividends, and interest income generated by the investments held in your 401(k) or 403(b) plan are not subject to income tax until they are withdrawn. Over time, this can result in much more wealth for you! Consider this: $10,000 invested annually each year for 40 years would grow to $3.97 million if the profits were taxed at 20 percent capital gains rates at the end of every year. If the same investment were held in a tax-advantaged account, however, and all of the profits were subject to ordinary income taxes of 35 percent at the end, the portfolio would grow to around $5 million! Why the drastic difference? In a

Crash Alert

Bear in mind that when you leave a job you have only 60 days to shelter your 401(k) before the IRS swoops down on it. Even though changing jobs is hectic, make sure you either transfer it to your new employer's 401(k) or to a rollover IRA.

tax-advantaged investment vehicle such as a 401(k), there is more money working for the investor in the form of deferred taxes.

◆ **Researched Investment Options.** The menu of investment options your employer offers through its defined contribution retirement plans has been carefully chosen and is probably quite solid. Managers of mutual funds and other investments compete intensely to convince corporations to offer their funds as 401(k) plan options.

◆ **The Employer Match.** Many employers offer to match a percentage of employee contributions in order to encourage saving for retirement. Do the math; if your employer matches you dollar-for-dollar on the first 4 percent of your salary and you contribute $1,000, it will deposit an additional $1,000. You have instantly made a 100 percent return on your investment. There is no other way you can so quickly and safely increase your net worth.

Can I Borrow from My 401(k)?

Can you take or borrow money from your 401(k)? Yes, but only under certain conditions enforced by the employer (and dictated by the federal government). If you borrow, you will have to pay competitive interest rates established by the employer. It is strongly recommended that this option be utilized only for a dire emergency, and that any sum borrowed be repaid ASAP!

You are required, ordinarily, to repay your 401(k) loan within five years. If you are using the money to purchase a home, however, you may be able to extend the repayment period over the length of the mortgage—up to 30 years. Of course, there is one catch (besides the fact that you are taking away money that could be compounding, tax-advantaged as *pretax dollars*, for the next several decades): if you cease to work for your employer—either voluntarily or involuntarily—you will only have two months to repay the loan. *If you are unable to repay during this window of time, the loan balance will be taxed (and charged a 10 percent penalty fee) as if it were a withdrawal!*

def•i•ni•tion

The money that is deducted from your pay before taxes are applied is called **pretax dollars**. This enables you to avoid paying taxes on whatever you contribute to your 401(k) or 403(b).

What If I Change Employers?

What happens to your 401(k) if you leave your employer? Following are your options:

◆ You could leave your 401(k) with your old employer. Some employers allow you to maintain your account in their 401(k).

◆ If your old employer won't allow you to do that, or you don't want to, you could transfer your 401(k) assets into your new employer's 401(k) plan. No tax will be generated by this transfer.

◆ You could establish a separate IRA account and transfer your assets to this account. You have 60 days to do this before the assets will be taxed and subject to a 10 percent penalty. Because you are *rolling over* your assets into another account, this is called a rollover IRA.

◆ Finally, you could cash out your IRA (after your employer deducts taxes and penalties) and buy a new car. But would we recommend that? Noooooooo!

 Crash Alert _____

We've seen several instances where employees had money in company stock and the company went bankrupt, leaving them with nothing. We're not trying to scare you, and you may work for one of the biggest and sturdiest companies in the world, but history is littered with fallen giants that were once thought untouchable—the Great Atlantic & Pacific Tea Company, the Pennsylvania Railroad, PanAm, and Kmart, just to name a few.

Once you create a rollover IRA, you can't move those funds to a traditional IRA or a 401(k) plan in the future.

Contribution Limits

Like all good things, Uncle Sam restricts the amount of *pretax dollars* you can contribute to your 401(k) or 403(b) plan. Take a look at the limits that are currently in place.

Annual Deferral Limits for 401(k) and 403(b) Plans

Year	All ages (no distinction between under/over age 50)
2008	$15,500
2009	$16,500

Why would the government put limits on the maximum amount you can save for your retirement? This is to prevent the very highest salaried employees from being able to shelter a much larger share of their income than lower salaried employees can. It also encourages companies to offer a higher level of matching funds. If the fat cats at the top of your company could shelter huge chunks of their salaries in retirement accounts and the company had to pay them, say, 50¢ on every dollar they saved in their 401(k) plans, pretty soon the company might decide it can only afford to pay 25¢ on the dollar, thus lowering the retirement benefit for everyone.

Should You Put All Your Eggs in the Company Basket? Ask the Folks at Enron …

Often, a company will offer its employees an opportunity to buy its stock as part of the menu for its 401(k) plan. At first glance, this might seem like a pretty good idea. Why not have your company act as a stockbroker for you? You give them your blood, sweat, and tears, why not let them work for you? This is not such a great idea. Even if the stock is being offered to you at a discount, you'll be putting all of your eggs in the company basket. Your future is already heavily invested in the success of your company—you work there!

When Enron, the energy conglomerate, came under investigation by the SEC in 2002, about 62 percent of the funds held in the 401(k) plans of 11,000 employees were invested in Enron stock. That money was wiped out when Enron's stock tanked, and so were the retirement dreams of many employees. Surprisingly, it's not unusual for company employees to hold so much company stock. According to a survey by DC Plan Investing, General Electric employees are 77 percent invested in G.E. paper, and Procter & Gamble's fund is almost 95 percent company stock. Common, yes. Smart, no.

If you do want to own some company stock in your 401(k), you should limit it to what you would invest in if you were creating your own equity portfolio. And don't worry—your employer can't punish you for taking minimal or no participation in the company stock option. There are laws against that. Don't let 'em pressure you (it was widely rumored that Enron execs were pushing their employees to buy more Enron stock while dumping it out of their own retirement accounts). One advantage of share ownership, though, is that it entitles you to receive annual reports and other information that goes to stockholders, so you can keep current on your company and its fiscal healthiness (or lack thereof), if you so desire.

What About Stock Options? Go for It.

If your company offers you *stock options*, as opposed to stock, go for it. These can be very profitable. You'd be amazed how many top executives in corporate America own little or no stock in their companies, but have large stock option grants.

Because there is no risk—you don't exercise your option unless the exercise price is less than the current price and you can make a profit—stock options are really a form of compensation.

If you are eligible for stock options, there are two things you can do with them:

◆ **Buy and sell on the same day.** You immediately exercise your option because the strike price is less than the current price and you can make a profit. You purchase the shares and sell the shares on the same day. This saves you the trouble of having to raise the money to buy the stock. You simply go to your human resources department and say you want to exercise your stock option (this may not be necessary because many companies establish services with brokerage firms that allow employees to manage their options directly over the Internet). Your profit is taxed at ordinary income tax rates. You pay tax on the capital gain resulting from the difference between the exercise price (sometimes called the "strike" price) and the sales price.

def•i•ni•tion

A **stock option** is the right, but not the obligation, to buy a stock at a fixed price after a specified period of time (usually 12 months) for a fixed period of time (10 years). Prices and time periods are all specified in the option contract.

◆ **Hold on to the stock now, sell later.** You can buy the stock and hold it, hoping that its price will go up and you can sell at a profit. First, you'll need the money to buy the stock. It can come either from your own savings or by borrowing from your friendly banker. Then you exercise your option, or buy the stock. If you hold the stock for at least one year, you are taxed at capital gains rates (maximum of 20 percent), which is probably lower than your income tax rate.

What would we do? Well, we prefer the bird in the hand rather than trying to search through those darn bushes, so we'd probably choose the same-day transaction and deal with the ugly income tax. But, hey, this is your decision. You know your inclination, you know the company's prospects, and you know your personal financial situation. Take all of these factors into consideration before you make your decision.

Individual Retirement Accounts

What's an IRA? Nope, it's not the Irish Republican Army, although it can pack the same punch. Instead, it's a retirement account that you set up for yourself, as opposed to a 401(k) or 403(b) which would be set up by your employer.

The IRA itself is not an investment; it's a tax-sheltered account into which you put money that you can then invest as you choose. That money can be used to buy stocks, bonds, mutual funds, certificates of deposit, real estate, and other investments. The IRS does not permit you to use your IRA to purchase collectibles (fine art, gems, etc.) or life insurance contracts. An IRA can be set up with a bank, a brokerage firm, or a mutual fund company.

There are several different kinds of IRAs, each with its own quirks and purpose. We'll discuss a few of them in-depth, but for now, here's a quick overview:

- **Traditional IRA.** Developed in 1975 to help people who were not covered by an employer-sponsored retirement plan to save for retirement; contributions to a traditional IRA are tax-deductible. Your money grows in the account until you are 59½ years old; at which point you can begin to make regularly scheduled withdrawals without incurring a 10 percent penalty fee. You must begin withdrawing funds by age 70½. As the funds are pulled out, the proceeds are taxed as ordinary income.

- **Rollover IRA.** Used to shelter retirement savings that have been taken out of a 401(k) or cash pension due to a job change.

- **Roth IRA.** Created by the Taxpayer Relief Act of 1997 in order to give people more flexibility when saving for retirement, buying a house, or financing a child's education.

- **Simple IRA.** The Savings Incentive Match Plan for Employees is another option for small employers, including those who are self-employed, that has been growing in popularity because it is very easy to use. An employer can match up to 3 percent of your total compensation or your contribution, whichever is less. (Remember, if you're self-employed, *you* are the employer and the employee!) Contributions are presently limited to $10,500.

Old Faithful: The Traditional IRA

There was once a time when the traditional IRA was the only kid on the block. The old faithful is still a very good option for individuals who do not qualify for a Roth IRA. Here's what you need to know:

- **Tax Deduction.** Contributions to your traditional IRA can be deducted from your taxes. According to IRS Publication 590, however, this deduction begins to be phased out if you are covered by a retirement plan at work and your adjusted gross income (AGI) is:

  - Between $83,000 and $103,000 for a married couple filing a joint return or a qualified widow(er)

  - Between $53,000 and $63,000 for a single individual or head of household

  - Less than $10,000 for a married individual filing a separate return

- **Tax Deferral.** All of the dividends, interest, capital gains, and other income generated by your investments while they are parked in a traditional IRA will grow tax-deferred. When you begin to make withdrawals, the proceeds are taxed as ordinary income.

- **Withdrawals.** You can begin making withdrawals from your traditional IRA at age 59½. If you make withdrawals before this age, you will pay taxes as well as a 10 percent penalty. You *must* take withdrawals by the age of 70½—otherwise, you could end up paying a 50 percent excise tax on the undistributed portion of your assets!

The Flexible Roth IRA

Less than 10 years old, the Roth IRA offers extraordinary flexibility when compared to its stodgy, more rigid sibling.

◆ **Tax Deduction.** Unlike a traditional IRA, contributions to a Roth IRA are not tax-deductible.

Crash Alert

If you make a contribution to your traditional or Roth IRA and suddenly realize you have gone over the Congressionally approved limit for the year, you can generally withdraw the cash with no tax consequences as long as you do it before the date of your tax filing for that year. If you fail to correct the situation on time, however, you will be subject to a 6 percent excise tax on the excess contribution!

◆ **Tax-Free Growth.** All of the dividends, interest, capital gains, and other income generated by your investments while they are parked in a Roth IRA—brace yourself for this—will *never* be taxed as long as you make a qualified distribution ("qualified" meaning either after the age of 59½ or one of the specific exceptions permitted, which we'll discuss in a moment).

◆ **Passing Along the Wealth.** If you don't need the money you put into your Roth IRA to keep you in golf balls during retirement, the Roth offers an amazing tax break for your heirs. First, you don't have to start taking distributions at 70½, like you do with the traditional IRA. So you can leave your kids quite the tax-sheltered pile.

If you name a child (or children) as beneficiary, the monthly distributions from a traditional or a Roth IRA will go to that child upon your death. With the traditional IRA, the distributions are taxable. With the Roth, they aren't. And, of course, the money passed on to them continues to grow tax-free.

◆ **Withdrawals.** There is no age at which you must begin to make mandatory withdrawals. In practice, this means you could be 105 years old and still compounding your wealth into the stratosphere. Another huge benefit is that you can withdraw contributions to your Roth IRA without penalty, at any time.

For example, you have a Roth IRA and you contribute $4,000 to it this year, never touching it again. Five years later, your IRA has grown to $6,500. You face an emergency and want to take cash from your account (not a good idea, but hey …). You could withdraw up to the amount of your contributions (in this case, $4,000) without penalty. The $2,500 in profit, however, is subject to the customary rules, restrictions, and red tape.

◆ **Income Restrictions.** If you are married and filing jointly and have an adjusted gross income (AGI) of $169,000 or more, or you are a single, head of household, or married and filing separately with an AGI of $116,000 or more, you cannot contribute to a Roth IRA. No exceptions. It's tragic, we know. Attempt to console yourself with your six-figure income or run for Congress to change the law.

Avoiding the 10 Percent Early Withdrawal Penalty

The members of the United States Congress, being the kind souls that they are, permitted a handful of exceptions to the 10 percent penalty on early withdrawals. Here are a few ways cash taken out of your IRA can escape this dastardly fate (note that withdrawals from your traditional IRA are still subject to ordinary taxes):

◆ Proceeds are used to pay medical expenses that are not reimbursed and exceed more than 7.5 percent of your adjusted gross income.

◆ You become disabled and unable to secure gainful employment due to your injuries.

◆ You die (in which case, you probably don't care about the 10 percent early penalty anyway …).

◆ You are receiving distributions in the form of an annuity.

◆ The distributions are used for qualified higher education expenses—such as tuition, fees, books, supplies, and required equipment—for you, your spouse, your children, or other family members.

◆ You buy or build a first home for yourself, your spouse, your or your spouse's child, grandchild, parent, or other ancestor. There is a $10,000 lifetime limit to this exemption.

If you are considering taking an early withdrawal from your IRA, head over to www. irs.gov, read IRS Publication 590 and consult with a tax professional so you don't run afoul of the law and find yourself faced with a hefty penalty.

Which IRA Is Right for Me?

If you qualify, it is better to go with a Roth IRA due to its added flexibility and superior tax treatment. If your income fluctuates, you may want to set up both a Roth and a traditional IRA. That way, you can contribute to the Roth IRA in the years your income is low enough for you to qualify and contribute to the traditional IRA when your income is higher.

Traditional and Roth IRA Contribution Limits

Regardless of which type you ultimately choose, both the traditional and Roth IRA share the same Congressionally mandated contribution limits.

Year	49 and Younger	50 and Older
2005	$4,000	$4,500
2006	$4,000	$5,000
2007	$4,000	$5,000
2008	$5,000	$6,000
2009	$5,000	$6,000

The Least You Need to Know

◆ If your employer matches your 401(k) contributions, take advantage of this free money—even if you are currently in debt!

◆ If you have a defined benefit plan, ask human resources to help you figure out your monthly pension.

◆ If you take a lump-sum retirement payment, invest it in something that will generate income for you to live on.

◆ Don't over-invest in your company's stock.

◆ Stock options can be very profitable employment benefits.

◆ In general, the younger you are and the less money you make, the more attractive the Roth IRA option is.

Chapter 7

Solving Debt and Credit Problems

In This Chapter

- Checking your credit history
- Building good credit
- The five components of your FICO score
- Paying off debt versus investing

Credit can be either a tremendous boon to your financial life or a dangerous drain, depending upon how wisely you use it. Human beings have struggled with its temptations for centuries.

Credit preceded the coining of money by more than 2,000 years. Coinage is dated from the first millennium B.C.E., but old Sumerian documents, circa 3000 B.C.E., reveal a systematic use of credit based on loans of grain by volume and loans of metal by weight. These loans often carried interest.

About 1800 B.C.E., Hammurabi, a king of the first dynasty of ancient Babylonia, gave his people the earliest known formal code of laws. A number of the chief provisions of this code regulated the relation of debtor to creditor. The maximum rate of interest was set at 33⅓ percent per annum for loans of grain repayable in kind, and at 20 percent per annum for loans of silver by weight. All loans had to be accompanied by written contracts witnessed before officials. Land and other assets could be pledged against a debt. So could the creditor, as well as his wife, concubine, children, or slaves (and you thought you had it bad!). According to Sidney Homer in *A History of Personal Interest Rates*, personal slavery for debt was limited to three years.

Creditors may no longer be able to take your firstborn, but nothing can screw up your financial goals more than a whopping debt or a bad credit report. In this chapter, we show you how to avoid credit mishaps so you can get into great investing shape.

What Does Your Credit Report Say About You?

Before a credit card company issues you a card or a bank lends you money, they will check out your credit report. There are credit-reporting agencies (CRAs) that do nothing but gather information about you from bankers and other creditors and sell that information to banks, stores, and other issuers of credit.

Fiscal Facts _____

When you apply for a credit card, a bank loan, or any other form of credit, you typically sign something that gives permission to the creditor to obtain your credit history. The creditor subscribes to credit reporting agencies, which forward your credit report. The information on the credit report is based on what other creditors have reported about you.

If you've ever defaulted on a student loan, failed to pay off a charge account at a department store, or forgotten to pay a bill because you moved, rest assured that these transgressions are on your credit report in black and white. In addition, your report carries your Social Security number, your past and present addresses, and any other details of your financial life the credit-reporting agency has been able to snag. Pretty creepy, huh?

CRA Horror Stories

Nothing can be more upsetting than to discover—the hard way—that you have a bad credit report. Whenever you are turned down for credit, you can contact the credit agency whose information was used to turn you down and get a copy of the report for free. Ed was shocked when he was turned down for a credit card. He exercised his right to request a free copy of his credit report.

Ed's report was clean as a whistle, except for one little detail: a state tax *lien* of $130, filed on June 10, 1997, for the transfer tax on a home sold back in 1991. The actual tax was a measly $25; the $105 was interest.

Ed made a slew of phone calls. Finally someone at the state tax department explained that the state had gone after both the buyer and seller of Ed's house, but the buyer never responded and the seller (Ed) did not have a current address in their system. So the state filed the lien. It's a good thing Ed and his wife found this out before they refinanced their mortgage several months later, because it took a month to clear up.

What about you? Do you have something like this lurking in your report? Want peace of mind to know you haven't been the victim of identify theft? Do you want to wait until you try to buy a car, a house, or a gym membership to find out?

def•i•ni•tion

A **lien** is a legal right to take someone's property and hold it until the owner pays a debt.

How to Check Your Credit Reports

We recommend that you look at your credit reports from at least the top three CRAs every year. These are:

- TransUnion: www.transunion.com

- Experian: www.experian.com

- Equifax: www.equifax.com

By law, you are entitled to request a free copy of your credit report from each of these agencies once every 12 months. You can find information and complete the process at www.annualcreditreport.com. If you discover a discrepancy, you can use the contact information we provide in Appendix A to reach the appropriate CRA who can then help you resolve the problem.

If you own a business, you will want to run a credit check on it periodically, too. You might also want to be able to check on your customers' credit. The top credit-reporting agencies in this field are:

- Dun & Bradstreet: www.dnb.com

- Experian: www.experian.com

How do you get a copy of your report? Each CRA has slightly different policies, but basically you will have to answer several security questions, such as the originator of your outstanding loans, Social Security number, and address. Our information is accurate as of May 2009 but you can always contact the Federal Trade Commission. The FTC website is www.ftc.gov.

Don't make the mistake of thinking that because you've never used credit, you have good credit. What you have is no credit, and if you have no credit, you'll have a difficult time getting approved for mortgages or auto loans. Many *credit card* companies won't approve you, either. You need to establish a personal credit history that shows you can make regular payments on a debt over time.

Super Strategies

To establish good credit you must show that you can make regular payments on a debt over time. If you take out a loan, for example, and you get an unexpected inflow of cash that enables you to pay it off all at once, that's fine, but it doesn't demonstrate your ability to make regular payments, and thus won't improve your credit history.

---

def•i•ni•tion

A **charge card** allows you to "charge" an item, or buy it without paying cash at the time of purchase. You are expected to pay the purchase off within 30 days, whereas with a **credit card** you can make monthly minimum payments indefinitely.

Although banks and credit card companies tend not to lend to people with no credit history, department stores are usually willing to let someone with no credit history open a *charge card* account. A charge account lets you buy something without paying cash for it at the time of purchase. You are expected to pay the purchase off by the end of the month. Some charge accounts let you pay off only a minimum balance monthly and charge you interest on the remaining balance.

When you get your first charge account, make a few purchases each month and pay for them by the end of the month. Never miss a payment or pay late.

Finally, make sure your efforts to establish good credit are being reported to the CRAs. Check your reports six months after using a charge account or other credit regularly and if no positive information has been reported, ask the issuer of the credit you're using to send a report to the CRAs. Request a copy for yourself, also.

Debit Cards: A Better Choice?

Debit cards enable you to make purchases with a direct deduction from your checking account rather than a charge to a credit card account. They are often packaged together as a combination cash card (which can be used for deposits and withdrawals at banks or ATMs) and debit card.

Debit cards are very convenient, and you do avoid interest charges by using them instead of credit cards, but they can make it even more of a hassle to balance your checking account. You have to keep track of every little purchase you make with your debit card and enter it into your check register. You can quickly lose control of your balance and run into overdraft and service charges.

def•i•ni•tion

A **debit card** can be presented like a credit card when you make a purchase, but the cost is deducted from your checking account at the time of sale.

To avoid the risk of overdraft charges or bounced checks, open a line of credit with your checking account. Typically, there is no charge unless you actually use the line, whereupon the rate is around 11 to 12 percent. Guess what, though? If you apply for a line of credit, your bank will check your credit report. If there are any problems, you will be turned down for overdraft protection.

Credit card or debit card? The choice is yours. But if you opt for the debit card, keep close tabs on your checking account balance. This includes communication and coordination with your significant other! Also (and perhaps this is the most important part), your debit card is not going to be reported to your credit agency. This means that it will do absolutely nothing to improve your FICO score.

The Mysteries of Your FICO Score

A good credit score, also known as your FICO score (short for Fair Isaac Credit Organization), can make purchasing a home, financing an education, buying a car, or obtaining capital for your own business easy. Yet many individuals don't have a clue how their FICO score is calculated—or even worse—where they fall in the spectrum.

Range of FICO Scores (Chart)

500 to 559 (Worst)

560 to 619

620 to 674

675 to 699

700 to 719

720 to 850 (Best)

The FICO system is tiered; in practical terms, this means that if you have a 725 score, you are going to get the same deal as someone with an 830. Your score is determined by five variables, each weighted differently. These are discussed in the following sections.

Paying Your Bills on Time (35 Percent)

Whenever you make—or miss—a payment, it is reported to the credit bureaus. This data allows potential creditors to gauge the probability of you making your payments on time. If you haven't paid your bills in the last few months, for example, no one is going to lend you money at a reasonable rate because they can surmise that you are headed for trouble.

Ratio of Debt to Total Credit Limit (30 Percent)

Say you have several credit cards. You don't carry a balance on any of them; none have annual fees. Still, you decide you want to improve your credit so you cancel all but one. Smart move? Wrong! You have single-handedly taken a chainsaw to your credit score and the damage can take years to repair. (We know it doesn't sound logical, but that's how the system works! It's based on the theory that if other people are willing to lend you money, you are a better risk.)

Here's why: the second largest component of your credit score is the ratio between your debt balance and your available credit. If you carried $2,000 on one credit card and had six other cards with credit lines totaling $20,000, your debt-to-credit-limit ratio would be 10 percent ($2,000 balance divided by $20,000 available); very favorable. If, however, you cancelled all of these cards but the one—which had, say, a $3,000 limit—your ratio would skyrocket to 67 percent! Your FICO score is going to get hammered, driving up the interest rate you pay on your existing variable debt and any future borrowings.

An ideal solution is to leave all the accounts open, but cut up all but one of your cards. This way, your credit ratio remains unaffected, yet you also don't tempt yourself to use more than one card.

Length of Credit History (15 Percent)

The third largest component of your FICO score is the length of credit history. All else being equal, the longer your accounts have been open and in good standing, the higher your score. This is another reason you don't want to cancel your credit cards—doing so could hit you with a double-whammy on both the ratio of debt to total credit limit *and* the length of credit history components.

New Accounts, Credit Inquiries, and Recent Applications (10 Percent)

Each time you request a new credit card or apply for a new loan, this is noted on your credit report. If there is a lot of activity in a short amount of time—say, the most recent six months—this negatively affects your score. Lenders are wary of anyone who attempts to get a lot of credit quickly; they assume you may be in financial trouble. In order to protect this component, only request credit when absolutely necessary and you've done your research.

Mix of Credit Cards and Loans (10 Percent)

Fixed charges are far less attractive from the standpoint of a lender. The reason is simple. If you get into trouble, you can make smaller payments on your revolving accounts, such as credit cards. You don't have this option when writing the check for your car payment, student loans, or mortgage. That's why the type of debt you carry—fixed or revolving—affects your score.

Should I Pay Off My Debt or Invest?

With even small decisions affecting your credit score, how should you determine if you should pay off your debt or invest? As with all financial quandaries, the question can be answered using simple math. The secret? If you can earn a higher after-tax return on your investments than the after-tax interest expense on your debt, you should invest. Otherwise, you should pay off your balance.

Super Strategies

Even if you are paying astronomical interest rates on your credit cards, you should contribute to your 401(k) up to the point of your company's match. The reason? By taking the match—which is completely free money—you are instantly earning a 100 percent return.

Generally speaking, there are two categories of debt: good and bad. "Good" debt is debt which carries a low interest rate and, in many cases such as student loans and mortgages, the interest expense is tax-deductible. When put to the test, this type of debt will, more often than not, result in diverting cash to build your portfolio instead of paying off your balances. "Bad" debt, on the contrary, is subject to high, often nondeductible, interest; the archetype being credit cards. Except in extraordinarily rare cases, this kind of debt should be eliminated as soon as possible.

Let's take a look at two examples:

- **Example 1:** Ruby has $10,000 in credit card debt. The interest rate on her cards is currently 18 percent; it is not tax-deductible. She has 20 years until retirement. Should she pay off her debt or invest?

  First, we see that Ruby has a long-term horizon. Thus, she has the luxury of riding out the volatility of the stock market and earning a rate of return in the neighborhood of 10 to 12 percent. None of this money is in a tax-advantaged account, such as a 401(k) or an IRA, making her actual, expected after-tax return somewhere between 8 and 9.6 percent.

  It is clear that she has no reasonable hope of generating a return on her investments anywhere near that which she is paying on her debt. As a result, she should stop contributing to her investments and, instead, pay off the balance of her credit card entirely.

- **Example 2:** Aaron, a recent college graduate, has $20,000 in student loans, currently consolidated at a fixed rate of 2.5 percent. He just landed a new job with a starting salary of $50,000. He is wondering whether he should start building his portfolio or pay off his debt first.

  Student loan interest is tax-deductible. Assume Aaron's effective tax rate is 25 percent; lowering his after-tax interest expense to 1.875 percent. Because he has his entire career ahead of him, he expects to earn 10 percent after-tax on his investments through his equity investments in the stock market.

  Clearly he should make the absolute minimum payment on his student loan and stretch out the term as long as possible. In this case, the benefit for doing so is even more compelling because his cost of borrowing—in effect, the cost of keeping that $20,000 capital at work in his portfolio—is less than the historical long-term rate of inflation (3 percent). Thus, in actual *economic* terms, he is actually being *paid* 1.125 percent to not pay off the loan! (Here's the math: 1.875 percent after-tax interest expense minus 3 percent inflation = (1.125) percent interest;

how can you have negative interest? He is paying off the loan with dollars that are less valuable than they were the previous year. This wouldn't be possible if the interest rate were variable as opposed to fixed).

The Least You Need to Know

◆ Nothing can screw up your financial goals more than a bad credit report.

◆ Check your credit history once a year to catch errors.

◆ No credit is not the same as good credit; you have to use credit to build a credit history.

◆ If you want to use a debit card, get overdraft protection.

Chapter 8

Home Ownership: What You Need to Know

In This Chapter

- ◆ Down payment do's and don'ts
- ◆ Timing the real estate market
- ◆ Owning versus renting
- ◆ Choosing between fixed-rate and adjustable-rate mortgages
- ◆ Interest-only mortgages

Most everyone starts adult life renting rather than owning. Initially, you may not even be able to afford to rent on your own, hence your roommates and their socks on the living room floor. But some 5 to 10 years after you enter the workforce, with perhaps marriage and children either present or on the way, you may want to buy your first home. In this chapter, we run you through key questions to ask yourself before you make the big life change from lowly renter to king or queen of your castle.

The Down Payment

The halcyon days of no-down-payment, subprime mortgages vanished with the financial crisis of 2008. You will probably need to put down at least 10 percent, and in some cases up to 20 percent, of the purchase price of the home you want to buy in order to obtain mortgage approval. There are also some first-time homebuyer programs that don't require such high down payments—for example, VA loans and HUD programs.

Here are the best sources for your down payment, in order of preference:

◆ **Savings.** You planned ahead by putting aside the savings for 10 percent down, and you're ready to go.

◆ **A loan from good old Mom and Dad (or your spouse's mom and dad).** "We can pay it back at our convenience? At 0 percent interest?" Or how 'bout: "It's a gift? We couldn't possibly … well, if you insist!"

◆ **Tapping your retirement plans (Roth IRA, 401(k), etc.).** Borrowing from the Roth IRA is preferable. If you borrow from your 401(k), it's considered a loan that you must pay back.

> **Super Strategies**
>
> Consider moving through a series of steps toward owning your dream home. Most people end up doing this: rental to condo to town house to starter home to the big comfy house in the 'burbs. Skipping any of these steps may leave you financially strapped.

Do not borrow the money for your down payment. The cost of carrying what amounts to a first and second mortgage will most likely overtax you financially. If you approach your mortgage banker already carrying a debt like that, you might be turned down for the mortgage anyway.

Timing Is Everything

The next question to ask is: what's the real estate market like? Hot, medium, or cold? If it's hot, you run the risk of paying inflated prices, potentially coming in at the top of the market. This translates to a higher down payment and higher monthly payments (principal, interest, and, in many cases, real estate taxes). If you then have to move for any reason, you run the risk of having to sell at a loss.

If possible, follow your local real estate market for several years before even considering home ownership. Most local newspapers carry charts or tables that show you whether home sales in your area are trending up or down, and to what degree. You can also get a feel by going to open houses and requesting sales literature on around a dozen homes that might meet your needs.

Specifically, you'll want to observe two indicators:

◆ Has the asking price been reduced, and, if yes, how much and how many times?

◆ How many days has the house been on the market?

In a "hot" market, homes are gobbled up in a matter of days, and the buyer pays the asking price. In a really hot market, with two or more buyers vying for the same property, the "winner" ends up paying more than the asking price. You definitely do not want to make your first home purchase in this environment.

You should also check out mortgage interest rates, but home prices are a more important indicator of whether or not it's the right time to buy.

> **Super Strategies**
>
> A good rule of thumb: if you can handle the monthly payments on the home you want and you think it's selling at a good price, don't concern yourself with mortgage rates. Just focus on home prices. Don't forget, you can always refinance your mortgage if and when rates fall.

Re-Fi Mania

Refinancing a mortgage can be an effective way to reduce household expense, but banks are largely unwilling to refinance at the low interest rates we've seen since the 2008 crash. It's still wise to understand when and how you should refinance. You want to ensure your savings will make up for the additional costs within a year or two, or it's not worth doing. Here's how to figure that out:

1. Total all your closing costs (document fees, appraisal, title, etc.). Exclude the one month interest you'll be charged (interest is paid in arrears), because you'll make that up with a one month "holiday" on the new mortgage.

2. Deduct the new proposed monthly principal and interest payments from the existing P & I.

3. Divide item 2 into item 1. If the number is 12 (one year) or less, go for it. If above 24, forget it (remember, the average person only lives in his/her home for five years).

Evaluate Your Mortgage-Worthiness Before a Banker Does

After you start to keep tabs on the real estate market, make it a point to sit down with a mortgage banker and determine what he or she looks for in a successful applicant so you can compare that profile to your present situation. If you can't find a mortgage banker willing to do this, go to a knowledgeable and experienced real estate broker. If you present your personal balance sheet and income statement (which you learned how to create in Chapter 5), the expert can tell you if you could qualify for a mortgage and how large a mortgage you could handle. If you don't qualify, you can spend the next few years both following the local real estate market and getting in better financial shape.

Compare Renting to Owning

If you are thinking about buying a home, sit down and calculate the total cost of home ownership versus renting. When you rent, you pay a monthly rental fee and utilities. You may also pay for parking and laundry. That's about it. Home ownership, on the other hand, is not just about a monthly mortgage payment and taxes. There are many expenses you may not have considered, such as:

- ◆ Outside maintenance—yard work, painting, and equipment such as a lawn mower and leaf and snow blowers.

- ◆ Inside maintenance—carpet cleaning, floor sanding and coating, appliance maintenance, plumbing repairs, painting, and papering.

- ◆ Major repairs and replacements—Retain an inspection service to ascertain the expected life of your hot water heater, roof, siding, deck, etc. People stay in one home an average of five years, so for anything that will probably need to be replaced within five years, determine the cost and divide it by 60. Add this cost to your monthly payments.

On the bright side, your interest and taxes on a home are deductible, and you are gradually building up equity (ownership!) in your home. In addition, you won't be hit with yearly rent increases.

Over Time, Owning Should Save You Money

It's hard to come up with a specific example that is applicable to everyone, so let's make some broad assumptions and compare renting to owning over a 60-month (five-year) time frame:

Per Month	Rent	Purchase
Rent: $2,000 × (4% annual increase ÷ 2) =	$2,217	
Parking	160	
Utilities	100	$200
Laundry	24	12
Principal and Interest*		1,231
Transportation	50	50
Maintenance		250
Homeowners Insurance		50
Repairs		250
Taxes		300
Totals	2,551	2,343

*Assumptions: $225,000 purchase price, 10% down, the balance financed at 6¼ percent over 30 years.

Fiscal Facts

The Consumer Price Index (CPI) is a group of prices that are followed by economists in order to gauge whether inflation is on the rise or waning. The CPI is probably the most well-known and widely reported inflation number we have. What is not well known is that housing prices for both rental and owned residences make up 40 percent of the benchmark.

In this example, we have a pretty clear-cut case favoring purchase on cash flow basis alone. Considering you also own an asset that now has the potential to appreciate in value while building equity, and there is no question that owning is a better choice. Your case may be different.

Renting Pluses

Although it's generally considered preferable to buy, continuing to rent is definitely preferable to buying the wrong home at the wrong price at the wrong time in the real estate market. That's why we suggest spending some time watching the market and getting a feel for what constitutes a bargain in your price range and your area.

Owning your own home has always been considered part of the American dream, but for people who bought when the real estate market peaked in the 1980s and suffered huge losses when they needed to move, the American dream turned into a nightmare. That may be the case right now.

Remember, you're in charge; you decide when the time is right, and another year or two in a rental is not the end of the world. Be cool.

How Much of Your Income Should You Spend on Housing?

Twenty-five percent of your gross income is a reasonable sum to spend on housing. Some experts use up to 33 percent or even 50 percent, but let's be conservative! Our recommendation means that someone earning $100,000 can afford roughly $2,000 per month for housing. Assuming a $6\frac{1}{4}$ percent mortgage rate and a 30-year mortgage, principal and interest would equate to roughly $1,539 per month on a $250,000 mortgage, leaving $461 per month for taxes. That feels about right. And with 10 percent down and closing costs, you're looking at a $275,000 purchase. Naturally, taxes vary, as do home prices and what you get for your money. That $275,000 probably buys you a lot in Nebraska or North Dakota, but little (if anything) in San Diego, Boston, Chicago, or New York City.

Fixed-Rate vs. Adjustable-Rate Mortgage

Your mortgage banker may offer you a choice between the following:

◆ A fixed-rate mortgage that locks you into a given interest rate for the life of the mortgage, which is traditionally 30 years.

◆ An *adjustable-rate mortgage (ARM)*.

How long you intend to stay in the house is the key to your decision. An adjustable-rate mortgage can be a good deal if you plan to stay in your house for no more than five years, and if the rate is sufficiently below the rate for a 30-year fixed-rate mortgage. If the adjustable rate is not at least 200 basis points (2.0 percent) below the 30-year rate, it's not worth the risk of escalating interest rates to commit to it. Right now, for example, short-term and long-term interest rates are all very low and there's not much difference between them, so fewer new homeowners are taking out adjustable-rate mortgages

def•i•ni•tion

An **adjustable-rate mortgage (ARM)** is priced off the yield for the 10-year Treasury note. Since the yield on the note changes every six to twelve months, so will the interest rate on your ARM. And when short-term rates are lower than long-term rates, you may get a better deal with an ARM than with a long-term fixed mortgage. How much the ARM rate fluctuates over the duration of your mortgage depends on interest rates in general and the product itself. Most ARMs have a lifetime cap, above which the rate cannot rise.

You can also get three-year, five-year, or seven-year ARMs that lock in a fixed rate for three, five, or seven years, and then revert to an ARM. If you think rates are at or near their lows, these are much better than the traditional ARM with a "teaser" 6- to 12-month low rate.

I.O. for U?

IO (interest only) mortgages are another product in home financing. As the name implies, the monthly payments are for interest only, with nothing going to pay down the mortgage. In other words, you are going to be paying less each month but you are never going to make progress on paying down the principal. Here is a comparison of an IO versus an ARM. In each case, the principal amount being financed is $200,000, the mortgage rate is 5⅛ percent, and the fixed term is five years.

	IO	ARM	Difference
Monthly payment	$854	$1,089	–$235
Five-year totals	$51,240	$65,338	–$14,098
Mortgage reduction	—	$16,019	+$16,019

Even if we assume that the $235 monthly difference is invested at 5 percent per annum, the total of approximately $15,900 is still slightly below the mortgage pay down of the ARM. So are there any circumstances in which the IO would be preferable to an ARM? Yes, two:

◆ The IO allows you to qualify for a larger mortgage or a more expensive home. In some cases, it could be the only way you could qualify.

◆ If you have no other means to fully commit dollars to your 401(k), 403(b), 457 plan, IRA, or emergency fund, etc., then maybe this is a good option. But you risk just spending the difference. Be careful that the IO doesn't just become another IOU.

The Costs of Closing

Closing costs vary from state to state, depending on whether the state says attorneys are required to handle the closing and on real estate tax rates. Typically, you should be prepared to cover closing costs of around 3 percent of the price of the house before the keys are yours. In some cases, you can gain a concession from a motivated seller and convince them to pick up these expenses.

Following is a summary of a typical closing statement. As you can see, there are columns for the borrower (buyer) and seller. Looking just at the columns pertaining to the buyer, we see that the buyer ends up paying over $6,000 in closing/settlement costs.

Line:			
101	Contract sales price	$252,000.00	The amount you agreed to pay for the home
103	Settlement charges	6,384.81	Detailed below
120	Gross amount due from buyer	258,384.81	Total of lines 101 and 103
Less:			
201	Deposit of earnest	25,300.00	Down payment money
202	Principal amount of new loan	100,000.00	The buyer's new mortgage

| 220 | Total paid by buyer | 125,300.00 | Total of lines 201 + 202 |
| 303 | Additional cash from buyer | 133,084.81 | Sum buyer must come up with at closing |

Summary of Settlement Charges (Line 103)

802	Loan discount	2,000.00	Buyer paid "points" (two) to get lower mortgage rate
904	Three months real estate taxes	1,548.22	Three months real estate taxes
905		6.94	Property overlaps two municipalities
1107	Attorney's fees	950.00	For the "closing"
1108	Title insurance	1,708.00	Required
1201	Recording fees	70.00	Required
1204	Notice of settlement	16.00	Required
1303	Faxes	45.65	
1304	UPS	40.00	
1400	Total Settlement Charges	6,384.81	Lines 802–1304

Second Mortgages: Pros and Cons

Once you own a home, you will be bombarded with offers for a second mortgage. Second mortgages are tax-deductible, but they place you in a financial straightjacket. With a second mortgage, you sign for a fixed-rate loan for the full amount of equity in your home. You might not need or use all the money, but you sure are paying interest on it. A second mortgage is either a desperation step for someone who wants to finance a dramatic career shift, or a short-term means of coming up with the down payment on your first (starter) home. Do not enter into it lightly.

Typically, a home equity loan is a better deal because it is a revolving line of credit—you only pay for what you use (like a charge card), and you can still deduct the interest from your taxes. This has normally been a very convenient and relatively low-cost source of cash, but that has changed due to the credit crisis. Typically, your bank will extend a line of credit to you, representing the difference between the market value of your home and the size of your mortgage. In a rising home market, this differential just keeps getting bigger and bigger.

Well, the opposite is happening right now. If you have an unused or partially used equity line of credit, check with your friendly banker to see to what extent it has "shrunk." You could be in for a rude surprise!!

Pluses and Pitfalls of Paying Off Your Mortgage

Mortgage (or rent) represents the largest single expenditure for the average taxpayer. It's wise, therefore, to try to retire your mortgage before you retire yourself. There are three ways to accomplish this:

◆ Stay in your home for 15 to 30 years and pay off the mortgage.

Fiscal Facts _____

There is a capital gains tax exclusion on your home of $250,000 for an individual and $500,000 for a couple. But to qualify you must have lived in the house for at least two of the past five years. Are there any exceptions? Yes! For job (transfer) or health reasons. Simply divide the number of months you actually lived in the home by 24 months (minimum required). Now multiply that figure by either $250,000 (individual) or $500,000 (joint return) to get your exclusion. Want more info? Request IRS Publication 523.

◆ Pay off half the mortgage, sell your home, and buy a condo/town house at half the price of your former home.

◆ Benefit from escalating home values. If your home rises in value 50 percent in five years, for example, sell your home and buy a condo/town house at half the price. This is beyond your control.

All of that extra cash can improve your standard of living and provide investment capital for you to build your portfolio (and increase the size of the estate you ultimately bequeath to your heirs or charitable causes).

The biggest drawback, however, is that a lack of a mortgage can seriously affect the components of your FICO score. This could make it difficult for you to obtain financing for future purchases and possibly even increase the interest rate you are paying on your existing debt.

Should You Shorten Your Mortgage?

Moving from a 30-year to a 15-year mortgage can make a big difference. Here's an example using a 60-month occupancy assumption and a $200,000 mortgage. The figures are very rough and just for purposes of illustration.

30-year mortgage, 6¼ percent*, monthly principal and interest = $1,231

15-year mortgage, 5¾ percent*, monthly principal and interest = $1,660

Difference per month = $429

You can get a rough approximation by adding or subtracting $15 for each ⅛ percent rates go up or down.

In essence, making a bigger monthly mortgage payment goes a long way toward building equity and reducing the mortgage on your property. In addition, you're going to save a substantial amount of interest expense. For a $200,000 mortgage with a 6.5 percent rate, for example, the total interest paid over 30 years would amount to around $243,319; on the 15-year mortgage, the total cumulative interest would only be $108,672, a savings of $134,647.

The 15-year mortgage just forces you to save. Depending upon the interest rate you are paying, however, it might be more profitable to take the longer mortgage and its smaller mortgage payments and invest the $429 that you save each month into a tax-deferred investment. This way you get the tax break and the benefits of compound interest.

The Relocation Package

If you are moving to take a new job or because you've been transferred by a new employer, look into whether your firm offers a "relocation package." Some aspects of a relocation package may be classified as compensation, meaning you'll have to pay income tax on it, but that's still better than paying all moving expenses out of pocket. The "job relo" may include any or all of the following:

1. Prepaid moving services

2. Special financing rates

3. Purchase of your existing home (and/or the sub-leasing of an apartment for you in the new area until you sell your home)

4. A "buyer's broker" paid for by your employer

If you don't have a job relo, go to a reputable real estate firm and ask for a licensed realtor with at least five years' experience. Be specific about your housing needs, such as size, style, price range, transportation, and schools. If good schools are an important part of your decision, ask the realtor for the names of the best school systems and cross-check the list with your employer. And bore in on real estate taxes. Remember, it's not the current taxes on the home that matter, it's what your tax bill will be if you purchase the property.

Should you use a "buyer's broker"? Before answering that question, let's make sure you understand who pays and who receives residential real estate commissions. A typical real estate commission of, say, 6 percent is split 3 percent to the listing broker (and his/her firm) and 3 percent to the selling broker (and his/her firm). The home seller pays the 6 percent. The selling broker is a sub-agent who represents the seller, not you. You are free to go to as many brokers as you wish to be shown properties.

When you use a buyer's broker, on the other hand, you sign a written contract with a specific broker who will represent you, the buyer. You, in turn, agree to only work with that broker. That 3 percent selling commission still comes from the seller's proceeds, only it goes to your buyer's broker. We think tilting the odds a little away from the seller and toward the buyer makes sense, so we recommend that you use a buyer's broker.

> **Crash Alert**
>
> Choosing the 30-year over the 15-year mortgage is financially sound if you really, truly have the discipline to invest what you would have had to pay monthly on the 15-year mortgage in your retirement account. If you find you're just spending that extra few hundred dollars a month, then opt for the 15-year mortgage.

Renting Out Your Home When You Move

Nobody wants to temporarily own two homes: the one you just purchased and the one that hasn't sold yet. But that situation arises more often than not. And if the prospective buyer knows your situation, you've lost some negotiating leverage.

What to do? Well, it depends primarily on market conditions and secondarily on your particular property. If the market is strong (or even stable), the economy is decent, and you have a tract home, one to two months of patience will probably pay off. Check with your broker to make sure your home is competitively priced; this is no time to be reaching for top dollar. Chances are, you know by the number of "showings" and offers (if any) whether or not you have a problem. If the market or the economy is weak, or if you have an atypical home (say, an offbeat architectural style or a less-than-accessible location), you may want to consider renting it out or renting it with an option to buy.

If you decide to rent your property, plan on offering a one- to two-year rental; shorter-term rental tenants are less likely to take care of your property. And remember, your end objective is still to sell your home. The complication is that you have to maintain your property while being geographically removed.

Unless you already have a willing tenant, you'll need to retain a broker to list your property as a rental. Typically, they will receive, up front, 10 percent of the yearly rent.

Real Estate Agents

We've all heard stories about how Jack and Mary sold their home themselves and saved $6,000, $12,000, or $18,000. What you don't hear about are the Bills and Nancys who overpriced their home, were excluded from multiple listing and relocation sources, and had no marketing plan. Their home sat on the market for months with few showings and no offers.

Not only do you waste time in this situation, you get a reputation for having an overpriced home. When you do get showings, it may simply be brokers using your home to show how attractive another property is on a price basis. We strongly urge you to get a broker; just be sure he/she is experienced. Ask for references and determine how much property the broker has sold during each of the previous three years. A good broker is worth more than the cost of the commission. Make sure your house is presentable, and don't restrict access to potential buyers.

If you are buying, by all means sign up with a buyer's broker. As we said, it's the only way to at least partially even the odds.

Closing the Deal

In a seller's market, you will get one or more offers at or very close to your asking price in a very short period of time. Lucky you! Make sure all parties agree to your closing terms, and let the process sort out the highest bidder.

In a buyer's market, you (and your broker) will have to "walk up" the bid. A low bid may be insulting, but don't let personal feelings get in the way of a business deal. Come down a little on your asking price and see what the prospective buyer does. Chances are the buyer was just trying to judge your level of desperation. After a few more rounds of this, your broker will offer this famous phrase: "Let's split the difference." Now, your soul-searching begins. Yes … no … maybe? It's a fine line between keeping the negotiations going and killing the deal. Listen to your broker, and good luck!

The Least You Need to Know

- ◆ Don't borrow the money for your down payment; you might get turned down for a mortgage.

- ◆ Try to follow your local real estate market for several years before buying a home.

- ◆ Evaluate your mortgage-worthiness before a banker does.

- ◆ Continuing to rent is definitely preferable to buying the wrong home at the wrong price and time.

- ◆ Retire your mortgage before you retire yourself.

- ◆ Use an experienced broker to sell your home—the money you might save trying to sell your home yourself will not be worth the headaches and hassle a good broker can prevent.

Funding Your Own (or Your Child's) Education

In This Chapter

- ◆ Setting up educational funds
- ◆ Withdrawing from a Roth IRA to pay for college
- ◆ Coverdell Education Savings Accounts
- ◆ Evaluating qualified tuition programs

When it comes to educating yourself, your children or your grandchildren, there's both good and bad news. The bad news is that college expenses continue to grow by at least two times the overall inflation rate in this country and the average family income. The good news is that an increasing percentage of college enrollees are getting financial aid. In addition, several options, such as 529 Plans and Coverdell Education Savings Accounts, make saving for college easier than ever.

An Overview of College Costs

Expenses for college vary dramatically, depending upon whether your child attends a state school or a private college or university. Between 2000 and 2005, the average cost of tuition for students attending four-year public universities jumped 40 percent. Private school tuitions, in contrast, only rose about 19 percent. Currently, the average state school tuition is $5,836, and the average private school tuition is $22,218.[1] When you add such expenses as fees, room and board, books, and supplies, of course, your total nut gets larger. Here are some figures from Sallie Mae, the United States' largest college student loan company:

◆ **Two-year colleges**. Average published tuition and fees at public schools in 2007–2008 are $2,361, $95 (4.2 percent) higher than in 2006–2007.

◆ **In-state students at public four-year colleges and universities**. Average published tuition and fees in 2007–2008 are $6,185, $381 (6.6 percent) higher than they were in 2006–2007. Average total charges, including tuition and fees and room and board, are $13,589, 5.9 percent higher than a year earlier.

◆ **Out-of-state students at public four-year colleges and universities**. Average published tuition and fees in 2007–2008 are $16,640, $862 (5.5 percent) higher than they were in 2006–2007. Average total charges are $24,044, 5.4 percent higher than a year earlier.

◆ **Private four-year colleges and universities**. Average published tuition and fees in 2007–2008 are $23,712, $1,404 (6.3 percent) higher than they were in 2006–2007. Average total charges, including tuition and fees and room and board are $32,307, 5.9 percent higher than a year earlier.

These figures give you an idea of the magnitude of the challenge faced by families trying to put several kids through college.

An Investment That Really Pays

One of the best investments you will ever make in your life is an education. On average, a person who holds a Bachelor's degree will earn $1 million more over the course of their lifetime than someone who graduated from high school only; a very real return on both time and capital employed. More important, an education will provide you with an improved ability to think, analyze, and study—traits that can make it easier for you to spot opportunities.

[1] *Washington Post, "College Costs Rise, But Not As Much," November 25, 2007*

You've already learned the difference between "good" and "bad" debt. Student loans are certainly one of the most attractive types of debt available thanks to the relatively low cost, the ability to lock in an interest rate through consolidation, the deductibility of interest expense for income tax purposes, and the subsequent increase in earnings that results from a higher education. Still, for those of you who want to start your life off with little or no debt, we're going to give you the lowdown on the investing options available to you so you can be prepared to write a check when the bursar calls.

> **Super Strategies**
>
> Involve your child in the decision about where to go to college by getting him or her a copy of *The College Handbook*, published by the College Entrance Examination Board. The handbook profiles 3,215 colleges and will definitely get you and your soon-to-be campus star excited and motivated.

Put Your Financial Security First

Maybe you're a parent who wants to start planning for your child's college education. That's a fine, noble goal. However, it should be the last thing on your list. Contributing to your retirement plan, building an emergency cash fund, purchasing a house, paying down debt—all of these should come first. There are numerous loans, scholarships, grants, work-study programs, and other options to help your child attend school. There are not, however, any special financial programs to help you fund your retirement. In other words, your child has many options at age 18: college first; work, then college; work-study program; no college; the military; and so on. Your retirement only has two options: either you have the money to retire or you don't. And don't forget two other issues:

♦ Where your child goes to college is driven more by his or her academic and extracurricular accomplishments than by your checking account.

♦ Your child is capable of contributing to his or her college education via summer or part-time work, and probably will be a better person for doing so.

Establishing an Education Fund

There are three questions that need to be answered when setting up funds for a college education.

1. What is the most appropriate investing vehicle for your education fund? Your best options include:

    ◆ Traditional or Roth IRAs.

    ◆ *Coverdell Education Savings Accounts (ESAs).* These used to be called Education IRAs.

    ◆ 529 Plans or QSTPs (Qualified State Tuition Programs).

    ◆ Patriot Bonds (formerly EE Savings Bonds)

2. What scholarships, grants, and loans are available for student expenses or reimbursement? Presently, programs available include:

    ◆ Hope Scholarships

    ◆ Pell Grants

    ◆ Lifetime Learning Credits

    ◆ Student loans

    ◆ Employer-paid educational assistance

3. Finally, should the securities or other assets you intend to save be in your name or the child's name?

def•i•ni•tion

The Education IRA was introduced in 1998. It has since been renamed **Coverdell Education Savings Accounts (ESAs).** The contribution limit was raised from $500 per year per child to $2,000. You can make contributions annually until your kids hit 18. Withdrawals for qualified educational purposes are tax-free.

Using a Traditional or Roth IRA to Save for College

The 10 percent additional tax on withdrawals from a traditional or Roth IRA before age 59½ can be waived for qualified higher education expenses. "Qualified" expenses include tuition, room and board, books, fees, and supplies.

Coverdell Education Savings Accounts (ESAs)

Like the Roth IRA, the Education IRA was introduced in the late 1990s. It has since been renamed the Coverdell Education Savings Account (ESA). Contributions are tax-deferred but not deductible, and are limited to $2,000 per year, per beneficiary. You can make contributions annually until your little rascal(s) turn 18. Withdrawals for qualified educational purposes are tax-free. The income eligibility for married contributors was raised by the 2002 tax law changes to $190,000. As a couple's income increases from $190,000 to $220,000, which is double the range for unmarried persons, their contribution limit phases out.

Qualified Tuition Programs (Section 529s)

Public or private schools may establish tax-exempt prepaid tuition programs, also referred to as Section 529 Plans. Section 529 plans are accounts that may be established by anyone—parents, other relatives, or friends of the family. The investment grows tax-free and distributions are tax-free when used to pay for tuition and other education expenses at any accredited college or university.

This is a smart idea for grandparents, who can contribute up to $12,000 per year ($24,000 for couples) without triggering the federal gift tax. You can even make a one-time contribution of as much as $60,000 ($120,000 from a couple) and spread the gift tax exclusion over the next five years. Not a bad way for grandparents to help out and avoid estate and gift taxes.

Interestingly, unlike with ESA and custodial accounts, you don't give up control of the Section 529 plan when the child reaches 18. You still control when withdrawals are taken and for what purposes. A delight for the control freaks among us!

Prior to 1998, these programs had to be state-sponsored. Withdrawals from qualified programs may be made for tuition, fees, room and board, books, and supplies. And, thanks to the Tax Relief Act of 2001, these specific withdrawals are tax-free. You can't contribute to both qualified tuition programs and an ESA in the same year, however.

Here's how a typical plan, the UNIQUE College Investing Plan, sponsored by the State of New Hampshire and managed by Fidelity Investments, works:

◆ To fund your account, you can sign up for Fidelity Automatic Account Builder (FAAB), with automatic transfers from your checking account of as little as $50 per month. All contributions must be in cash (via check). Families who don't establish automatic contribution plans can start an account with as little as $1,000.

◆ Your funds are invested in "lifestyle" portfolios consisting of Fidelity Mutual Funds that automatically shift the allocation of your assets between equity and fixed income as the beneficiary (your child) ages. A newborn might be invested 88 percent equity/12 percent bonds, while at college age the ratios might shift to 20 percent equity/40 percent bonds/40 percent short-term bonds and money market instruments—freeing up funds to pay for college. The stock/bond ratio for your child would be dependent upon his or her age upon entering the program. Alternatively, you can invest in fixed asset allocations.

◆ Fidelity uses no-load mutual funds, so the account will be charged only for the operating expenses. In addition, there is a fee of 0.30 percent of your account assets per year and a $30 annual maintenance fee (waived for accounts over $25,000 or if you sign up for FAAB).

◆ You can increase your monthly contributions with FAAB at any time if you start earning more money or decide that you've underestimated potential education costs.

◆ Earnings grow tax-deferred until they are distributed. If the distributions are for qualified education expenses, they are exempt from federal income tax; check with your state to determine state tax status.

◆ There are no adjusted gross income (AGI) restrictions or qualifications.

◆ Multiple accounts can be opened for your child by grandparents and other relatives. Joint accounts are not allowed, however. You cannot contribute more than the amount necessary to provide for the qualified education expenses of the beneficiary.

◆ You can change the beneficiary to another child. If you distribute the assets to someone besides the designated beneficiary, however, or if the funds are not used to pay qualified education expenses, you will be socked with state and federal taxes, as well as a 10 percent penalty.

◆ Contributions are considered completed gifts, so the value of an account won't be included in the donor's estate when he or she dies. You can also give up to $55,000 ($110,000 if filing jointly) in one year without gift tax as long as you opt to apply the $11,000 annual exclusion over five years.

◆ You can invest in both a UNIQUE Plan and a Coverdell ESA in the same year. Your child can also benefit from Hope Scholarship and Lifetime Learning Credits, which are discussed later. If you claim these credits, however, you cannot make a tax-free withdrawal to pay for the same expenses. If you do, your 529 withdrawal may be taxable.

◆ You can use the assets to pay for qualified education expenses at any accredited institution of higher learning, not just New Hampshire schools.

◆ Qualified withdrawals may also be tax-free at the state level if you are a resident of that particular state.

◆ Qualified education expenses include tuition, fees, room and board, books, and supplies.

This is just a summary of the UNIQUE Plan. You will want to delve more deeply into the matter before proceeding, but it looks pretty nifty to us.

Fidelity, Vanguard, TIAA-CREF, and Salomon Smith Barney are just some of the institutions offering 529 plans.

Each plan has different fees, so shop around. We suggest you start by contacting your State Treasurer's office. You can also mine the State Treasurer's website at www.collegesavings.org. Alternatively, check out www.savingforcollege.com.

Pros and Cons of 529 Plans

Just so we are on the same page, you understand that 529s are for college and university expenses, right? Good (just checking to make sure you're awake)! Now a quick summary of the pros and cons:

Pros

◆ Contributions qualify for annual gift tax exclusion.

◆ Assets enjoy tax-free growth.

◆ You have the option of accelerating the annual gifting provision fivefold (e.g., $11,000 × 5 = $55,000).

- Distributions can cover tuition, fees, books, equipment, and room and board.

- The donor (you) has the power to change the beneficiary.

- Payment does not have to be made directly to the school; you can reimburse the beneficiary.

Cons

- A penalty is assessed if the funds are used for any purpose other than education.

- Contributions must be in cash.

- Although you can change the beneficiary, there may be gift tax consequences.

- Whatever you give for the 529 must be deducted from your annual max ($11,000) or the five-year max ($55,000).

- Be careful if you mix 529s with the Hope or Lifetime Learning Credits we will discuss in the next section.

Tax Breaks for Education Expenses

As we said at the beginning of this chapter, there are all kinds of ways to defray expenses for college—and more are coming on-line all the time. Here's a breakdown of the ... breaks!

The Hope Scholarship Credit

Started in 1998, the Hope Scholarship Credit allows parents to take a credit against federal income taxes for tuition and related expenses. The credit is limited to the first two years of undergraduate education and consists of 100 percent of the first $1,000 of qualified expenses, and 50 percent of the second $1,000. Thus, the maximum credit you can take in the first two years is $1,500 per year. Warning: the credit is phased out for married taxpayers filing jointly with a modified AGI between $85,000 and $105,000 ($42,000 and $52,000 for individual filers). These amounts are adjusted for inflation.

Lifetime Learning Credits

Lifetime Learning Credits were also introduced in 1998. These are credits you can take for education expenses that are not eligible for the Hope credit. Included are expenses incurred to acquire or improve job skills. The credit is 20 percent of expenses up to $10,000 per year. The Lifetime has income credit AGI phaseouts identical to the Hope.

Mix and Match Carefully

Assume you are looking at a $3,000 tuition bill (obviously, your kid is going to a state school!), and you take the Hope credit, which reduces your income taxes. But you still have to come up with $3,000. Use the 529? Wrong! You can use the 529 for the first $1,000, but the other $2,000—equal to the Hope credit—must come from someplace else: your pocket, your checking account, Aunt Martha …. If not, you owe taxes and a 10 percent penalty on the amount involved.

The Education-Loan Interest Deduction

Those of you with a modified AGI of less than $65,000 (individual return) or $130,000 (joint return) may be eligible to deduct the interest paid on your student loans. This deduction can decrease your income taxes by up to $2,500. Incidentally, the interest paid is deducted "above the line," meaning you do not have to itemize to claim the deduction. What's the best choice? Be guided strictly by your AGI. If you qualify, go for the Hope/Lifetime credits; otherwise, use the tax deductions.

Patriot Bonds (formerly EE Savings Bonds)

Following the events of September 11, 2001, EE Savings Bonds were renamed The Patriot Bonds. These savings bonds can be either plugged into Coverdell ESAs or Roth IRAs, or used on their own to save for college. There are some disadvantages to using savings bonds, however:

◆ The yield is fixed at 90 percent of a five-year Treasury note, and is recalculated every six months. If Treasury note rates fall, so does the rate on your bond. If the five-year Treasury note is yielding 3.25 percent, the Patriot Bond is yielding 2.925 percent. But if six months later the Treasury note yield drops to 2.75 percent, your bond starts earning only 2.475 percent. Of course, the yields could go up, too!

- Although you can redeem (cash in) a Patriot bond after six months, you will pay a three-month interest penalty unless you wait at least five years to redeem it. To avoid the penalty, you have to really plan ahead when using savings bonds for college. You'll need to stop purchasing the bonds five years before the last college bills come due.

- You also have to deal with a limit of $15,000 purchase price per purchaser per year.

Patriot savings bonds do have some great advantages:

- You can purchase them for as little as $25 ($50 face value).

- They make great gifts from relatives.

- The interest income on an EE savings bond is free of state and local taxes. The federal taxes on interest income are due only when the EE savings bond is redeemed. In some instances, there is a tax exclusion if the proceeds are being used for postsecondary education.

Cool, but how does this work? First of all, the exclusion is limited to tuition and required fees. In this case, it may not be applied to room, board, or books. Second, the bonds must be registered in the name of the taxpayer, not the child, although the child can be named as beneficiary.

In addition, the qualified tuition and fees paid must be equal to or greater than the amount of money received when the bonds are redeemed. If you pay tuition and fees of $5,000 and the bond proceeds are no more than $5,000, you're qualified for the exclusion. If tuition and fees are $4,000 and the bond proceeds are $5,000, you can deduct only that ratio ($4,000 – $5,000 = 80 percent) of the interest income on the bonds (not the principal). Don't you love how confusing this stuff is?

Fiscal Facts _____

You can get more information on Patriot Bonds and other U.S. Treasury issues at www.savingsbonds.gov.

Finally, to qualify for the tax exclusion, you have to earn less than the modified AGI limits. Currently, benefit is phased out for modified adjusted gross incomes of $89,750—$119,750 for couples filing jointly and $59,850—$74,850 for single filers. In other words, you can get full exclusion if you earn under $89,750, and partial exclusion scaling down to zero once you earn over $119,750. Did you notice that we tucked in the word "modified"?

In this case, modified AGI is AGI plus the interest earned on the redeemed bonds. Ah, the tax code! But wait: there's another neat way to use EE savings bonds for a child's college expense. Buy the bonds in the child's name and file a tax return with the child's Social Security number. Then report the accrued (earned but not received) interest income on the bonds for that year. You won't need to file again and no tax is due unless or until the child's total income exceeds the threshold for taxes owed ($650). If tax is owed, it is at the parent's rate for children under age 14 and at the child's rate at age 14 or older.

It is unfortunate that the regulations on EE savings bonds are so complicated because they have a lot to offer parents saving for college. But that's the Feds for you.

Other Options

We have no intention of exploring every conceivable option for financing an education in this chapter. Our intention was to primarily explore investment options.

But do take a look at two other important prospects:

- ◆ **Student loans or so-called Stafford loans.** These are available from the government's "Sallie Mae" program (www.salliemae.com, 1-888-2-SALLIE). Stafford loans are for 10 years and the interest rate is set annually on July 1, based on the last 91-day T-bill auction in May. Also, you can take one opportunity to consolidate any outstanding Stafford loans.

- ◆ **Scholarships.** First, check with the college your child wants to attend to find out whether he or she is eligible to apply for any scholarships. Definitely call local organizations such as the Rotary Club or Kiwanis, which often sponsor scholarships for deserving students. Remember that grants or scholarships do not have to be repaid, loans do. Your college can also help you determine whether your child qualifies for financial assistance in the form of Pell grants or other government-sponsored grants. Financial aid is defined in terms of demonstrated need; total college expense less family contribution equals demonstrated need.

Sorting Out All the Options

Now, how do you sort out all these complicated alternatives? It seems that the best tax-incentive alternatives are available to low-income parents, who may also be most likely to obtain scholarship dollars for their child.

On the other hand, these parents face a level of complexity that would challenge an accountant. Parents over the AGI limits, meanwhile, can feel very frustrated. Let's list the alternatives we've discussed on a best-to-worst basis, both for those with a qualifying AGI and those above it.

If you earn at or below the AGI minimum:

- Coverdell Education Savings Account—Benefit specific (education) and ideal for larger families.

- Roth IRA—Not education specific, but same qualifications and benefits.

- EE savings bonds—Register in your name; also request gifts in child's name. Not all education expenses covered.

- Scholarships—Must pursue and apply shortly before matriculation.

- Hope/Lifetime Credits—If you have to borrow, use these tax deductions.

- Student Loans—Last resort.

If your earnings are over the AGI minimum:

- 529 Plans (qualified tuition programs)—Choose the variable option over the fixed one; this gives you a better shot over time at making more money.

- Traditional IRA—Use the education expense option.

- EE savings bonds—Keep in child's name; ditto for gifts; don't bother with annual tax filing.

- Taxable portfolio—Invest in index equity funds or passive equities; mix with EE bonds.

- Hope/Lifetime Credits—See if you qualify.

- Student Loans—See Sallie as a last resort.

In Whose Name?

Parents ask us all the time whether they should keep education funds in their name or in the kid's name. This issue revolves around taxes versus trust. If the assets are put in the child's name, the tax bite is going to be less. But if the assets are in the child's name, the child can choose to cash them in and move to Bali to study puppetry, rather than attend your alma mater. The very thought sends some parents into a spin. Then again, the young woman who designed the award-winning sets for Disney's Broadway production of *The Lion King* went to Bali to study puppetry, to the probable mortification of her parents, and she's doing awfully well! On the other hand, if the assets are in the child's name, it can reduce a child's financial aid eligibility.

We come down on the side of holding taxable education assets in the child's name for the lower tax hit. If you are concerned that your child might abuse these assets, your problems are far greater than financing a college education.

The Least You Need to Know

- ◆ We've said it before, we'll say it again; don't jeopardize your retirement to pay for your kids' education.

- ◆ Put your education savings in traditional and Roth IRAs, and Coverdell ESAs and EE savings bonds.

- ◆ 529 College Savings Plans (QTPs) are tax-exempt, prepaid tuition programs; one of the most interesting is the UNIQUE College Investing Plan.

- ◆ Several income tax credits are now allowed by the IRS for education expenses.

- ◆ Hold taxable education dollars in your child's name for a smaller tax bite.

Part 3

Investing 101

It is not the return on my investment that I am concerned about; it is the return of my investment.

—Will Rogers

You've made it this far, and now you're ready for the meat and potatoes! Part 3 will endow you with a thorough understanding of the investments that are likely to make up a majority of your portfolio—common and preferred stock, fixed income securities, mutual funds, and real estate investment trusts. We'll even tell you what you should look for in a broker.

Sit back, relax, grab a big cup of coffee and a highlighter ... we're about to demystify that venerable place called Wall Street. Part 3 explains how stocks and bonds and mutual funds work. You'll learn how to pick up the phone and order research material that'll make sense to you. You'll know how to contact and use a broker. You'll be ready to start designing a sturdy investment portfolio that will help you meet your investment objectives.

Chapter 10

What Are They Up to on Wall Street, Anyway?

In This Chapter

- What you need to know about Wall Street
- How to read stock tables
- Understanding P/E ratios
- Rebalancing and dollar-cost averaging
- Choosing a broker

Corporate America is not only a key employer of many of the citizens of this country, but it is owned by them. Corporations sell stock in exchange for ownership. The stock market represents this ownership, and, as we were reminded by the market's reaction to the wave of corporate scandals in 2002, when corporations go bad, that's bad for America.

Investors watched billions of dollars in stock market holdings collapse as Enron imploded, WorldCom filed for bankruptcy, and Global Crossing, Adelphia Communications, and Tyco scandals came to light, followed by SEC inquiries into stalwarts like Johnson & Johnson.

Congress promptly passed a corporate-oversight bill designed to discourage "creative" bookkeeping, diminish conflicts of interest, and crack down on financial abuses. It was watershed legislation—perhaps the most important since the 1930s laws enacted after the Great Depression that brought much-needed regulation to the stock market. Others questioned whether it would really have much impact.

It was useful legislation, but nonetheless in 2008 investors suffered through another stock market crash, this time brought on by a bursting housing bubble and the resultant credit freeze. The nerves of investors were understandably frayed by the wild swings in the stock market. The losses were certainly painful. Nonetheless, we live (and hope to prosper) in a capitalist society, and the capital is largely provided by the stock market. Historically, the market has recovered from worse times and has gone on to make investors wealthy. If you learn how it works, you'll learn how to protect yourself from its volatility and still earn great returns on your investments.

The Purpose of Wall Street

Wall Street is a financial district in lower Manhattan where the New York Stock Exchange and the American Stock Exchange are located, as are the headquarters of many investment banks and brokerage firms. In the vernacular, however, Wall Street is used to refer to the investment community at large. "The Street," as it is known, has two components, each with its own purpose: the primary market and the secondary market.

The Primary Market

Imagine you own a chocolate company. After years of building the business, you've increased sales to $100 million and net income to $25 million. You continue to reinvest the profits and occasionally use bank loans to expand, yet you find it difficult to get enough capital to go to the next level. Frustrated, you don't know where to turn.

You're in luck, my friend! Wall Street may have the answer. You can call an investment bank, and begin the process of "going public." Here's a simplified version of what is going to happen. First, your investment banker is going to value your business; in your case, they may tell you the chocolate company is worth $300 million. After some discussion, they decide they want the opening stock price to be $25 per share, so they cut the company up into 12 million shares ($300 million divided by $25 = 12 million shares).

At this point, you will decide how much of your business you want to sell and how much you want to keep. You may, for example, decide to sell 45 percent of the company, or 5.4 million shares worth a collective $135 million, to the public. The investment banker you worked with throughout the process (known as the "managing house" or "lead underwriter") is going to call several other investment bankers on Wall Street and form a syndicate. This syndicate will then purchase those shares from the company.

During this time, the underwriting syndicate holds the bag—that is, if the market collapses, it doesn't matter to the company because the underwriter is the one that owns the securities, albeit temporarily. In exchange for this holding risk and other services rendered, the investment banker will be paid a fee; normally around 7 percent of the gross proceeds raised during the initial public offering ("IPO"). In exchange, the business is going to receive a $100-million-plus check for the proceeds of the offering. Now you have capital to open new stores, build new factories, hire additional employees, acquire other companies, or any other activity that management believes will generate attractive returns.

The underwriter is going to sell the shares it has purchased of your chocolate business to the general public through any number of methods; best-effort basis, competitive *bid*, negotiated purchase, privileged subscription, or direct sale, to name a few. This placement—investors purchasing directly from the underwriter—is known as the "primary market."

def•i•ni•tion

> The ask price is the lowest price a seller is willing to accept for a stock. The **bid** is the highest price a buyer is willing to pay for the stock. The spread is the difference between the ask price and the bid price. If a NASDAQ trader has a seller who is willing to sell a stock for 30 and the trader can get a buyer to bid 30¼, the trader can keep the ¼ as his profit. That quarter point is the spread.

The Secondary Market

Investors who purchased your shares on the primary market may sell them on the open stock market—a secondary market that facilitates trades by matching buyers and sellers. This is "the stock market" most of us think of and hear about on the nightly news.

The Stock Exchanges

The stock market in this country is comprised of a number of exchanges, plus the NASDAQ over-the-counter market. The exchanges include:

♦ Boston Stock Exchange

♦ Chicago Board Options Exchange

♦ Cincinnati Stock Exchange

♦ New York Stock Exchange

♦ Pacific Stock Exchange

♦ Philadelphia Stock Exchange

Fiscal Facts

How the broker who handles a securities trade is compensated can vary. On the New York Stock Exchange, for example, the system is "plus commission," whereas on the NASDAQ over-the-counter market, it's "ex-commission." If you buy 100 shares of ABC stock via NYSE for $90 each, you will pay $9,000 for the shares plus a commission of $25. Your total transaction price is $9,025. If that stock were traded on the NASDAQ, the stock would be priced at $90.25, with the commission built in. You'd still pay a total transaction price of $9,025, but you wouldn't be aware that the extra $25 is commission.

Organized in 1790, Philadelphia is the oldest exchange. The New York Stock Exchange, also known as "the Big Board," is the most well known. Today, roughly 2.1 billion shares worth roughly $87 billion are exchanged daily on the floor of the NYSE. There are currently around 2,805 companies listed on the exchange with a capitalization of nearly $20 trillion. To be listed on the New York Stock Exchange, the company must have in excess of 2,200 shareholders with an average daily trading volume of at least 100,000 shares. Generally, the company must have a total capitalization of $750 million or pretax earnings in excess of $10 million.

The organization that became the NYSE began trading stocks under a buttonwood tree at what is now 68 Wall Street on May 17, 1792. On March 8, 1817, the traders wrote a constitution and the name "New York Stock Exchange Board" was adopted. The name was changed to "New York Stock Exchange" on January 29, 1863.

Some years later, a rival exchange, the New York Curb Exchange, was founded. While NYSE members had moved indoors, "the Curb" literally traded outdoors until 1921. In 1953, the New York Curb Exchange changed its name to the American Stock Exchange. Although the short name is "the Amex," old-timers still refer to it as "the Curb." It became the exchange for companies too small to be traded on the NYSE. On October 1, 2008, the Amex was acquired by NYSE Euronext and renamed NYSE Alternext U.S.

The NASDAQ *(National Association of Securities Dealers Automated Quotations)* is an American stock exchange that was founded in 1971 by the National Association of Securities Dealers (NASD). In the 1990s it became the market of choice for high-tech businesses and today it is the largest electronic screen-based equity securities trading market in the United States. With approximately 3,200 companies listed, it has more trading volume per day than any other stock exchange in the world. After buying the Scandinavian "operated exchange" OMX, and forging an agreement with the Borse Dubai, NASDAQ has become a transatlantic market. It operates the NASDAQ stock exchange in New York City—the second largest exchange in the United States—eight stock exchanges in Europe and holds one third of the Dubai Stock Exchange.

The Securities and Exchange Commission (SEC)

The markets are regulated by the Securities and Exchange Commission. Its mission is to protect investors and maintain the integrity of the securities markets. Appointed by President Roosevelt in 1934, the first Chairman of the SEC was Joseph Kennedy; father President John F. Kennedy.

The SEC requires companies to provide certain disclosures and information to all investors—whether a multi-billion-dollar pension fund or an elderly retiree with only a few hundred dollars. It has authority over nearly every institution involved in the securities markets: stock exchanges, mutual funds, investment advisors, brokers, dealers, and public utility holding companies.

The key to enforcement success is simple—the SEC carries a very, very large stick. It has the ability to bring action against individuals and entities that engage in insider trading, securities fraud, or a host of other verboten activities. It can even seek to ban individuals who have engaged in such activities from serving as officers of publicly traded companies for the rest of their lives!

What's With All the Animal References?

There's an old saying on Wall Street: "Bulls make money, bears make money, but pigs get slaughtered." But what's a "bull" and what's a "bear"? Bulls are people who believe a stock or the stock market is going to increase. Bears believe the price of a stock and/or the stock market is going to decrease.

Of course, the question that remains is where did these particular names originate? There are two explanations that are usually bandied about. The first is based on how each animal attacks: the bear by raking down with his large sharp claws, the bull by tossing up his large sharp horns. The second explanation comes from *The Wall Street Journal Guide to Understanding Money and Markets* (by Kenneth M. Morris, Fireside, 1999) and is a little fancier. According to the *Journal*, the term "bear" comes from sellers of bearskin who had a penchant for selling the bearskins before the bears were caught. Later, the term morphed to represent speculators who, on a hunch that the price would drop, agreed to sell shares they didn't own. Their next move would be to quickly buy the now lower-priced stock and sell it for the previously agreed higher price.

Because bull and bear baiting were once popular sports, bulls came to mean the opposite of bears. Bulls were those who bought heavily, expecting a stock price to increase.

Whatever explanation floats your boat, the words have carried down through the years, and people to this day describe themselves as bullish or bearish, depending upon their outlook.

But What Do All Those Numbers Mean?

Have you ever ventured onto the stock pages of *The Wall Street Journal* or your local paper and been utterly overwhelmed and confused? Well, we're here to prep you so you can dive back in with total confidence. Those rows and rows of tiny numbers are called stock tables and are loaded with useful information, if you know how to read them.

Stock tables vary slightly from publication to publication. We have included the explanation for the daily table from *The Wall Street Journal*. The first stock listed in the August 2, 2002, table was AAR. Reading from left to right, here's an explanation for each figure:

Ytd% Chg	52-Week Hi/Lo		Stock	(Sym)	Div	Yld%	PE	Vol 100s	Close	Net Chg
-8.2	17.45	6.96	AAR	AIR	.10	1.2	Dd	570	8.27	-0.47

1. **-8.2**. This is the year-to-date percentage change in the stock price.

2. **17.45 6.96.** The number on the left is the highest price at which this stock has traded for the last 52 weeks, excluding the last day of trading. The number on the right is the lowest price the stock has sunk to during the last 52 weeks. If there is a triangle symbol pointing up or triangle pointing down in this column, it indicates that there was a new 52-week high or low on the last day of trading.

   An S before the price change would indicate that there was a stock *split* or stock dividend amounting to 10 percent or more.

3. **AAR.** This is the name of the stock. It's usually abbreviated so it can fit into these minuscule rows; e.g., AutDataProc is Automatic Data Processing.

4. **AIR.** This is the stock or "ticker" symbol. When you enter an order to buy or sell AAR, you would say, for example, "Buy 100 AIR." Stock tickers were first introduced on the NYSE back on November 15, 1867.

5. **.10.** This is the annual cash dividend (10¢), based on the most recent quarterly declaration. For every share of this stock you owned, therefore, you would get 2.5¢ as a dividend payment every quarter (every three months).

6. **1.2.** This is the yield. Yield is derived from dividing the cash dividend of 10¢ by the closing stock price, which the table tells us farther down is $8.27.

7. **dd.** This is where you would typically find the price/earnings ratio. It is the stock's market price divided by the company's earnings. It is a measure of the absolute and relative value of the company because it makes it easy to compare the company's performance to that of other companies with stock outstanding. In this case we see "dd," which is a note indicating that the company suffered loss in the most recent four quarters.

   Although the company's earnings are not listed in this table, we can derive them from the P/E ratio and the price (P). P/E ratio is a key concept to master because it tells you whether a stock is over- or undervalued. Remember, a stock that is undervalued will probably rise in price to its proper value, so when it's undervalued it could be a good buy.

8. **570.** This is the volume, or number of 100 share (round lot) trades. So 570 means 57,000 shares traded that day.

9. **8.27.** This is the closing price for the last trading day. This is the price used in the P/E ratio.

10. **–0.47.** This is the net change in price for the last trading day (net change from the previous day).

Now you are ready to dazzle your friends and neighbors by whipping open the financial pages and commenting intelligently on the performance of Coca-Cola (abbreviated in the stock tables as KO) or Microsoft (MSFT) stock.

The Key to Your Stock Knowledge: Price-Earnings Ratios

If you want to understand the stock market, Price-Earnings—or P/E—ratio is a key concept to master. The P/E ratio is price divided by earnings; the resulting number indicates what investors think of the earnings performance of the company.

The P/E ratio is probably the most popular and useful measure of a stock's value. You can use it to compare the performance of a particular stock to the performance of the market as a whole, or to the stock of other companies in the same industry. Or you can compare current P/E to historical P/Es. It's like today's temperature: You can compare it to yesterday's temperature, the temperature on the same day last year, or the highest and lowest temperatures on record. There are two caveats or adjustments that need to be made to the *E* part of it:

1. Some companies experience big swings in earnings. During a year of low earnings, the stock will have a very high P/E ratio. For example, assume a stock with $.10 in earnings is selling at $20 per share. This stock would have a P/E of 200! ($20 × .10 = 200.) Anyone looking at the P/E ratio might conclude that this is a greatly overvalued (or overpriced) stock. But what if this represented the low in the company's business cycle, or the company just suffered a long strike? For this reason, analysts will "adjust" the earnings, either by using normalized earnings (what the company should earn in an average or normal year), or by estimating prestrike earnings. Let's assume that in either case, these normalized earnings amount to $2.00 per share. Now the P/E ratio is a more realistic 10 ($20 ÷ $2 = 10).

2. Some companies experience earnings during a year or quarter that will never happen again. Let's say the company in the previous example sells one of its divisions and reports earnings of $4.00. If we didn't adjust for these one-time earnings, the resulting P/E ratio of 5 ($20 ÷ $4 = 5) might mislead investors to assume the stock was very underpriced and a really good buy.

Look into My P/E Crystal Ball

P/E ratios are very useful because they allow us to examine how a company has performed over time and make intelligent decisions about whether to buy or sell its stock. For instance, we can compare current to historical P/E ratios. We can also compare a company's current P/E ratio to the performance of the market as a whole (using the S&P 500's P/E, for example). This comparison is called the relative P/E. All of this information is listed in the newspaper.

Let's look at a simple example: Scooby Inc. makes Scoobies, and although the demand for Scoobies ebbs and flows (it's especially high just before Christmas), it doesn't fluctuate enough to require us to make an adjustment or normalize earnings.

Scooby Inc.

10-Year P/E Range	10-Year Relative P/E Range
20–10	1.2–0.8
Current P/E	**Current Relative P/E**
12	1.0

Take a look at the first column. Over 10 years, the P/E for Scooby Inc. has varied from 20 to 10. The current P/E is 12. So we can conclude that Scooby is selling close to its historical low P/E of 10. Hmm … this might be a good time to buy, because we can expect that Scooby stock will bounce back from this low.

The second column, however, tells us that the relative P/E of 1.0 is smack in the middle of the historical relative P/E range of 1.2 and 0.8. Hmm … maybe Scooby Inc. won't bounce back from this low. We'll have to do more research before deciding whether or not to buy this stock. We'll need to investigate whether earnings are increasing or decreasing, for example.

If you are going to get involved with trading individual stocks, an understanding of P/E ratios is crucial. The point is that the P/E is only useful when compared to other P/Es—be they historical or market figures. It's not a stand-alone number.

Should You Play with the Big Kids or Just Get a Piggyback Ride?

Before you dive headlong onto the trading floor, let's think for a moment about how much time you're willing to invest in, well, investing. Only you can decide how much time and energy you're willing to devote to it. The great thing is you have options. Let's take a look at them now.

Take the Easy Route

If you want to buy individual stocks, you'll be competing with full-time professionals who live and breathe P/E ratios and have the latest research and the finest analysts at their disposal. Just because you like to drive, does it make sense to drive in the Indy 500? Not only are you very unlikely to win, but you also could get hurt.

Owning a single stock or a limited number of stocks subjects you to an unhealthy degree of market risk (as the Enron employees who invested their retirement savings in company stock learned, sadly). When the stock market is at an all-time high, there is always at least one stock that is selling at a new low for the year. Can you guarantee that you will not own that stock?

Fiscal Facts _____

Prior to 1957, Standard & Poor's service used two indexes, a daily and a weekly index of 90 stocks. In 1957, S&P scrapped these indexes for a modern index of 500 stocks, calculated by a high-speed electronic computer. It is based on 425 industrials, 25 railroads, and 50 utilities. The index is carefully weighted according to the importance of the various stocks used. The 500 stocks represent the prices of shares making up from 90 to 95 percent of the value of New York Stock Exchange common stock issues held by investors.

The best way to minimize market risk is to own a broadly diversified list of common stocks, spreading the risk out over 25 to 50 stocks. One bad apple out of 50 is acceptable; one out of one is not.

So when it comes to your IRAs, 401(k)s, and other tax-deferred investments, stick with stock mutual funds. When you buy into a mutual fund, you are buying shares in the fund, and the fund owns hundreds of stocks. Through the fund, you own those hundreds of stocks, too. Now, that's diversification. And you didn't have to do any of the hard work.

Creating Your Own Stock Index Fund

You can also consider buying and holding your own individual securities, with the emphasis on buying and holding. Remember, the more you trade your stock, the more taxable capital gains you could generate. You could wind up owing a lot of tax and really eating into your profits.

Above all, keep in mind that if you want to own individual stocks, the idea is not to compete with professional traders. Trust us: if you try, you'll give yourself an ulcer. Most professional traders have ulcers! Not to mention a pathological inability to sleep through the night without calling Tokyo.

Super Strategies

A better strategy might be to create your own personal index fund. An index fund is a mutual fund that mimics an index, such as the S&P 500, by buying the same stock in the same proportion as the index. The fund requires very little management: You simply buy the stock and hold it. No trades, no capital gains tax. You could purchase all 30 stocks in the Dow Jones Industrials index, for example, or the Dow Jones composite of 65 stocks (30 industrials, 20 transportation stocks, and 15 utilities). These appear in *The Wall Street Journal,* C Section, usually on page C2 or C4, under the heading "The Dow Jones Averages."

Just Buy Large-Cap Stocks

Similarly, you could select the 25 or 50 largest stocks in the S&P 500 index. By largest, we mean the stocks of companies with the most amount of money circulating in the stock market. This amount is called the market capitalization of a corporation. It equals the number of shares outstanding times the stock's market price. Exxon Mobile is currently the largest market capitalization stock (or large-cap stock) listed on the stock exchange, with over $385.62 billion of its stock outstanding (e.g. traded on the market) and a 4 percent weighting in the S&P index. General Electric is second and

Proctor & Gamble is third. The company with the largest market capitalization listed on NASDAQ is Microsoft, which has about $175.06 billion of its stock circulating.

You would be surprised at how much of the S&P 500 index you could own by just owning the 25 or 50 largest stocks in the index. The top 50 stocks in the S&P 500 index account for over half of the index's total value. So to set up your own index, you could just buy those stocks—rather than all 500 in the index.

You can find an up-to-the-minute listing of the companies in the S&P 500 that includes links to each company, and their prices and trading volumes, at www. bloomberg.com/markets/stocks/movers_index_spx.html.

How to Manage Your Index Fund: Leave It Alone!

Once you've created your personal index, what do you do? Nothing. Absolutely nothing. Don't execute a single trade. Just collect the dividends and invest them in a taxable or tax-free money market fund. One caution: this strategy only works if you are investing a large sum at one time. If you are investing $100 to $400 per month, you can't really buy 25 to 50 stocks at a time. If that is your situation, you can still participate in an index by buying an index mutual fund or ETF (exchange-traded fund).

The Best Ways to React to Blips

If you believe the newspapers, we should hold our collective breath every time the stock market takes a plunge and breathe a collective sigh of relief the minute the Dow Jones average heads back up.

As a long-term investor, though, you should have absolutely no interest in and no concern for short-term blips in the market. Just keep breathing, no matter what! Whether the market is up or down today, last week, or next month is irrelevant to your long-term game plan. In fact, ignore the financial section of the newspapers entirely (once you have shown everybody how you can read it).

By the same token, don't torture yourself following the daily ups and downs of your mutual funds. Just check on them once every three months. Each calendar quarter the papers publish quarterly mutual fund results. And you will most likely be able to assess each of your fund's quarterly reports.

Asset Allocation/Rebalancing

Rebalancing is a handy concept to help you keep your investments on target. When you invest, you allocate your money among various types of ventures according to percentages that you set as goals.

For instance, assume that last year you had a $100,000 portfolio and you decided to invest 50 percent in stocks and 50 percent in bonds. Obviously, you end up with $50,000 in both stocks and bonds. Let's say last year was a very good year for stocks, but not so good for bonds. Let's say that by now your investment in stocks has grown to $72,000, but you took a bit of a loss in bonds, and are left with $48,000 there. Your total portfolio is $72,000 + $48,000, or $120,000.

It's great that you've made money, but now your portfolio is a little out of whack. You definitely have more than 50 percent invested in stock and less than 50 percent invested in bonds. Time to rebalance. In this case, you need to sell some stock and buy some bonds in order to split your $120,000 50/50 between stocks and bonds. You should rebalance so you have $60,000 in stocks and $60,000 in bonds. You've figured out where the scales tipped and rebalanced your investments so you stay on track. Once a year, on your birthday (there's that day again), check to see if your stock or bond portion is out of balance and needs to be rebalanced.

How Much Stock Should Be in Your Portfolio?

According to Ibbotson Associates (a firm specializing in financial statistics), from 1926 to 2007, common stocks have provided an average return of 10.4 percent. This is more than twice the return for long-term Treasury bonds (5.5 percent average) and three times the average 3.7 percent return for T-bills. It's also more than three times the average inflation rate of 3.0 percent for the same period.[1]

So the evidence is overwhelming that you should keep a significant portion of your assets in common stocks—if you are at least 10 years from your planned retirement age. The simple rule is the longer time you have until you retire, the more you should have in common stocks. Here are some guides for how you should consider allocating your assets at different ages.

---

[1] *Source: Ibbotson Stocks, Bonds, Bills and Inflation R 2008 Classic Edition Yearbook. C 2008 Morningstar. All Rights Reserved. Used with permission. Copies of the Yearbook may be acquired directly from Morningstar. For more information, please visit global.morningstar.com/SBBIYrBks.*

	Age 17–35	Age 36–45	Age 46–55
Stocks	100%	70%	50%
Bonds	0	30	50
Bills	0	0	0

Another easy rule is: Multiply the number of years until you retire by two to get the percentage of your assets you should keep in stock.

Age	Years to Retirement = × 2 =	Stock %
Up to 25	40 × 2	80%
30	35 × 2	70
35	30 × 2	60
40	25 × 2	50
45	20 × 2	40
50	15 × 2	30
55	10 × 2	20

These two principles should guide your retirement investing:

1. The further you are from retirement, the more of your assets should be invested in stock.

2. Change your stock/bond ratio no more frequently than every five years. You're not a professional investor, so you shouldn't be reacting to every zig and zag in the markets. Stay the course and you'll do fine.

What if you're starting to invest just before a "change point"—at age 44, for example? Start with the allocation recommendations for the next closest age bracket—45 to 50, in this case.

Super Strategies

What if you reach a five-year mark and the table calls for you to cut back on stocks, but the market is weak and you are concerned that you won't get a good price for them? Because you're not a professional investor, go ahead and sell the stock anyway. If you're truly convinced that stocks have declined substantially and you wish to wait a year, go ahead, but don't defer your decision more than a year.

If you are over 55 or fewer than 10 years from retirement, you're dealing with the biggest risk in stocks, which is their volatility. Although over the long run stocks do very well, a dip right before you need your money can trash your retirement. You can only reduce this risk by reducing the percentage of your assets in stocks. On the other hand, only stocks offer some protection against inflation. And they can really grow. Therefore, it's wise to keep some equity in your portfolio even after you retire. How much? That's up to you. At least 10 to 20 percent is great, if you can swing it and are comfortable with that level of risk.

Dollar Cost Averaging, or How to Own Stocks and Stay Happy

But how do you avoid getting on the emotional roller coaster that the stock market can be? By staying well diversified and remembering that over the long haul, market ups are great and market downs are buying opportunities—so they're great, too. Ignore the histrionic reports in newspapers and on TV when the Dow Jones takes a dive. It will recover; it just may take a while. As long as you have the time to ride it out, your portfolio will be fine.

After all, market drops are great buying opportunities. Assume you invest $300 per month in stock mutual funds. Market goes up? Great, you're worth more. Market goes down? Great, you can buy more shares with the same amount of money (think of this as the financial equivalent of a white sale). Let's say you bought $300 of a $10 fund last month, or 30 shares.

The fund declines 10 percent: That means your $300 buys you 33 shares this month. Not too shabby.

The Two Secrets of Successful Investing

You now have under your belt two of the great secrets to successful investing:

1. Rebalance your portfolio from time to time.

2. Don't sweat the stock market's ups and downs. Use dollar-cost averaging to navigate these sometimes-treacherous waters.

Here's how you can "marry" these two great investment secrets: assume you are adding monthly sums to a taxable portfolio and it's time to rebalance. Simply divert all your monthly sums to the now-underweighted asset class (e.g., stocks or bonds) until the proper balance is regained. No tax consequences! What could be simpler?

Interest Rates and the Market

As you learned earlier, the Federal Reserve is our central bank, and is charged with the responsibility to keep the economy from growing steadily without steaming into inflation or falling into a recession. To do this, the Fed can expand or contract the money supply and cut or raise the discount rate banks must pay when they borrow directly from the central bank. This, in turn, affects the rates banks charge you to borrow money for a mortgage or to use your credit card.

Interest rates directly affect the financial markets. The longest-term U.S. Treasury obligation is considered by the financial community to be the "risk-free" interest rate. That is, the investor is always going to get his money back because the United States can tax and/or turn on the printing presses to ensure that the principal is repaid.

All investments are compared and valued against this risk-free rate. An insurance company may decide it wants a 3 percent risk premium for a corporate bond; therefore, it would only buy the bond if it yielded as much as the long-term treasury rate plus 3 percent. If the Feds increase the risk-free rate by 1 percent, for example, the corporate bond now only offers a 2 percent risk premium. Investors aren't interested so they will sell the bond until the price falls far enough the yield increases to provide a 3 percent-over-risk-free premium once again. This relationship between risk-premium and the risk-free interest rate is the key to understanding why the markets react so strongly when the Federal Reserve takes action. By influencing the direction of rates, the Fed can literally change the value of every asset in the country.

Choosing a Broker

Before you can begin investing, you will have to open a brokerage account. This account will allow you to buy and sell securities. Each time you execute a trade, you will pay your *broker* a commission. Depending upon the type of brokerage firm with which you have an account, your commissions can be very low (as little as $8.95 per trade or less) or very high (hundreds of dollars, depending upon the size of your transaction).

Traditional vs. Discount

A traditional or *full-service broker* offers clients individual attention from a broker who is familiar with your portfolio and can provide research, products, and investment advice. All of this comes at a price, of course. Commissions and fees for traditional brokerage accounts can be many times as much as you would pay at a discount broker.

A *discount broker*, on the other hand, performs a single task: he or she executes your trade. In some cases, you don't even talk to a person! The advantage of a discount broker is a lower commission rate. Period. No free toasters, hand-holding, or "hot tips."

How do you know which type of broker is right for you? It depends upon your personality, your investing experience, and the complexities of your trades. If you feel capable of making investment decisions on your own and don't want input from an outside party, go the discount route. If, on the other hand, you feel more comfortable with (and are willing to pay for) an advisor, you may want to go with a traditional broker.

def•i•ni•tion

A **broker** will act as an intermediary between you and the stock market. He or she will seek out buyers for stock you want to sell and find sellers of stock you want to buy. **Full-service brokers** also provide research and make recommendations. **Discount brokers** simply execute trades.

Check Out Your Broker's Background

In most cases, snooping isn't considered polite. When choosing a broker, however, you want to do the intellectual equivalent of dumpster-diving. On Wall Street, the dumpster is the Central Registration Depository. The CRD database contains information about individual brokers and brokerage firms. Through this system, you can quickly discover any complaints that have been filed against your broker or regulatory compliance issues, check his or her education and employment histories, and verify whether the broker and the firm are properly licensed. Why is this important? If you open an account with an unlicensed brokerage firm and it goes under, you may not be able to recover your assets; not the kind of surprise you want.

To tap into the CRD, contact your state securities regulator or the National Association of Securities Dealers (NASD) Broker Check service at 1-800-289-999 or pdpi. nasdr.com/PDPI. It's completely free!

SIPC Protection (or What If My Broker Goes Bust?)

There's one last thing you must do before opening an account: Check to make sure that your brokerage firm is part of the Securities Investor Protection Corporation (SIPC) by visiting www.sipc.org/who/database.cfm. This program ensures that if your broker goes out of business, you will recover up to $500,000 in assets, $100,000 of which may be in the form of cash. SIPC participation does *not* protect you against declines in the market value of your investments. Many firms will purchase additional insurance to give their clients added peace of mind.

If you are still not appeased by the idea that your account could go up in smoke should your broker fail, you can enter into a custodial agreement with your local bank. When you execute a trade, your broker will contact your bank, which will transmit the funds necessary to complete the transaction. The broker will then deliver the securities purchased to your bank for safekeeping. The custodian may also perform other functions, such as collecting dividend and interest income on your behalf and monitoring corporate actions (e.g., stock splits). Despite the added expense, this is a good option if your assets are considerable.

> **Super Strategies**
>
> If you want to deal with a single financial institution only for all of your banking and brokerage needs, an asset management account may be the ideal solution.

Placing a Trade with Your Broker

Regardless of which type of broker you choose, most of the trades you place are going to fall into one of three categories:

- **The Market Order.** This type of order instructs the broker to buy or sell at whatever the current market price is, no matter where it goes before your order is filled. You can expect that your broker will complete trades of 1,000 shares or less at or very close to the last trading price recorded. Such orders are typically executed electronically. You can usually get your price confirmed before you hang up after placing the order. Larger orders of 25,000+ shares may have to be "worked." For example, if ABC stock is moving up and you place an order to buy 50,000 shares of that stock when it was trading at 45, you may receive a report from your broker that you purchased that shows:

10,000 shares at $45\frac{1}{8}$

15,000 shares at $45\frac{1}{4}$

10,000 shares at $45\frac{3}{8}$

At this point, your broker may say: "I can fill the balance at $45\frac{3}{4}$." Now it's your decision: do you want to fill at that price or step aside and see if the price declines? If you go ahead, your broker would most likely report the balance of the trade as:

100 shares at $45\frac{1}{2}$

100 shares at $45\frac{5}{8}$

14,800 shares at $45\frac{3}{4}$

Your average stock price (before commissions) would be $45.40.

- ◆ **The Limit Order.** Using the previous example, you might conclude that ABC stock will settle down in price and instruct your broker to "buy 50,000 shares of ABC with a 45 limit." Next, you must tell the broker if this is a day order (i.e., either filled that day or canceled) or "good 'til canceled" (referred to as GTC). That means the order will stay open until the broker fills it or you cancel it.

  The problem with GTCs is you can forget you placed them. Maybe a few weeks later you'll buy alternative stock XYZ only to receive a follow-up call from your broker stating "we just filled your GTC on ABC." Whoops, a little short on money? It's easier to stay on top of things if you cancel and reenter your order each day, although your broker won't appreciate the extra work.

- ◆ **The Stop or Stop Loss Order.** Let's say you bought ABC stock at 30, saw it shoot up to $45\frac{3}{4}$, and it has now backed down to 42. At this point, you may be more willing to lock in a gain rather than roll the dice to see if it crests the $45\frac{3}{4}$ high again. So you instruct your broker to place a stop loss order to sell at $40. If the stock goes up, great; if it goes down, you're "out" at 40.

Unless you are a professional investor dealing with large orders, our advice would be to use market orders. Of the three, there isn't the margin of error that exists in the latter two choices. You're still getting in on the action, but you're letting a professional do most of the work.

Asset Management Accounts

In response to the stock market crash of 1929, Congress passed the Glass-Steagall Act. This legislation required a separation between brokerage services and commercial banks. For nearly seven decades, this restriction remained in place until, in 1999, President Clinton signed the Gramm-Leach-Bliley Act, which permitted the creation of "financial services" firms. Endowed with the powers to engage in both banking and brokerage activities, these firms created *asset management accounts*.

Here's how they work. When you make a deposit, the proceeds are automatically swept into an interest-earning money market fund. You can write a check or use your debit card to access the cash, just as you would with a regular bank account. You can also go online or call your bank and purchase stocks, bonds, mutual funds, and most other investments. At the end of the month, you will receive a single, consolidated statement detailing all of your transactions, both banking and brokerage.

There are a few downsides. Most asset management accounts require at least $15,000 for an opening balance, while a regular brokerage account typically requires $1,000 or so. The fees are higher than those charged by discount brokers, although they are usually lower than traditional broker fees.

Asset management accounts (AMAs) are particularly appealing if you want to call the shots with your investments. They are a good alternative to having a financial advisor or broker manage your investments for you. Assume you have a $250,000 IRA and a $50,000 taxable account at Bank of America Investment Services, for example. First, you pay no annual asset fee for either account (financial advisors typically charge 1.0 percent per annum). Second, the fee or commission per transaction is only $7.00. The taxable account at BofA is called a Money Manager account, and includes free checking. If the above appeals to you, call BofA Investment Services at 800-926-1111.

AMAs are also a very good choice if one or more of your portfolios are in the form of a trust (such as a Living or Inter Vivos Trust, a Testamentary Trust, a CRT, a CLT, etc). More on trusts in Chapter 23.

Financial Advisors

If you don't want to direct your investments and are interested in a financial advisor/ planner, you can find one at fpanet.org or napfa.org. If the advisor/planner wants to charge you for your initial consultation, take a hike. To find an advisor/planner who charges on an hourly basis, go to www.garrettplanning.com. For fee-only planners/ advisors, go to fpanet.org. "Fee-only" means they should not be receiving any additional income at your expense (e.g., by selling you an investment).

When you find an advisor you like, ask him or her to give you forms ADV 1 and 2. These are disclosure forms that require the advisor to disclose whether he or she will receive commissions from companies that they may be recommending to you). Finally, call the Financial Regulatory Authority hotline at 800-289-9999 to see if any disciplinary action has been taken against the financial advisor or firm.

The Least You Need to Know

- ◆ Corporations sell stock in exchange for ownership. The stock market represents this ownership.

- ◆ A bull is someone who believes stock prices are going to increase; a bear believes stock prices are going to decrease.

- ◆ The primary responsibility of the SEC is to preserve the integrity of the financial markets.

- ◆ The best way to minimize market risk is to own a broadly diversified list of common stocks, spreading the risk out over 25 to 50 stocks.

- ◆ Before you open a brokerage account, check with the CRA database to see if the broker and brokerage firm are licensed. You should also make sure the broker participates in the Securities Investor Protection Corporation.

- ◆ An asset management account allows you to keep both your bank accounts and investment accounts at one institution.

How to Invest in Individual Stocks ... Not That We Recommend It!

In This Chapter

- ◆ Commonsense trading tips
- ◆ How to spot a quality company
- ◆ Finding reliable and affordable research
- ◆ Analyzing a company's annual report
- ◆ Diversifying your holdings
- ◆ Using DRIPs to build your portfolio

As you learned in the previous chapter, the best way to meet your financial goals and minimize the risk of losing your hard-earned cash is to own a broadly diversified list of common stocks, spreading the risk out over 25 to 50 stocks. Unless you have the scratch to buy, say, 100 shares each of 25 to 50 broadly diverse companies (that's a lot of scratch!), stick with stock mutual funds.

If you are an amateur investor, there are only three reasons to actively trade the stocks of individual companies:

1. Your employer is a publicly traded company, and you want to own a few shares so you can keep current on company developments. If this is the case, see if your employer offers a stock purchase plan (which usually sells the stock at a discount price). Buy the minimum number of shares.

2. A relative passed away, leaving you shares of ABC Corporation with this admonition: "Whatever you do, don't sell ABC Corporation." If your conscience won't let you sell, give the shares to your favorite charity and take the tax deduction.

3. You love the action. Some people play the horses, some people play poker or the office pool, and you play the stock market. Okay, we all have our vices; admit it to yourself (and your spouse), control it as best you can, and get on with your life. Just don't call what you're doing investing. It's entertainment—pay for it out of your entertainment budget.

Trading Tips

Still not persuaded? Still want to try some trading? Okay, we'll tell you what you need to know.

Do:

- Use your broker to execute your trades, not to do your research. Paying full commission to a broker is like paying list price for a car.

- Negotiate your broker's commission before, not after, placing the order.

- Do you really need a full-service broker? If you feel you are getting your money's worth from a full-service broker, God bless, but you probably don't need or want the broker's suggestions and reports. At least, not enough to pay for 'em. Try a discount broker instead.

def•i•ni•tion

Penny stocks are stocks that are selling for a very low price—typically one, two, or three dollars.

- Avoid speculative securities. Initial public offerings (IPOs), *penny stocks*, and "hot tip" stocks aren't worth the risk. Even the best traders don't buy all their stocks at low prices; mistakes are part of the business. But good quality stocks recover and eventually go on to new highs; losers just curl up and die. Here's the real deal on

IPOs: The "hot" ones go to large institutional customers; the little people might get a few shares if they're lucky. If you are offered a good chunk of an IPO, odds are the broker was unable to unload all the shares to institutional customers and is calling with a "hot tip" because he's got to get rid of them somehow.

When the hot tip gets all the way down the chain to you, it'll be lukewarm at best. If an investment seems too good to be true, it *is* too good to be true.

When Should You Buy Stock?

It depends on how much money you have and how much time you want to devote to managing your individual stock holdings. We're going to assume your answer to both questions is: "Not much."

If you have selected your stocks but can only afford to purchase a round lot (100 shares) of each, go ahead and buy. If you can buy 200 shares of each, buy 100 now and the rest:

- On your anniversary date—usually your birthday

- Or if the stock declines 10 percent from your purchase price, whichever comes first

---

Super Strategies

If you set aside an additional sum each year to purchase stocks, or if you plan to reinvest your dividends, pick an annual portfolio anniversary date. Avoid vacation months, holiday months, or January, which is generally a strong month for stock prices because institutions are buying stocks for their pension and profit-sharing plans then. Pick your birthday month, or, if your birthday clashes with any of the above stipulations, an "interim" time like late October—early November.

If You Buy It, You'd Better Love It

Ideally, you should buy stocks that you never have to sell because every time you sell stock, you generate a tax bill. If you hold a stock for more than a year, and then sell it, you must pay a 15 percent capital gains tax on the profit. If you decide after a year that you want to sell $15,000 of stock to buy some "better" stock, for instance, you would only have $14,250 to reinvest after paying the 15 percent capital gains tax.

If you sell the stock before a year is up, you have to pay the short-term capital gains tax, which depends on your income tax bracket and can go as high as 35 percent. In addition, there are commission costs for both the sale and the subsequent purchase. Not to mention state and local taxes.

Super Strategies

Obviously, there are good reasons sometimes to sell a stock. Maybe you made a mistake in the first place, or the company has fallen apart. But your best bet is to buy the stocks of stable, high-quality companies that you'll feel comfortable owning for a long time. If they pay a modest but growing cash dividend, so much the better.

The Biggest "Do" of All: Invest in Quality

Here's the "Big Daddy Do" for amateur investors: Limit your investments to quality companies. What's a quality company? Below are the characteristics that make a company worthy of your precious investment dollars:

1. **Market leadership.** If you want to buy stock in a certain industry, buy the market leader—buying number two or number three is not worth the aggravation. How can you tell if a company is the market leader? When size, marketing power, and cost control make it the most profitable company in its industry; when its new products or services are more readily accepted in the marketplace than the competition's; when it's the name investors buy when they want to participate in the industry; and when it's the last stock to be sold (if it ever is sold) when investors look to reduce industry exposure.

def•i•ni•tion

In the late nineteenth century, stock quotes were transmitted over telegraph lines to ticker machines. As the information was received, the machine would print it on a small strip of paper known as ticker tape.

Although computers came to replace ticker machines, stocks are still tracked by short combinations of letters known as **ticker symbols.** Coca-Cola, for example, has a ticker of KO; the Washington Post, WPO; General Electric, GE; Walmart, WMT; Microsoft, MSFT; Hershey, HSY; and so on. If you wanted to purchase shares of Hershey, you would call your broker and say, "Buy 100 shares of HSY."

2. **A strong balance sheet.** Professional investors don't like to be blindsided by a company that suddenly develops credit problems. A strong balance sheet (more assets than liabilities) ensures a high credit rating, which in turn ensures that the company pays low interest rates when it does borrow. A strong balance sheet also enables the company to quickly take advantage of acquisition opportunities.

Ideally, an industrial company would have no debt, but this is a rarity. To evaluate a company's debt position, take a look at its debt to total capitalization ratio. This ratio is found in the annual report and should be between 25 and 30 percent. To figure it out for yourself, use this formula:

long-term debt divided by

long-term debt + preferred stock + common stock + *retained earnings.*

Fiscal Facts _____

Profits reinvested in the business are known as **retained earnings.**

3. **A consistent and seasoned track record.** Any company whose stock you seek to own should have at least a 10-year public (not private) record to analyze. Look for how well or poorly the company did in previous industry and/or general economic downturns. Do revenues and earnings increase each and every year? Nine years out of ten? At least four years out of five?

Be careful of companies with above-average earnings growth (+10–20 percent) but only average or below average (+3–5 percent) revenue growth. This may indicate that management is trying to improve the bottom line by raising prices or cutting costs. This will only keep the company profitable for so long if revenues aren't increasing.

Crash Alert _____

Be leery of corporations that buy back shares each year, irrespective of stock price levels. When a company buys back its own shares, it's artificially forcing up the stock price by decreasing the amount of stock outstanding. Sometimes management will do this to protect a stock that has been pummeled by investors for what management believes to be short-term or transitory reasons. The company may even borrow money to buy the stock. This is just a maneuver to improve the stock price.

Here's a neat rule: Look for companies where unit sales (e.g., the number of widgets sold per year) are growing at least 50 percent faster than the real, or inflation-adjusted, gross domestic product (GDP) in this country. The GDP is reported quarterly in newspapers and on TV newscasts.

4. **A high reinvestment rate.** What does the company do with the money it makes? Does it pay out a significant sum to shareholders in the form of cash dividends? Companies that pay out a high percent of earnings to stockholders as cash dividends are telling you, by their actions, they do not view the future of the company with much favor. If they did, they would reinvest those dollars back into the business.

Researching Individual Stocks

There are good research resources available to the individual investor, many at your local library. In addition, if you do hire a full-service broker, you can avail yourself of his or her research department.

In our opinion, the two most basic, cost-effective, and objective research tools are the *Value Line Investment Survey* (www.valueline.com) and *Standard & Poor's Stock Guides* (www.standardandpoors.com). Both may also be available at your local library.

The Invaluable Value Line

The basic Value Line service covers approximately 1,700 stocks. For each stock, Value Line provides two rankings: timeliness and safety. Of the two, pay particular attention to safety. Stocks are ranked on a 1 to 5 basis, with 1 being the safest. Don't consider any stock with less than a 2 rating.

Value Line also provides scores for four other key indicators:

- Financial strength
- Stock price stability
- Stock price growth persistence
- Earnings predictability

Value Line includes, in addition to the rankings and key indicators cited above, a great deal of relevant statistical and narrative information. Value Line reports are updated regularly. The individual company write-ups will take some getting used to, but after a while you will find that you can easily determine a company's earnings growth rate and the consistency of that growth rate.

Use Value Line to help you select at least 25 stocks that:

1. Are safe or very safe (remember, that means a ranking of 1 or 2)

2. Are growing at an above-average rate

3. Are growing consistently and steadily

What does "above average" mean? We suggest you look for a minimum of 8 percent and, ideally, 10 percent growth. And keep an eye on consistency. For a 10 percent grower, 10 percent a year is perfect but rarely achieved. A range of 8 to 12 percent is very consistent. From 6 to 14 percent is acceptable. But if the company's earnings swing between 0 percent and 30 percent, for example, it's too volatile to be in your portfolio.

S&P Stock Guides: Another Great Tool

Standard & Poor's Stock Guides (Bond Guides are also available) are an excellent research tool. The guides come out monthly and cover the stock of approximately 5,000 U.S. companies and 3,200 outside the U.S., as well as mutual funds and variable annuity/life investments.

The Best Newspapers for Stock Info

Finally, two newspapers, *Investors Business Daily* (www.investors.com) and *The Wall Street Journal* (www.wsj.com), do an excellent job of tracking the stock market and individual stocks. Either may be available at your local library.

If you simply must follow the market during the day, both CNBC and Bloomberg Information TV do a good job of keeping you current. For a nightly wrap-up, check out PBS's Nightly Business Report.

All the News That's Fit to Print: Company Annual Reports

The most valuable research you can get your hands on is provided by the companies themselves. Once you purchase individual equities, the company (or your brokerage firm) will begin stuffing your mailbox with quarterly and annual reports.

If you want those reports before you purchase a stock, check the stock tables in *The Wall Street Journal*'s Section C. You will find a symbol next to those companies that provide a free annual and free current quarterly report. To obtain these reports, call *The Wall Street Journal*'s Annual Reports Club at 1-800-965-CLUB.

Annual reports and quarterly reports are like report cards. Avoid the verbiage and the pretty pictures, and you'll be able to tease out trends from the financial statements. The *10-K* is the annual report equivalent filed with the *SEC*. It's sometimes more revealing than the corporate reports to shareholders and comes without the rosy verbiage.

Finally, the *8-K* form is a report that a corporation's managers must file with the SEC within 30 days of any event that might affect the financial status or share price of the company.

def•i•ni•tion

A corporation issues an *annual report* once a year that includes the company's financial statements—income statement, balance sheet, cash flow statement, etc. The company is also required to file a **10-K report** with the Securities and Exchange Commission (SEC). The 10-K is the same information in the annual report, minus pictures and narrative. A company must also file an **8-K report** with the SEC within 30 days regarding any event that could affect the company's performance.

Analyzing a Company's Annual Report

When that annual report arrives in the mail, skip all the narrative and pictures and turn straight to the income statement near the back (also called the profit/loss statement). It's similar to your own personal income statement. Below is a guide for how to analyze each item.

1. **Gross or Total Revenues.** For quarterly reports, how do revenues compare with the previous quarter and the same quarter in the previous year? For annual reports, how do they compare to last year, 5 years ago, 10 years ago? You are looking for changes or breaks in the normal patterns, up or down. If you find any, scan the text for explanations. If you aren't satisfied with them, call the company, ask for the investor relations officer (IRO), and introduce yourself as a shareholder with questions. If there is no IRO, or you are still not satisfied, go progressively up the line: treasurer, financial vice president, president. Remember, you are an owner; act like one.

2. **Gross Profit.** This figure is the result of subtracting the cost of goods from the actual revenues. Cost of goods sold is the cost of making each additional unit of whatever's being sold. Gross profit is an indication of the company's efficiency: Is it improving or deteriorating? Again, compare the numbers for previous years and quarters. If you really want to get fancy, divide gross profit into revenue and multiply by 100 to get a percentage called "gross profit margin." You can analyze every item on the income statement this way—by dividing it into revenue. This way you can see how each item looks as a percentage of revenue. If gross profit is only 5 percent of revenue, for example, where's all the revenue money going? Why isn't gross profit higher?

3. **Selling, General, and Administrative Expense (SG&A).** Again, compare to past periods. Any big changes? Divide this expense (SG&A) into revenue.

   If the resulting percentage is very high, maybe that's your answer for why gross profit is low—because the company has very high expenses.

4. **Research & Development (R&D).** Sometimes this item is included in SG&A; sometimes it's broken out separately. For some companies (such as technology companies), this is a critical expenditure; it could make or break future growth opportunities. Look to see if R&D is rising in line with revenues; if not, the company may be shortchanging its future to keep its current earnings looking attractive.

5. **Earnings Before Interest, Depreciation, and Amortization (referred to as EBIDA and pronounced "E-bah-dah".** Used to measure a company's profitability and efficiency.

6. **Pre-Tax Earnings.** Earnings before taxes; again, divide into revenues to obtain pre-tax margins.

7. **Tax Rate.** Is the tax rate rising or falling? If falling, management may have manipulated it to cover up declining revenues.

8. **Net Income.** Income after taxes. Any cash dividends on common stock will be paid from this sum.

You're now your own security analyst! As you go through this exercise for the first time, think how each of these categories relates to your personal income statement.

Analyzing the Balance Sheet

Just like your personal balance sheet, a corporate balance sheet is broken down between assets and liabilities, and each of these categories, in turn, are divided into short- (or current) and long-term assets and liabilities.

Assets	Liabilities
Current Assets	*Current Liabilities*
Cash & Marketable Securities	Accounts Payable
Accounts Receivable	Debt due withing 12 mos.
Long-term Assets	*Long-term Debt*
Plant	Mortgages
Equipment	Debentures
Other	*Shareholders Equity*
Goodwill	Preferred Stock
	Common:
	Par Value
	Paid in Capital
	Retained Earnings

The statement is called a balance sheet because:

Total Assets = Total Liabilities + Shareholder's Equity

The balance sheet contains all the information you need (i.e., is the company carrying lots of debt? What kind of cash is available?) to analyze a company's financial strength and financing strategies. Analysts look at several ratios when examining a balance sheet. These ratios indicate the amount of long-term debt the company is carrying and how it relates to the amount of equity outstanding.

Debt-to-Equity ratio: Total Debt/Total Equity

Debt ratio: Total Debt/Total Assets

Current ratio: Current Assets/Current Liabilities

Analysts also watch for increases or decreases in cash, accounts receivable, and accounts payable.

Dividends: How Companies Share the Wealth

As an owner of a company, you are entitled to a share of its profits. To distribute profit to the shareholders, a company will pay a *cash dividend.*

Generally speaking, a profitable company's board of directors has two choices: It can either reinvest the funds in the business or it can send you a check in the mail. Profits reinvested in the business are called *retained earnings.* Profits paid to shareholders in cash are *dividends.*

Most companies pay dividends quarterly. If you open *The Wall Street Journal* and see that a corporation pays a $1 dividend, it is likely that you are going to receive $0.25 per share, four times a year (Jan. 1, Apr. 1, July 1, and Oct. 1, for example). Some businesses, on the other hand, pay dividends annually or semi-annually.

On rare occasions, a Board of Directors may declare a special dividend. These are one-time distributions normally arising from excess funds that have accumulated or unusual, non-recurring sources, such as the sale of a business or an award from litigation.

Common sense tells you that if a company has earnings per share of $2, yet it is paying a dividend of $3, this unfortunate state of affairs cannot endure forever. Only purchase companies that have "earned" the dividend several times over. If Jemima's Diner Company is paying a $1 dividend, for example, make sure it has an earnings per share of more than $1.

There may be some years when a company reports a restructuring charge or a loss. If this is an isolated incident and not part of an ongoing trend, you probably don't need to be concerned about the safety of the dividend. Most management teams understand that investors depend upon the dividend, and are unlikely to do away with it unless absolutely necessary.

The Truth About Stock Splits

Notice that we haven't mentioned stock splits as a way to make money on stock? A lot of novice investors think that when a stock splits, it's good for their portfolio. In fact, it's the financial equivalent of getting two $10 bills in exchange for the $20 you have in your pocket. It does not increase your wealth. Here's an example:

The Missouri Tea Company has 100,000 shares outstanding, each trading at $30; giving the business a market capitalization of $3 million. Last year, MTC had a net income of $250,000, or $2.50 per share.

The Board of Directors declares a 2-1 stock split because it thinks that $30 per share is too expensive for the average investor. It prints an extra 100,000 shares. It then distributes them to the existing shareholders (if you owned 100 shares, you would receive 100 shares of the newly created stock).

The result is that the shareholders now hold twice as many shares. But the entire company is still the same size! The $250,000 profit is being split by 200,000 shares instead of the 100,000 that existed previously, cutting the earnings per share (EPS) in half to $1.25. The result is that the stock price—which was $30 per share—gets cut in half to $15 per share. Before, you had 100 shares at $30 each generating $2.50 per share in profit. Now you have 200 shares at $15 each generating $1.25 per share. At the end of the day, you are still in the exact same economic position.

If you look at the stocks you've purchased, they probably fall into a few different categories. For instance, some might be "energy" (i.e., oil, gas, and utility companies) or "technology" (i.e., software manufacturers). These categories are called sectors. A *sector* is a particular segment of the economy. Now, when your portfolio anniversary comes up, take a look at how each stock you hold in each sector has performed.

Now, stick with us here. We're going to tell you to do something that might not seem like the obvious choice: If you plan to purchase more stocks, put more money into the stocks that did poorly. Why? So that you maintain positions for each sector that are comparable. This is another example of dollar cost averaging.

Let's say you started with $10,000 and split it evenly, buying $2,500 worth of stock in each of four different sectors: technology, health care, energy, and finance. By the end of the first year, maybe your technology stocks are now worth $3,000, health-care stocks dropped to $2,000, energy shot up to $4,000, and your finance stocks held steady at $2,500. Your portfolio is now worth $12,000, but you no longer own an even 25 percent in each sector.

$3,000	(technology)
+ $2,000	(health care)
+ $4,500	(energy)
+ $2,500	(finance)
= $12,000	

We're suggesting that you rebalance your portfolio so that you again own 25 percent in each sector. With a $12,000 portfolio, that would mean holding $12,000 × .25, or $3,000, in each sector. You'll have to sell off some of your energy stocks to beef up your holdings in health care and finance.

Professionals might disagree with this approach, arguing that you should pour more money into your "winners" and less into your "losers." This is fine for professionals whose job it is to carefully research their holdings. Right now, you're a rookie and your one big asset is time. As long as you stick with top-quality investments, the time you invest in them is more than likely to pay off. You may not have as many big winners, but, by the same token, you should have fewer (and maybe no) losers.

Diversifying Your Stock Portfolio: How Many Holdings Are Enough?

You need at least 25 stocks to achieve an acceptable degree of diversification. That doesn't mean that owning 25 drug stocks will give you diversification, however! You need diversification by number (25+), and by sector or type.

Let's look at how the S&P 500 is weighted by sector, and compare this to four tax-advantaged portfolios we've set up:

Sector Weighting (10/31/08)	S&P 500	#1	#2	#3	#4
1. Basic Materials	3.1%	0	4	4	2
2. Industrials	11.0	8	4	8	4
3. Consumer Discretionary	8.2	8	6	8	14
4. Consumer Staples	12.9	16	10	20	18
5. Energy	13.1	8	4	0	0
6. Finance	14.9	20	28	0	10
7. Health care	13.9	12	20	36	32
8. Technology	15.8	20	14	24	20
9. Telecommunications	3.3	8	10	0	0
10. Utilities	3.8	0	0	0	0
Total	100.0	100.0	100.0	100.0	100.0

As you can see, our four model portfolios own stock in at least 6 of the 10 sectors that are available in the market. This is so we won't be zigging when the market is zagging.

If you select individual securities for your portfolios, be sure to line them up by sector as shown above to make sure you have good diversification. For each of the five biggest sectors of the S&P 500, try not to own more than two times the percentage amount of stock that the S&P 500 owns. And make sure you don't own less than half of what the S&P 500 owns in each of those same five sectors.

Okay, if you want to play with stocks, at least we've done our best to goof-proof you!

We're Not Talking About Leaky Faucets: Investing Through DRIPs

Most corporations offer a Dividend Reinvestment Program, or DRIP for short. DRIPs are the best way for you to build a position in a company at a very low cost over a long period of time. Advantages of these programs include:

- In most cases, there is little or no fee for shares purchased through a DRIP. This lowers your cost basis and can increase your returns substantially over long periods of time.

- You can purchase additional shares of stock directly by sending in a check or having funds withdrawn from your checking/savings account. Most of the time, additional investments can be as small as $10 or $25.

- You can establish automatic, regular withdrawals from your bank account to purchase shares. This is an easy way to establish a dollar cost averaging program, which you will learn about in Chapter 20.

- Fractional shares can be purchased. Say you receive $15 in dividends, yet the current stock price is $50. Through a DRIP program, you will actually be able to purchase 0.3 shares. This isn't possible through a broker.

Want to know how to get started? First, check and see if the stock you fancy offers a DRIP. You can either find the phone number for the investor relations department on the company's website or head over to www.equiserve.com.

Next, buy a single share through your broker and then request that he send you a stock certificate; you can also order a single certificate through a special gift service such as OneShare.com. This makes you eligible for participation.

Finally, fill out and mail in the paperwork provided to you by the investor relations department or Equiserve.

Violà! You've done it! Sit back and relax. Without any additional work, the amount of shares you own will increase as your dividends are reinvested.

Changed Your Mind About Being Your Own Securities Analyst?

What if you don't have the time or the inclination to get involved with analyzing each and every company you are considering for purchase? Stick to these simple steps:

1. Make sure you understand the company's products or services. This will enable you to decide for yourself if you think the company's outlook is favorable (better than the economy as a whole), neutral (like the economy) or unfavorable (worse than the economy).

2. Determine the PEG ratio (price/earnings multiple divided by the estimated growth rate). Less than 10 is favorable; 20 or higher is unfavorable.

3. Ask: Will the company you are considering further diversify your stock portfolio, or merely add to sectors you already own? If you already own a similar company, you probably don't need this one.

4. Take our original advice and don't buy individual stock. Invest in stock index funds for far greater diversification than you could achieve on your own!

The Least You Need to Know

- Investment returns arise from two sources: appreciation in the price of the security and dividends.

- The payout ratio is the percentage of a company's profit that is distributed to the shareholders as cash dividends.

- DRIPs offer an easy, low-cost way to build a position in a company.

- Excellent businesses possess certain characteristics such as the ability to pass on cost increases to consumers, sensible management with reasonable compensation, a Board of Directors with significant personal holdings, open and honest communication, little or no debt, tons of free cash flow, a history of share repurchases, market leadership, and an attractive price.

- You always want to read a company's annual report, 10K, and proxy statement before investing.

- The tax considerations and unpredictable nature of Wall Street make market timing extremely difficult.

Slow and Steady Wins the Race: Fixed-Income Securities

In This Chapter

- ◆ What are fixed-income securities?
- ◆ Using fixed-income securities to protect your portfolio
- ◆ How to buy Treasury bills and bonds
- ◆ Knowing when to add bonds to your portfolio
- ◆ Adding savings bonds, STRIPS, and agency debt

Maybe you're not the type that likes to take big chances. You like to know what's coming around the corner, and, if you can't, you at least like to have a back-up plan to deal with life's little boomerangs. If this is you, there are two words you need to remember: fixed income. A fixed-income security entitles you to regular, fixed payments of interest income on your investments. In this chapter, we're going to give you the lowdown on these securities and how they can benefit you.

What Are Fixed-Income Securities For?

Bonds and *notes* are fixed-income securities that corporations and governments issue in order to borrow money. When you buy a bond or note, you are agreeing to lend the company issuing the bond or note a sum of money. In return the company gives you a fixed-income security and promises to make specified interest payments to you and return the full amount borrowed when the security matures. The amount of income, the timing of the payments, and the *maturity date* are all spelled out in a document called the *indenture*.

def•i•ni•tion

Bonds, notes, and bills are all IOUs that corporations and governments issue when they want to borrow money. The borrower promises to pay you interest as well as return the principal amount you lent it at a specific date in the future (this is known as the **maturity date**). In the case of the United States government, these IOUs are called bonds when the specified date is longer than 10 years from the date the bond is issued. When the maturity date is between 1 and 10 years from issuance, the IOU is a known as a note. When it's one year or less from issuance, the IOU is called a bill.

When corporations raise money using fixed-income securities, it's called debt financing. When they issue stock to raise money, it's called equity financing.

It may surprise you to learn that, although the stock market receives more coverage on the nightly news, the bond market is far, far larger!

Bonds and other fixed-income securities balance out the risk of carrying stocks in your portfolio. Unless you lend money to a borrower with lousy credit, you can count on getting your money back when the fixed-income security matures. Plus, you earn all that interest income in the meantime.

When the stock market is tanking, it can be a great relief to know that you have some of your money in nice, safe bonds. Even better, when the stock market is performing miserably, the bond market tends to do really well, and vice versa. This seesaw effect keeps your portfolio on an even keel when you own both stocks and bonds.

When Do You Get That Groovy Interest Income?

In the United States, most, but not all, fixed-income securities pay interest twice a year; on the annual anniversary of the original issue date, and again six months later (in Europe, most bonds pay interest annually). For example, five-year U.S. Treasury notes pay interest in May and November each year. Plus, the Treasury will pay you back the amount you lent it (your principal) on the maturity date.

Super Strategies

To paraphrase Will Rogers, "It's not the return on your principal, it's the return of your principal ...." When buying fixed-income securities, don't just look for notes and bonds with the highest yields. If a borrower is willing to pay high interest rates, its credit must not be very good. Junk bonds, for example, are high-yielding bonds from corporations with lousy credit ratings. They may pay a lot of interest, but the risk that you will never be paid back part or all of your principal is also very high.

Beware the Call Feature

Some fixed-income investments include a "call" feature. What is this? Well, let's say you have a home mortgage. This is essentially a fixed-income security you sold to your bank. You, as the borrower, agreed to make fixed monthly payments and to pay off the principal by a final maturity date. You have, however, the right to pay off your mortgage in advance and to refinance your mortgage to take advantage of declining interest rates. This right is the "call" feature. You can "call" your mortgage anytime and pay it off. Some U.S. government bond issues and the vast majority of corporate and municipal issues also have call features. These give the issuer/borrower the right to pay off ("redeem") the bonds issued.

Why would the borrower want this right? Well, let's go back to our example of Treasury notes paying 6.625 percent interest and pretend the issue is callable. What if interest rates declined to 3 percent? The Treasury would love to be able to pay off the note at 6.625 percent and issue a new note. It would save billions of dollars in interest expense!

This would be a drag for you, though, because now you no longer have a 6.625 percent note. Sure you got your principal back, but now if you want to reinvest it, the best you'll do is a new Treasury note at 3 percent. Your interest income has been drastically reduced by this swift move and there's not one thing you can do about it!

Now, let's assume that rates increase to 8 percent. You would be very pleased if the Treasury would call your note so you can reinvest at the higher rate, but the Treasury sure doesn't want to pay 8 percent when it's got you locked in at 6.625 percent.

In this case, the Treasury would not exercise the call right.

Crash Alert

Call features only benefit the original issuer; they never benefit the purchaser or owner. Therefore, either don't buy any issues with a call feature, or be very careful about incorporating them into your bond portfolio.

Sinkers

Now, let's return to the example of a mortgage. Your monthly payments may stay the same over the life of the mortgage, but as you get closer to maturity less of the monthly payment is interest and more of it reduces the principal balance. The amount of interest income going to the bank is declining. Some corporations issue bonds that do the same thing—the part of the payment that is devoted to interest gets smaller and smaller as the bond gets closer to maturity. These are called sinking fund payments, or "sinkers."

Here's an example of what you receive each six months for a $100,000 purchase of a 6 percent corporate bond due in 10 years with a mandatory sinking fund starting in year five.

Year	Interest		Principal	Total
4/30/02	1A	(Issue Date)		
	1B	$3,000	$3,000	
4/30/03	2A	3,000	3,000	
	2B	3,000	3,000	
4/30/04	3A	3,000	3,000	
	3B	3,000	3,000	
4/30/05	4A	3,000	3,000	
	4B	3,000	3,000	
4/30/06	5A	3,000	3,000	
	5B	3,000	3,000	
4/30/07	6A	3,000	$10,000	13,000
	6B	3,000	3,000	

Year	Interest		Principal	Total
4/30/08	7A	3,000	10,000	13,000
	7B	3,000	3,000	
4/30/09	8A	3,000	10,000	13,000
	8B	3,000	3,000	
4/30/10	9A	3,000	10,000	13,000
	9B	3,000	3,000	
4/30/11	10A	3,000	10,000	13,000
	10B	3,000	3,000	
4/30/12	11A	3,000	50,000	$53,000
		$60,000	$100,000	$160,000

Is this a good deal for you? Well, because you are getting some of your principal paid back before maturity, you are faced with the reinvestment rate issue. Unless you are living off the principal and interest, you have to reinvest your interest and sinking fund payments back into the bond market. If rates go down, it's a bad deal for you. If rates go up, it's a good deal for you.

Fiscal Facts _____

Each of the two world wars occurred just before a major turning point in the history of bond yields. World War I was accompanied by high and rising yields, and so was every earlier great war of modern times. World War II, in contrast, was accompanied by low and declining bond yields. World War II ended one year before bond yields reached their lowest point this century. In 1946, one issue of the long government bond sold yielding only 1.93 percent. (Source: *A History of Interest Rates*, pg. 335)

The Wonderful World of Bond (No, Not James)

The bond is a popular fixed-income security. But in the world of finance, you've probably heard the term tossed around with stocks as if they're one and the same: "Stocks-n-bonds, stocks-n-bonds." Well, obviously, they're not.

For one, when you buy a stock you are buying equity—ownership in the company that issued the stock. You are now an owner, entitled to share in the profits and to suffer the losses of the company. The company may or may not pay you dividends, depending on whether or not profits rise. The price of the stock you own may or may not rise. If it does, you could sell it and get your investment back many times over. But when you buy a bond, you are buying debt. You are not an owner; you are lending money to the company (or government) and it has agreed to pay you interest and to pay you back at a certain date. You are promised a specific return (the interest) on your investment, as well as the eventual return of your investment. Because you are not an owner, you are not entitled to a share of the company's profits, nor are you expected to suffer its losses. No matter how bad things get, the company is expected to honor its promise to pay you interest and return your principal at maturity.

Unlike bondholders, stockholders are not guaranteed a specific rate of return and they might not even get their investment back. On the other hand, stockholders might make a huge return on investment if the company in which they invested skyrockets. A bondholder does not share in that possibility. Stocks are riskier investments than bonds, but offer the possibility of higher returns.

When Do You Want Bonds in Your Portfolio?

There are three reasons to own bonds:

- To meet current income needs. Bonds provide high current income. This is why, as you approach and eventually reach retirement, bonds will play an increasingly important role in your portfolio. You should be able to live off the income they generate when you no longer earn a salary.

- To reduce the volatility or risk in your portfolio.

- In the unlikely event of another depression like the one that decimated stock prices between 1929 and 1932, having bonds in your portfolio can cushion the blow when your stocks take a hit.

Let's look at an example. Say there are two portfolios: one is invested 100 percent in equities, and the other has 20 percent in bonds that pay 6 percent annual interest and 80 percent in stocks.

Portfolio One (100% Equities)				Portfolio Two (20% Bonds/80% Equities)			
Bond Return	Equity Return	Total Return	Index Nos.	Bond Return	Equity Return	Total Return	Index Nos.
-	+10	+10	+1.010	+6	+10	+9.2	+1.092
-	0	0	+1.10	+6	0	+1.2	+1.105
-	+20	+20	+1.32	+6	+20	+17.2	+1.295
-	−10	-10	+1.188	+6	−10	−6.8	+1.207
-	+30	+30	+1.544	+6	+30	+25.2	+1.511
Total Return		+50				+46	
Average		+10.0%				+9.2%	
Compound Annual		+9.1%				+8.6%	

The portfolio with bonds returns 8.6 percent. The portfolio invested exclusively in stock earns 0.5 percent more (9.1 percent), but it is much more volatile. Is it worth forgoing that small 0.5 percent difference to invest in bonds and have a more stable portfolio—especially as you get closer to retirement age? For many people, the answer is "absolutely!"

How Inflation Erodes Bonds

Bonds are definitely safer than stocks … unless you are in a period of high inflation, that is. When the cost of living is going up rapidly, an all-bond portfolio carries a wipeout risk that makes the gyrations of the stock market look mild.

Stock prices typically rise with inflation, so the value of stock you own is somewhat protected from inflation. Bonds, on the other hand, offer no protection against inflation because a $1,000 bond bought today will only pay the bondholder $1,000 at maturity. If that $1,000 only buys $750 worth of groceries due to inflation, the value of the bond has been eroded by inflation. This is why bond prices typically decline when investors hear economic news that causes them to worry about inflation.

In 1971, for example, the year-end yield on long-term government bonds was just below 6 percent. Say you invested your entire net worth—$100,000—in these fixed-income securities at that time in order to generate current income. That year, inflation was running at 3.36 percent making your real return 2.64 percent. Now take a look at what happened throughout the remainder of the decade:

Year	Rate of Inflation	Inflation-Adjusted Value of Investment	Nominal Interest Income	Inflation-Adjusted Interest Income
		$100,000		
1972	3.41	$ 96,590	$6,000	$5,795
1973	8.80	$ 88,090	$6,000	$5,285
1974	12.20	$ 77,343	$6,000	$4,640
1975	7.01	$ 71,921	$6,000	$4,315
1976	4.81	$ 68,461	$6,000	$4,107
1977	6.77	$ 63,826	$6,000	$3,829
1978	9.03	$ 58,063	$6,000	$3,483
1979	13.31	$ 50,335	$6,000	$3,019
1980	12.40	$ 44,093	$6,000	$2,645
1981	8.94	$ 40,151	$6,000	$2,409

(Source: Ibbotson Associates, Inc. Stocks, Bonds, Bills and Inflation © 2004 Yearbook. All right reserved. Used with permission.)

By the end of the decade, nearly 60 percent of the real purchasing power of your initial investment had been obliterated! To add insult to injury, the $6,000 you received in interest income each year now only buys you the equivalent of $2,409 worth of goods and services. Although your portfolio still has $100,000 worth of bonds paying you $6,000 per annum, the true economic net worth would be less than it was when you began investing; a terrific tragedy.

Instead you'd much rather own shares of outstanding corporations. Why? Think back to the list of traits exhibited by an excellent business that we discussed in the previous chapter. A good enterprise is capable of passing on cost increases to the customer in the form of a higher selling price without affecting sales. Likewise, because it is not capital intensive, it doesn't have to worry about replacing huge factories that now cost more. The net result is that inflation inflicts far less damage. The moral: an all-bond portfolio can actually be riskier than an all-stock portfolio in real, honest-to-goodness economic terms during periods of high inflation.

A Simple Rule for Deciding How Much of Your Portfolio to Keep in Bonds

Many books have been written on the subject of how to allocate the assets in your portfolio between the three major investment classes: cash, stocks, and bonds. Cutting through the blather, the simplest rule is this: subtract your age from 100. The difference is the amount you should hold in stocks. A 60-year-old, therefore, should keep 40 percent of his or portfolio in stocks and the rest in bonds, with a portion in cash for an emergency fund.

You can "ladder" or stagger bonds to help protect your portfolio in times of financial crisis. The idea is to have some bonds maturing (returning your principal to you) every year. Ladder securities with 1- to 10-year maturities so you have one maturing every year. You can then keep the maturing principal safely in Treasury bills if you think interest rates are going to rise (which drives bond prices down). Or you can use the money to purchase a new 10-year Treasury, thereby retaining the "ladder."

Now combine this with the simplified asset allocation formula. For a sixty-year-old who has invested 60 percent in bonds and 40 percent in equities, over the past 12 months (ending 10/24/08), the portfolio's return would be as follows:

Equities = $40 × -35 percent = $26

Fixed Income = $60 × 10 percent = $66 (includes interest income)

Total fund = $26 + $66 = $92

So this account is down 8 percent over the past 12 months; not too shabby, considering the dizzying drops in the stock market.

Bond Ratings

Bonds are rated by *rating agencies* such as Moody's and Standard & Poor's. Fixed income analysts pour over financial data provided by the issuers of bonds and assign grades to help investors determine the level of risk a bond issue poses. The higher the credit quality, and thus rating, the lower the yield. The reason is simple: companies that are high-risk have to offer higher interest payments to compensate for the greater probability of default.

Investment Grade	Moody's	Standard and Poor's
Highest Quality	Aaa	AAA
High Quality	Aa	AA
Tier-1 Medium	A-1, A	A
Tier-2 Medium	Baa-1, Baa	BBB
Noninvestment Grade or Junk		
Speculative	Ba	BB
Extremely Speculative	B, Caa	B, CCC, CC
In Default	Ca, C	D

As an individual investor, you should relegate your purchases to the upper levels of investment-grade securities. Otherwise, you might find yourself in the unhappy position of losing your entire investment.

How to Read a Bond Table

Like stocks, bonds are also listed in tables in the financial section of newspapers. Bond tables are useful for two reasons:

◆ If you own a bond and want to sell it, chances are the price is going to be different than what you paid for it. You need to know how different.

◆ Most bonds are purchased from the secondary market. The table allows you to research and compare current yields for various issues.

A bond table is a handy way to adjust to changes in bond yields and/or prices. When bonds are first issued, they are priced to sell at *par*, or 100. As they trade, their price moves above or below 100, depending on the demand for the bonds. If a bond's price falls below 100, it is considered to be selling at a *discount*. If it rises above 100, it is selling at a *premium*. Bonds trade in "32nds"; $\frac{1}{32}$, $\frac{2}{32}$ price movements. For example, in May of 2002, the Treasury sold five-year notes that matured in May 2007 and paid 4.375 percent interest. By August 1, 2002, the notes were trading at a *premium* price of $104\frac{12}{32}$ with a yield of 3.37 percent.

def•i•ni•tion

Par is the original price of a bond, note, or bill. It is also the amount that the security will pay back at maturity and is referred to as "100" (e.g., a $1,000 par value bond that increased in price to $1,100 due to a fall in interest rates would be quoted as "110" in the bond tables). Between issuance and maturity, a fixed-income security may be bought and sold, with its price rising or falling depending on interest rates and other factors. If a bond's price is over 100, the bond is said to be trading at a **premium**. If the price falls below 100, the bond is trading at a **discount**.

If the yield fell 30 basis points (.30 percent), what would the price of the bond be? Looking in a bond yield book (your broker or banker will have one), you would look down the yield scale to 3.07 percent and then over to 4 years 10 months to maturity to read a price of 105.87. Alternatively, if the yield increased 30 basis points, you would look up to find the price of 103.12. Know the price but want to find the yield? Just reverse the process!

Corporate Debt—An Unwise Choice for Small Investors

Corporations issue bonds and notes—both *mortgage* (*secured* debt) and *debentures* (*unsecured* debt)—but these are not wise investments for individual investors. Why not? Well, since you asked so nicely …

◆ Corporate debt typically includes call features—a must to avoid. Some corporations also issue a hybrid security called a convertible *debenture*. A convertible claims to give you participation in both the bond market and the stock market. Unfortunately, you just get two watered-down products: (1) a coupon that pays less interest income than a plain old bond and (2) a chance to buy the company's stock that doesn't kick in unless the stock price increases at least 20 to 25 percent. Avoid convertibles and leave the field to the experts who specialize in these securities.

def•i•ni•tion

A **mortgage bond** is a bond backed by actual collateral, either in the form of real estate or property that can be liquidated in the event of default. Mortgage bonds are also known as **secured bonds**. On the other hand, **debentures** are bonds backed only by the promise of the company to repay; also known as **unsecured bonds**.

- Most corporations have fluctuating credit ratings. You might buy bonds from a company with a triple-A rating, only to find that a few years later the company has made some bad business decisions and has had its credit rating downgraded to A or even triple-B. Yikes, now you have to worry about whether the company will be able to honor its promise to give you back your principal at maturity.

- Outstanding corporate debt typically sells in individual units of 100 bonds ($100,000). Do you want to sink that kind of money into one company's bonds? Not unless you have millions to invest, in which case you don't need this book, you need your own private financial advisor.

- Corporate debt is primarily traded over the counter instead of on the New York Stock Exchange or American Stock Exchange, which are more accessible to individual investors. The NYSE might trade around $10 million in bonds on any given day. Amex only does around $750,000. Meanwhile, roughly $100 million a day in corporate bonds is traded in the over-the-counter market. That's a market that small investors don't really have access to, and those bonds aren't quoted in the newspaper bond tables, either.

For all these reasons, corporate bonds are not a good choice for individual investors—meaning you. The higher yields are not worth the added risk and aggravation. Stick with Treasuries and agencies.

Treasuries—Smart Alternative to Corporate Debt

Don't feel too bad about staying away from the tantalizing array of corporate debt out there. The U.S. Government issues plenty of options that are much healthier for your portfolio. The best part? Uncle Sam's obligations are considered risk-free. That is, you are always going to get your interest and principal because the debt is backed by the full faith and credit of the United States government. In practical terms, if the Treasury runs short, the Feds can either turn on the printing presses and print more money or simply raise taxes to increase revenue.

U.S. government debt is issued by:

- The Treasury Department
- Government and Quasi-Government Agencies

U.S. Treasury debt takes one of three forms:

- ◆ Treasury bills (out to one-year maturity)

- ◆ Treasury notes (2- to 10-year maturities)

- ◆ Treasury bonds (maturities beyond 10 years)

There are also two other forms of Treasury debt:

- ◆ Treasury STRIPs are Treasury notes and bonds "stripped" down to their individual coupons and maturity. These are sold at a discount like Treasury bills, and are very useful if you know you will need a sum of money by a certain date (college tuition, for example).

- ◆ Treasury debt also appears as inflation-indexed notes and bonds. These include an inflation adjustment, which you get when the bond matures. So if you buy a $10,000 inflation-indexed bond and inflation has risen by 10 percent by the time the bond matures, you'll get your $10,000 principal back plus a $1,000 inflation adjustment.

How to Buy Treasuries

Treasury securities are easy to purchase at regular Treasury auctions. You can participate online via Treasury Direct (www.treasurydirect.gov). There are weekly T-bill auctions, monthly one-year T-bill auctions, and quarterly Treasury note and bond auctions. Check your local newspaper or *The Wall Street Journal* for advance notices, which usually appear five to seven days before an auction. You can also deal directly with your nearest Federal Reserve Bank or ask your banker or broker to make purchases for you for a small service fee of around $25. The minimum purchase is $1,000 and all bids must be made in $1,000 lots.

Buying Outstanding Treasuries

Besides buying Treasuries at auction, you can also buy outstanding Treasuries on the market. They will be trading either at a discount or a premium (although you will receive your principal back in full at maturity, the par value of a bond will fluctuate in the interim due to changes in interest rates; as rates decrease, bond prices increase and vice versa).

Fiscal Facts _____

Patriot bonds are a type of zero-coupon bond. Instead of sending you your interest payments periodically, the investment is issued at a discount to par. As a result, you received your interest in the form of an appreciation in the price of the bond, rather than interest checks in the mail.

What does this mean to you? Well, a bond or note is selling at a premium because it pays a higher interest rate than current new notes or bonds. So if you buy an outstanding Treasury at a premium, you will get higher interest income than you would from the new Treasuries being auctioned. On the other hand, you don't get all of your principal back when you buy a Treasury that is trading at a premium. Remember, the principal is the amount that the borrower originally borrowed. If you buy a $10,000 Treasury note at a premium, it'll cost more than $10,000, but $10,000 is all you get paid back at maturity.

A discount bond works in just the opposite manner. Let's say you purchase a Treasury bond trading at 96, or $9,600. You'll receive $10,000 at maturity, for a gain of $400. However, you'll get interest income from this note for around $400 to $600 less than the current rate. Is it worth it to receive less income in return for greater principal return? That depends on what's more important to you—some people want income, some want a greater return in the long run. If the answer to either question is no, just buy at the auctions.

A final reason for buying and holding individual Treasury securities, as opposed to a typical bond fund, is illustrated by the 2008 financial panic. The typical bond mutual fund is laced with corporate bonds (of varying credit quality). In the current environment, however, investors demand absolute safety of principal. Therefore, investors have a tendency to redeem their bond fund shares, which causes the bond fund manager to sell some of his bonds to meet the redemptions, thereby pressuring the value of his fund. As other shareholders do the same in other bond funds, and as corporate bonds drop in value versus Treasuries, the net asset value of typical bond funds decline. You really don't want to be stuck in _that_ vicious cycle during another financial crisis.

An Old Favorite: Savings Bonds

Savings bonds—the kind you received from your grandparents when you were a kid—can actually be a great option for the average investor. Like treasuries, savings bonds are backed by the full faith and credit of the United States government.

Patriot Bonds (Formerly EE Savings Bonds)

Following the events of September 11, 2001, EE Savings Bonds were renamed Patriot bonds. They are purchased for half of their face value (e.g., a $10,000 savings bond will cost you $5,000) and come in denominations of $50, $75, $100, $200, $500, $1,000, $5,000, and $10,000. Patriot Bonds, a type of *zero-coupon bond*, are simple, straightforward, and absolutely safe. There are some disadvantages, however:

- The yield is fixed at 90 percent of a five-year Treasury note, with the yield recalculated every six months. If Treasury note rates fall, so does the rate on your bond. If the five-year Treasury note is yielding 3.25 percent, the Patriot Bond is yielding 2.925 percent. But if six months later, the Treasury note yield drops to 2¾ percent, your bond starts earning only 2.475 percent. Of course, the yields could go up, too!

- Although you can redeem (cash in) a Patriot bond after six months, you will pay a three-month interest penalty unless you wait at least five years to redeem it. To avoid the penalty, you have to really plan ahead when using savings bonds for major expenditures such as a college education. In other words, you'll need to stop purchasing the bonds five years before the last college bills come due.

- You also have to deal with a limit of $30,000 face value ($15,000 purchase price) per purchaser, per year.

Patriot savings bonds do have some great advantages:

- You can purchase them with as little as $25.

- They make great gifts from relatives.

- The interest income on an EE savings bond is free of state and local taxes. (Remember, we promised way back in Chapter 9 to get to this!) The federal taxes on interest income are due only when the EE savings bond is redeemed. And in some instances, there is a tax exclusion if the proceeds are being used for postsecondary education.

Here's how the exclusion works: first of all, it is limited to tuition and required fees. In this case, it may not be applied to room, board, or books. Second, the bonds must be registered in the name of the taxpayer, not the child, although the child can be named as beneficiary.

In addition, the qualified tuition and fees paid must be equal to or greater than the amount of money received when the bonds are cashed in. If you pay tuition and fees of $5,000 and the bond proceeds are no more than $5,000, you're qualified for the exclusion. If tuition and fees are $4,000 and the bond proceeds are $5,000, you can deduct only that ratio ($4,000 ÷ $5,000 = 80 percent) of the interest income on the bonds (not the principal). Don't you love how confusing the IRS can make things?

Finally, to qualify for the tax exclusion, you have to earn less than the modified AGI limits. Currently, the range of modified adjusted gross income is $89,750 to $119,750 for couples filing jointly and $65,000 to $80,600 for single filers. In other words, you can get full exclusion if you earn under $98,400, and partial exclusion scaling down to zero once you earn over $128,400. Did you notice that we tucked in the word "modified"?

In this case, modified AGI is AGI plus the interest earned on the redeemed bonds. Ah, the tax code! But wait: there's another neat way to use EE savings bonds for a child's college expense. Buy the bonds in the child's name and file a tax return with the child's Social Security number. Then report the accrued (earned but not received) interest income on the bonds for that year. You won't need to file again and no tax is due unless or until the child's total income exceeds the threshold for taxes owed. If tax is owed, it is at the parent's rate for children under age 14 and at the child's rate at age 14 or older.

It is unfortunate that the regulations on EE savings bonds are so complicated because they have a lot to offer parents saving for college. But that's the Feds for you.

I Bonds

Series I bonds were first issued by the Treasury in September of 1998 and provide built-in inflation protection (remember our discussion about how inflation can erode a bond's value?). The earnings rate of an I bond is a combination of two separate rates: a fixed rate of return and a variable semiannual inflation rate. The fixed rate remains the same throughout the life of the I bond, whereas the semiannual inflation rate is adjusted every six months based on changes in the *Consumer Price Index*. The semiannual inflation rate is combined with the fixed rate to determine the I bond's earnings rate for the next six months.

def•i•ni•tion

Published monthly, the **Consumer Price Index** (CPI) tracks the cost of a basket of goods that includes housing, food, transportation, and more, in an attempt to measure inflation.

You must hold I bonds for at least six months to get your original investment and earnings; however, if you cash out before five years, you'll lose three months of interest. With six-month CDs offering their lowest rates in almost 20 years, I bonds are not a bad parking spot for your savings.

Agency-O-Rama

The Treasury is not the only government agency that issues debt. There are a host of government agencies and quasi-agencies (agencies created by an act of Congress, like FNMA) out there borrowing money. Following are some of them:

♦ The Federal National Mortgage Association (known as "Fannie Mae"). FNMA is a quasi-agency. Its debt is an implied (but not a guaranteed) obligation of the federal government. The agency's stock trades publicly on the New York Stock Exchange under the ticker symbol FNM.

♦ Federal Home Loan Mortgage Corp. ("Freddie Mac"). Like Fannie Mae, Freddie Mac is a quasi-agency/private corporation with stock listed on the New York Stock Exchange under the ticker symbol FRE.

♦ Student Loan Marketing Association ("Sallie Mae"). Officially known as SLM Corporation, Sallie Mae is the third and last of the three public/private corporations. Its ticker symbol is SLM.

Fiscal Facts

The difference between general obligation and revenue municipal bonds is the source of repayment. GOs rely on the taxing power of the issuer, whereas revenue munis are operations of an enterprise such as a hospital.

◆ Government National Mortgage Association ("Ginnie Mae") issues bonds that return both principal and interest, just as you pay your monthly mortgage in a single sum to cover both principal and interest. GNMAs are federally guaranteed. This is the only quasi-agency that enjoys this privilege. "Ginnie Mae" bonds are an example of a class of bonds called mortgage-backed securities (MBS). The MBS is a debt instrument with a pool of real estate loans (perhaps your mortgage included) representing the underlying collateral. As principal and interest payments are paid into the pool, they, in turn, are paid out to GNMA bondholders. Mortgage-backed certificates are issued by banks and insured by private mortgage insurance companies.

◆ Resolution Funding Corporation (RFC). These bonds are guaranteed as to principal, but not interest, and were issued to help resolve the Savings & Loan crisis of the late 1980s/early 1990s.

CDs: A Viable Alternative to Government Debt

If you want the guarantee of the federal government but aren't willing to venture into buying Treasuries, consider your old pal the certificate of deposit. After all, CDs can be purchased in maturities up to 10 years, and for specific sums once you clear the minimum (usually $1,000). The first $100,000 is completely guaranteed by the federal government.

As we mentioned earlier, though, CD rates are currently quite low, so this might be a good time to gather up your courage and visit the Treasury online and learn how to purchase Treasury notes. It's really not that tough, we promise!

Nevertheless, CDs offer an interesting alternative to shorter maturing government securities. And, if you buy at your local bank, you have the added convenience factor. CD rates tend to be competitive with government paper, especially Treasury bills, but you may need to shop around to determine which bank offers the best deal. The only problem with CDs is the penalty you incur (usually three to six months of interest, depending upon maturity) if you sell prior to maturity. Unlike the new I bonds, they don't offer any protection against inflation.

Municipal Bonds

Municipal bonds are issued by city, county, and state governments. The proceeds of the issue are often used for projects such as building a hospital, facilities for public schools, or improving infrastructure. Unlike corporate bonds, the interest income investors receive from "munis" are free from federal taxes; sometimes, even the state taxes are waived if the investor resides in the state that issued the bonds!

There are two broad categories into which municipal bonds fall—*general obligation* (GO) and *revenue*. The difference arises from the source of repayment. GO munis are backed by the power of an entity to tax, whereas revenue bonds rely on the operations of an underlying business such as a hospital or utility.

It is much more difficult to secure information on municipal issues than it is, say, the bonds of General Electric. As a result, you need to do two things:

◆ Examine the credit rating assigned to a municipal bond. Don't even think about buying something that is outside of investment-grade range.

◆ Some municipalities will lower their cost of borrowing by paying for bond insurance. The result is that you—the investor—can buy munis that are guaranteed by a third party; meaning that if the bond issuer defaults, the insurer steps in and foots the bill to ensure that you get your money.

Calculating Taxable-Equivalent Yield

There's a quick and easy way to compare the tax-free yields on municipal bonds to those offered by less advantaged issues. Here's the formula:

$$\frac{\text{Tax-Exempt Yield}}{1 - \text{Tax Bracket}}$$

Assume an investor in the 35 percent tax bracket is interested in acquiring a muni that is currently yielding 4.0 percent. Plug this data into the equation.

Step 1. $\dfrac{.04}{1-0.35}$

Step 2. $\dfrac{.04}{0.65}$

Answer = 0.0615, or 6.15 percent

The result tells us that the investor could either acquire a municipal bond yielding 4 percent or a fully taxable bond yielding 6.15 percent and come out in the exact same financial position once the bill to the IRS had been paid.

In almost all cases, investors that reside in high income tax brackets are going to find munis more attractive than other fixed-income securities. Likewise, municipal bonds make absolutely no sense for tax-advantaged institutions such as churches, universities, and other nonprofits.

Money Market Funds

Okay, for you purists out there, we realize that money market funds aren't fixed-income investments themselves. Still, because they are invested entirely in fixed-income securities, it makes sense to discuss the topic while we're here.

A money market fund attempts to keep its share price at exactly $1. The funds it receives from investors are placed into short-term, fixed-income securities such as *commercial paper*, Treasury bills with maturities of 30 days or less, and certificates of deposit. The income from these investments is paid out to the fund owners and may or may not be taxable depending upon the type of money market fund chosen.

def•i•ni•tion

Commercial paper is an unsecured obligation issued by companies with stellar credit ratings to help meet short-term funding needs. The typical maturity runs from 2 to 270 days. There is a very limited secondary market for commercial paper due to the extremely short maturities.

Although not insured by the FDIC, there is very little risk of loss because the SEC requires the average maturity of the investments held by the fund to be 90 days or less. If you are in between investments or simply looking for a safe place to park your cash, a money market is an excellent way to get a little extra yield without a substantial increase in risk.

The Least You Need to Know

- A fixed-income security pays you interest income when you lend a sum to a borrower, who promises to pay you back on a specific date called the "maturity date."

- When stock prices are falling, bond prices tend to rise, so having bonds in your portfolio can help to counteract declines in the value of your stock.

◆ Avoid call features, sinkers, and corporate debt.

◆ Buy Treasury bills, notes, and bonds and government agency paper for the fixed-income segment of your portfolio. Consider the new I bonds as alternatives to CDs.

◆ For most high-income households, municipal bonds make more sense than their taxable counterparts.

Preferred Stock: A Hybrid of Wall Street

In This Chapter

♦ Why preferred stock doesn't make sense for individual investors

♦ Cumulative versus noncumulative provisions

♦ Participating preferred issues

♦ Convertible preferred stock

Somewhere between common stocks and bonds lies a hybrid known as preferred stock. Although technically equity, preferred issues have many of the characteristics of debt. In this chapter, you learn why these commitments rarely make sense for the individual investor and—for those of you who choose to take the path less traveled—the terms to look for if you do decide to add them to your portfolio.

Fiscal Facts _____

The dividend for a preferred stock is usually stated as a percentage of par value. Put another way, when you are researching preferred stocks, you will notice in the title something like "ABC Company Cumulative 9 Percent Preferred"; this means that the dividend is going to be 9 percent of the stated par value. If, for example, those shares had a $100 par, the dividend would equal $9 annually; a par value of $25 would result in a dividend of $2.25.

What Do You Get When You Mix Stocks with Bonds?

First, let's examine three basic characteristics of preferred stock:

- **Higher Dividends.** The main attraction to preferred stock is that it offers dividends that are substantially higher than those available on the common stock (which may or may not receive any cash distributions). Unlike common dividends, which are declared in nominal per share amounts, preferred dividends are spelled out in a prospectus and normally stated as a percentage of *par value*.

- **Liquidation Preference.** In the event of bankruptcy, preferred stockholders rank beneath the bondholders and above the common stockholders. (For example, if there is anything left of the company after the bondholders' claims are satisfied, it will be distributed to the holders of the preferred stock. The common stockholders come last.)

- **No Residual Right.** In exchange for the higher dividend and liquidation preference, preferred stockholders forgo any residual right to excess profits. After they've received their juicy dividend, they have no further expectation of profit from the success of the enterprise—all of that bounty goes directly to the holders of the common stock.

It Just Doesn't Make Sense

As you can see, the preferred stockholder has all of the drawbacks of bond ownership (no residual right to profits) as well as all of the drawbacks of common stock ownership (subordinate rank in the event of bankruptcy). Why, then, would anyone purchase preferred stock? Believe it or not, it can be a great investment for corporations. To understand why, we must voyage into that Oz-like land of tax law. Here's all you need to know:

- When a corporation *issues* bonds, the interest it pays out to the bondholders is tax-deductible. When it issues shares of stock—whether common or preferred—the dividends are not.

- When a corporation *invests in* the bonds of another corporation, the interest income received is fully taxable. On the other hand, 70 percent of dividends received on equity investments—whether common or preferred—are excluded from the calculation of tax (unless the investor is an insurance company, in which case it can exclude only 59½ percent).

The result is that a corporation would generate higher after-tax rates of return by receiving dividend, rather than interest, income. Therefore, a corporation choosing between a bond and preferred stock issue, each yielding 5 percent respectively, would almost always opt for the latter despite the fact that it was subordinate to the bonds.

Prior to the Bush tax cuts, individual investors paid personal income tax rates on both interest income and dividends received. Now, dividends are taxed at a maximum rate of 15 percent. Absent this recent incentive to invest in equities, it makes more sense to purchase fixed-income securities; in addition to being at the top of the list in the event of bankruptcy proceedings, you have a greater chance of receiving your money on time. Believe us—although corporations loathe either scenario, missing a bond payment is a much more serious transgression than passing on a preferred dividend.

Bolstering Capital

The fact that preferred stock is more popular among corporate investors leads to many custom-tailored *private placement* issues created with specific goals and objectives in mind. Say you owned a chain of hotels and were low on cash due to rapid growth-driven expansion. Through a series of events, one of your competitors falls upon hard times and is interested in selling out to a larger concern: a once-in-a-lifetime opportunity. You'd love to jump at the offer but you have some hesitations. First, you don't want to issue bonds and increase your level of outstanding debt. Second, you don't want to issue additional common stock, diluting the ownership of your existing shareholders.

def·i·ni·tion

Private placements are investments sold directly to institutional investors such as corporations, insurance groups, pension funds, mutual funds, and investment partnerships. Private placements are not publicly traded and, in many cases, are nontransferable. Unlike public placements, registration with the SEC is not required.

You don't necessarily have to pass on the opportunity. You could approach a cash-rich corporation and offer to create a special class of preferred stock, tailored to the needs of both parties. You receive the proceeds of the sale, providing the capital necessary to complete the acquisition, and the other corporation gets the promise of earning higher rates of return than would otherwise be possible on its idle cash balances. As you'll see throughout the remainder of the chapter, the myriad of options available for customizing the issue are limited only by the imagination of the participants; cumulative vs. noncumulative, participating vs. nonparticipating, voting vs. nonvoting, convertible vs. nonconvertible, higher penalty rates in the event of nonpayment of dividends, and mandatory redemption provisions, just to name a few.

It's a Family Affair

Sometimes a company's founding family wants to go public to raise capital and expand the business, but doesn't want to pay out all of the earnings as dividends, slowing growth.

Throughout history, creating a special class of preferred stock has often been a solution to this problem. The new class of preferred shares could have a mandatory annual dividend (such as 5 percent of par) that is payable under all but the most dire circumstances. It could have voting power to elect a set percentage of the Board of Directors. In some cases, it may even be participating.

If you have any stake in a company—common stock, preferred stock, or bonds—you need to be aware of the existence of a capitalization structure, such as the one just described, that may cause the controlling family to have interests divergent with your own. This information isn't likely to be in the annual report. Instead, you'll have to turn to the 10-K.

What to Look for in a Preferred Stock

The odds are fairly good that you are neither a corporation, nor a member of a controlling family about to take a company public. That being the case, for those of you who are still interested in acquiring preferred stock for your portfolio, the least we can do is offer you a checklist of things to look for and/or avoid when searching through the minefields. All of these details can be found in the prospectus for the preferred stock issue you are considering. You can get a copy of the prospectus by contacting the Securities and Exchange Commission.

Cumulative vs. Noncumulative

As an investor, you expect to receive your dividends. On rare occasions (for example, a company facing the possibility of missing an interest payment to its bondholders) a board of directors may decide to withhold the dividend that would otherwise be paid to the preferred stockholders.

What happens when and if prosperous times return? If your preferred stock is cumulative, the dividend that you did not receive is known as *in arrears*. This means that before dividends can be paid on the common stock, the company must make up all of the past skipped payments to the preferred stockholders. If your shares were noncumulative, you would simply be out of luck; when the board of directors passed on the dividend, it was lost to you forever. Tough break!

It shouldn't be hard to see that the single most important consideration for a preferred stockholder is whether an issue is cumulative or noncumulative. Repeat after us: "I will purchase only cumulative issues." Now, say it again.

def•i•ni•tion

When a dividend is **in arrears,** it means that it is owed, but not paid, to the preferred stockholders. In order to protect the preferred shares, companies are often prohibited from paying dividends on their common stock until the balance has been paid in full.

Voting Rights

Most of the time, preferred stock has no voting rights. Sometimes, however, the prospectus may contain a provision granting voting rights to the preferred stockholders if dividends are not paid for a specific length of time.

Take Avalon Bay Communities, one of the largest apartment rental real estate investment trusts in the United States. The company has an 8.70 percent Series H Cumulative Redeemable Preferred Stock. Diving into the prospectus, you find just such a provision:

> "As a holder of Series H Preferred Stock, you will generally have no voting rights except as required by law. However, if we fail to pay dividends on any shares of Series H Preferred Stock for six or more quarterly periods, our Board of Directors will increase the number of directors of Avalon Bay by two. As a holder of Series H Preferred Stock, you will be entitled to vote, separately as a

class with the holders of all other series of preferred stock upon which like voting rights have been conferred and are exercisable, for the election of such two additional directors until we have fully paid all dividends accrued on the shares of Series H Preferred Stock (or until we have declared such full dividends and set aside a sum sufficient for the payment thereof)."

The presence of conditional voting power seems fair and desirable. It can provide you with reasonable assurance that management isn't going to pass on the preferred dividend simply to enlarge the empire.

Redemption Rights

Remember the call provision we discussed back in Chapter 12? When a stock is redeemable at the option of a company, it is never good for the preferred stockholder. In effect, it means that the Board of Directors could decide to cancel your certificates and send you a check in the mail at a predetermined price—even if you didn't want to sell the investment.

Some issues are redeemable at the option of the stockholder. This means that you could force the corporation to repurchase your shares at a previously agreed-upon price, most often during a small window of time every few years. These are almost always good for you. In effect, it can establish a floor to the stock.

Participating Provisions

Remember when we told you that preferred stock has no residual right to excess profits generated above its fixed dividends? That was true … unless, of course, the issue contains a participating provision!

Participating provisions allow the preferred stockholders to receive extra dividends, based upon a formula spelled out in the prospectus, when and if the dividend on the common stock exceeds a certain level. This potential for additional income is going to cause the preferred stock price to fluctuate far more than it would otherwise. Don't worry, though. As long as the fixed dividend is paid, it tends to act as a stabilizing force (unlike common stock, it's not probable your preferred stock would lose 70 percent of its value if the dividend is still being, and expected to remain, paid).

Adjustable Rate Provisions

Some preferred stock issues have adjustable rate provisions. Instead of a fixed dividend expressed as a percentage of par, the payout is determined by the movement in an established benchmark, such as U.S. Treasuries.

Unlike traditional preferred stock, the dynamic nature of the dividend payout on adjustable rate issues generally results in a relatively narrow range of market prices. Although this is good for you, it doesn't overcome one big shortcoming—you don't know how much you are going to receive in dividends each year! When investing for current income, you need to know how much cash you can expect to have in hand.

Riding with the Top Down: Convertible Preferred Stock

An entirely different beast altogether, convertible preferred stock offers the owner the option to convert their preferred stake into shares of common stock. The terms of conversion are determined at the time of issuance and are carefully spelled out in the prospectus. Consider the following hypothetical scenario:

> To raise capital, my company issued shares of $100 par value, 5 percent convertible preferred stock with the right to convert the security into 4 shares of common stock at $25 per share; at the time, my common stock was trading at $15 per share. By offering you the conversion privilege, I was able to get away with paying you a dividend that most investors would have otherwise rejected as insufficient.

> Upon issuance, the conversion privilege has little or no value (why would you convert a $100 preferred stock into 4 shares of common stock, effectively paying $25, when the current market price is only $15?). Instead, you hold your position because you are interested in the $5 annual per share dividend. The potential to profit from a move in the common stock without the associated risk is simply icing on the proverbial cake.

> A few years pass and the price of my common stock has increased to $40. Now, the conversion right offers some real gravy! An *arbitrager* could purchase shares of the preferred stock on the open market, convert them, and instantly experience a profit of $15 per share ($40 per share selling price – $25 per share cost = $15 per share profit). Due to the basic law of supply and demand, the resulting buying frenzy will cause the market price of the preferred stock to rise, say, to $160 per share. Here you are, sitting on your original shares, with a $5 annual

dividend arriving in the mail every year and a $60 unrealized capital gain due to the conversion feature. Life is sweet.

There's only one problem. You originally purchased your shares strictly for investment purposes—that is, you wanted current income in the most old-fashioned of ways. Your shares, which originally yielded 5 percent ($5 annual dividend divided by $100 per-share market value) now only yield 3.125 percent ($5 dividend divided by $160 market price) thanks to the conversion-driven increase in the market value!

Had you purchased your position before the conversion boom, you would be fine in the event of a collapse in the underlying common stock. Your investment would return to its former price and you would continue to receive your dividend check in the mail. Had you purchased the shares after the price contained some sort of reflection of the conversion privilege, however, you would have effectively been speculating in the common stock! The only redeeming factor is that the presence of the preferred dividend, in most cases, establishes a practical floor that protects you from losing everything.

There are portfolio managers who spend their entire lives specializing in nothing but convertible arbitrage. This is a field dominated by specialists. For those of you who insist on playing in this sandbox, remember that arrogance can be financially ruinous; seek the advice of professionals.

The Least You Need to Know

- ◆ Preferred stocks often make more sense for corporate investors than for individuals.

- ◆ Preferred dividends are usually expressed as a percentage of par value.

- ◆ Never invest in a noncumulative preferred stock.

- ◆ Check for the existence of capitalization structures that may cause the interests of a founding family or other entity to diverge with your own.

- ◆ Leave convertible issues to the pros.

Chapter 14

Navigating the Mutual Fund Universe

In This Chapter

◆ The difference between open-end and closed-end funds

◆ Avoiding unnecessary fees and expenses

◆ How to pick a winning fund

◆ The benefits of index funds

Although the first mutual funds were created before the 1929 stock market crash, mutual funds have truly exploded in popularity in the last 20 years.

Why did they become so popular? There are a few reasons:

◆ Mutual funds became the product of choice for 401(k) plans.

◆ Some mutual fund managers became cult figures who were frequently quoted and interviewed in major publications nationwide.

◆ With the downturn in the stock market in the late 1990s and the more recent turmoil, individual investors who got burned by holding only a few stocks realized that mutual funds offer much wider diversification than they could achieve on their own. Such diversification reduces the risk of investing in just one or several stocks. In addition, investors discovered the merits of bond funds, which offer diversification plus an alternative to the stock market!

def•i•ni•tion

An **index** is merely a list of assets used as a barometer. The Dow Jones Industrial Average, for example, is the most widely recognized index. It is a list of 30 blue chip stocks selected by the editors of *The Wall Street Journal* (a publication of the Dow Jones Company) price-weighted (that is, a stock that is $50 per-share would have a greater effect on the Dow than a stock that is $30). Other famous indices include the S&P 500, the Wilshire 5000, the Russell 2000, and the NASDAQ composite.

What Exactly Are Mutual Funds?

A mutual fund is a company that invests on behalf of customers. The "customers" may be individual investors like you, or even big companies. Either way, the mutual fund pools the money it collects and manages it with investment objectives that are carefully spelled out in a document called the *prospectus.*

def•i•ni•tion

A **prospectus** is a legal document sent out to potential investors. It describes a fund's objectives, strategies, risks, and other pertinent data designed to help investors determine if the fund is right for their personal needs.

For example, one fund might invest only in technology stocks. Another might invest in small, emerging companies; another in government securities, or in corporate bonds. There are funds that mimic the S&P 500 index or other indices; these are passively, not actively, managed—meaning that the fund's managers do very little. When you buy "shares" in a mutual fund, you own a piece of its investments proportional to the amount you've invested. Because the mutual fund is investing millions of dollars, it can develop a diversified portfolio—far beyond anything you could likely afford to create by yourself.

Open-End and Closed-End Funds

All mutual funds are registered with the Securities and Exchange Commission (SEC) under the Investment Advisers Act of 1940. Most mutual funds are open-end. This means that they are always open to accepting more deposits from more customers and can continue to grow in size with no limit to asset size. Some funds are closed, meaning they accept no more deposits after their initial offering. Closed-end funds only sell a fixed number of shares—similar to a corporation. And, like many corporations' shares, closed-end funds are primarily listed and traded on the New York Stock Exchange or the American Stock Exchange. Closed-end funds only hold around 2 to 3 percent of the total assets invested in mutual funds.

You can buy shares in a mutual fund by contacting its distributor. The price you'll pay for shares is based on the net asset value that day, provided your order is received and accepted before the close of business (currently 4 P.M.). Orders received after 4 P.M. are priced at the next day's *net asset value (NAV)* figure.

def•i•ni•tion

Net asset value (NAV) is the dollar value of all the marketable securities owned by a mutual fund, less expenses, and divided by the number of the fund's shares outstanding. When you want to buy shares in an open-end mutual fund, the price you will pay is based on the net asset value. Because the shares of a closed-end fund trade on the market, however, its share price may differ from its NAV.

 Crash Alert

Sometimes closed-end funds become open-end funds, thereby eliminating the discount that may have made them an attractive buy in the first place. You can check the current premium or discount by looking in Monday's *Wall Street Journal* (Section C near the end), and also in Sunday's *New York Times* "Money & Business" section (again, near the end).

With a closed-end fund, though, differences can develop between a share's net asset value and its market price because shareholders are competing to buy a fixed number of shares. If the shares are selling above the net asset value, they are selling at a "premium." In contrast, shares trading below NAV are said to be selling at a "discount." Some closed-end funds sell at a discount of 20 percent or greater.

If you buy shares in a fund that's selling at a hefty discount and later the fund's share price bounces back, you could make a tidy profit. So if you are interested in closed-end funds:

◆ Stick with discounts.

◆ Study the historical discount range to determine whether the current price is at the top, middle, or low end.

Why would a fund choose to be closed rather than open? Fund managers are concerned with sell-offs that could be triggered by bad news or other events. For this reason, emerging market equity funds, specialized equity funds, and municipal bond (especially state-specific) funds tend to be set up as closed-end funds because holders of the shares who wish to sell don't turn to the fund, but to the market. This protects managers from having to raise the money to buy back shares in the event of a sell-off.

Avoid Load Funds

Do you simply pay the NAV times the number of shares you want to purchase when you buy shares in an open-end mutual fund? Not always. Some funds deduct a sales charge from your principal; this is referred to as a "front-end load." Funds that charge this fee are called "load" funds. Loads currently make up 5.0 to 5.5 percent of your investment and go to whomever sold you the fund (your broker, for example); they do not go to the fund itself. Funds that do not charge this fee are called "no load" funds—and they are a much better deal. Here is a simple example of how a front-end load can hurt your investment. Let's say you purchase $10,000 of a fund with an NAV of $10 and a 5 percent load:

	Load Fund	**No-Load Fund**
Principal Amount	$10,000	$10,000
Less Sales Commission	$500	$0
Net Available	$9,500	$10,000
Net Asset Value	$10	$10
Number of Shares	950	1,000

If you buy the load fund, you lose $500, or 5 percent, of your principal before it even has a chance to work for you! Over time, the result can be millions of dollars in forgone wealth.

Some funds also charge you when you redeem (sell) your shares. This charge is referred to as a back-end or back-door load. It is also called a deferred sales charge. The intent here is to penalize investors who make frequent fund purchases and sales.

Back-end loads may run as high as 6 to 7 percent of the amount you sell in the first year, scaling down to zero by, say, the seventh year. This charge, if applicable, is deducted from your gross proceeds when you make the sale. Finally, many funds charge a shareholding servicing fee, often referred to as a 12b-1 fee. This fee, limited to .25 percent, is used as an inducement to brokers who have helped or may help sell fund shares. It is vital that you learn before purchasing shares in a fund whether it charges a front- or back-end load, and/or a 12b-1 fee. It's your money, after all! Simply ask your broker, call the fund company, or request a prospectus.

Index and Tax-Advantaged Funds

If you can shelter all the dollars you want to invest in IRAs and 401(k)s, great. But if you put some of your money directly into equity mutual funds without the shelter of an IRA, you will have to pay taxes on any gains the fund makes, even if you immediately reinvest them back into the fund. To avoid this situation, you can limit your mutual fund holdings to one of two types of stock funds—index funds and tax-advantaged funds:

- Index funds mimic the behavior of stocks in a particular index (such as the S&P 500). Because there are few trades, few capital gains are generated, meaning a lower tax bill for you. The irony is that most actively managed mutual funds (the "smart money") fail to beat low-cost index funds (the "dumb money") over long periods of time! The oldest, largest, and least expensive fund is the Vanguard Index 500, which mimics the S&P 500 Index. You can contact Vanguard at www. vanguard.com or 1-877-662-7447.

- Tax-advantaged funds make a conscious effort to minimize taxes by minimizing trading. The fund managers don't completely ignore opportunities to improve the portfolio by buying and selling, but they do it as little as possible to avoid generating taxable capital gains. The fund managers will also attempt to offset gains with losses whenever possible—again, to reduce taxes.

Exchange-Traded Funds

In addition to index mutual funds, you can now purchase and hold index funds that trade on an exchange (like closed-end funds). ETFs have grown like crazy since their introduction several years ago. Fund expenses are low, if not lower, than those for index mutual funds, and you can buy or sell at any time during normal trading hours. In contrast, regular mutual fund shares can only be traded after closing prices are reported. They work best, however, in a buy-and-hold mode because you do incur commission costs every time you make a trade. Mutual funds are priced after the market closes each day, whereas exchange-traded funds (ETFs) trade like individual stocks during the course of a normal trading day, giving you much more flexibility. However, ETFs are purchased via a broker, which means commission dollars for each transaction. If you are a frequent trader, mutual funds would be more cost-effective. Otherwise, ETFs might be the best way to go. If you can minimize commissions and are not a compulsive trader, ETFs are an excellent choice.

SPDRs

Think health-care stocks are poised to outperform the broad market? Maybe you like retail, instead. Now, thanks to an ETF known as SPDRs, you can instantly purchase a particular *sector* of the S&P 500. As of this writing, there were nine Select Sector SPDRs available:

def·i·ni·tion

A **sector** is a subset of the broad market. The financial sector, for example, consists of banks, underwriters, and insurance companies.

SPDR	Symbol
Consumer Discretionary	XLY
Consumer Staples	XLP
Energy	XLE
Financial	XLF
Health Care	XLV
Industrial	XLI
Materials	XLB
Technology	XLK
Utilities	XLU

If you were to purchase the consumer staples SPDR, for example, you would acquire ownership in over 30 separate companies; a lot of diversification with only one commission! As of Nov 30, 2008, your top ten holdings would consist of:

Company	Percentage
McDonald's	8.04%
Walt Disney	6.67%
Comcast	6.64%
Time Warner	5.44%
Home Depot	5.10%
Target	4.29%
Lowes	4.02%
News Corporation	3.19%
Nike	3.04%
Amazon	2.69%

For more information, visit www.spdrindex.com

iShares

With tiny expense ratios, iShares can be an excellent, low-cost way to achieve instant diversification across numerous asset categories. These ETFs allow you to invest by security (equities, fixed income, or real estate), style (value or growth), individual areas of the market (sector or industry), internationally (by country), or even in precious metals such as gold! Head over to www.ishares.com to check out your options.

HOLDRs: An Alternative to ETFs

Invented by Merrill Lynch, HOLDRs are trust-issued receipts that represent ownership of a basket of stocks. There are currently 17 different varieties: biotech, broadband, B2B Internet, Europe 2001, Internet, Internet architecture, Internet infrastructure, market 2000+, oil services, pharmaceuticals, regional banks, retail, semiconductor, software, telecom, utilities, and wireless. There are no management expenses, unlike a mutual fund. Instead, the investor pays an annual custodial fee—currently 8 cents per share—that is waived if dividends are not paid on the underlying stocks.

Here's how it works: you call your broker and purchase a round lot (100 shares) of the Regional Bank Holder (symbol: RKH). The most recent trading price was $78.57 per

HOLDR, so your entire investment equals $7,857. According to the most recent 8-K form filed with the SEC, here's what you would own:

Name of Company	Ticker	Share Amounts
BB&T Corporation	BBT	10
Bank of America	BAC	27.765
Comerica Incorporated	CMA	5
Fifth Third Bancorp	FITB	13.5
J.P. Morgan Chase	JPM	43.56
KeyCorp	KEY	13
Marshall & Ilsley Corporation	MI	6
Bank of New York Mellon	BK	14
National City Corporation	NCC	18
Northern Trust Corporation	NTRS	7
Piper Jaffray Companies	PJC	0.5683
Regions Financial	RF	9.57
SunTrust Banks, Inc.	STI	9
Synovus Financial Corp.	SNV	8
The PNC Financial Services Group, Inc.	PNC	9
US Bancorp	USB	56.83
Wachovia Corporation	WB	41
Wells Fargo & Co.	WFC	48

Had you bought these stocks individually, you would have paid 18 separate commissions!

Another great advantage of HOLDRs is that, unlike an ETF, you can actually take possession of the underlying securities. In exchange for a cancellation fee of $10 per round lot, the HOLDR trustee (the Bank of New York) will unbundle the stocks. Why would you want to do that? Maybe you need to sell off some assets to pay a tax bill or raise cash for a down payment on a home. You could dispose of the stocks you cared for the least, while retaining those you thought had above-average prospects.

For more information, check out www.holdrs.com.

What's out There in the Fund Universe?

With nearly 17,000 mutual funds in existence, how can you determine which ones fit your investment needs and objectives? As in most situations, the best thing you can do is turn to the experts. In the world of mutual funds, no one holds a candle to Morningstar.

Founded well over one hundred years ago in a Chicago apartment by a man named Joe Mansueto, Morningstar now reigns supreme in the business of mutual fund-ranking and analysis. Premium subscribers can use the firm's website (www. morningstar.com) to research individual funds, expense ratios, top holdings, annual turnover statistics, analyst recommendations, minimum investment requirements, and more.

There are over 9,000 open-end funds currently operating. Morningstar recently broke them down as follows:

Domestic Equity Funds	4,048
International Equity Funds	1,259
Taxable Bond Funds	1,924
Municipal Bond Funds	1,818
Index Funds & Others	252
TOTAL	9,301

Open-end funds are listed by the National Association of Securities Dealers (NASD) once they have at least 1,000 shareholders or net assets of $25 million. Money market funds, which we discussed in Chapter 3, number about 1,300, of which 875 are taxable and 425 are tax-free (either general or state specific).

Additionally, *The Wall Street Journal, Barron's,* Yahoo! Finance, and MarketWatch, participate in the Fund Info Service. Whenever you see a mutual fund listing at one of these sources with a "club" symbol next to it, you can contact a website or toll-free number to quickly obtain a prospectus, information kit, and an application. The financial information can be downloaded instantly or hardcopy versions can be mailed within 24 hours.

Why Funds Are a Great Investment Option

There are several key reasons why you should consider mutual funds:

♦ **Professional Management.** The manager of a given mutual fund may not be more intelligent or luckier than you, but he or she can devote full-time attention to what you can, at best, only give a portion of your time. Also professional investment management has access to research and to market information that would either not be available to you at all or only after a time delay.

In addition, corporate "road shows" stop off at various professional management offices to bring them up-to-date, but don't expect them to come knocking on your door. Finally, influential Wall Street professionals share their opinions first with large, commission-generating customers—like mutual fund managers.

♦ **Instant Diversification.** We're going to tackle the issue of diversification when we talk about asset allocation in Chapter 21. For now, realize that to achieve even bare-bones diversification on your own at a reasonable cost, you would need several hundred thousand dollars to invest.

♦ **Low Costs.** We've pointed out layered fund expenses such as front- and back-end loads and 12b-1 fees. Funds also charge management expense fees that approximate 50 to 75 *basis points* (0.50 to 0.75 percent), and go as high as 75 to 150 basis points for some equity funds. If you stick to no-load funds that keep expenses low, however, you'll find that investing in mutual funds is a great deal cheaper than investing in stocks on your own and paying commissions and transaction costs. Some index mutual funds have expenses as low as 7 basis points (0.12 percent). Try topping that!

def•i•ni•tion

There are 100 **basis points** in one percentage point. So 100 basis points = 1 percent.

♦ **Terrific Variety.** Whatever you want, the fund industry offers. Want to invest in Japanese companies? Health care? New Jersey municipal bonds? Indonesian utilities? There's a fund somewhere doing just that.

♦ **Ease and Convenience.** Usually, you can complete your transaction with one phone call and a bit of paperwork. And if you stay within a particular fund family, you can switch funds with no—or at the very least, minimal—expense, over the phone.

These are some of the more significant reasons why mutual funds have reached unparalleled popularity in this country (other than those primetime TV ads). You just have to use your head in making your selections. Start by requesting annual and quarterly reports and prospectuses from funds that interest you. And actually read them before you buy!

How to Pick a Winning Mutual Fund

How do you pick a fund? Well, for starters, don't read those glossy financial magazines with the eye-catching headlines screaming from the newsstand about can't-lose mutual funds. Okay, read them if you must, but take a look at who's buying the ads that keep these mags afloat. That's right: mutual funds.

We have a better suggestion. Simply apply the following criteria, and you'll make excellent choices.

- **Performance.** Is the fund rate of return above average for its category for the latest one, three, and five years? Notice that we are not recommending that you buy the funds with the highest return or even the ones in the top 10 percent. We prefer to sacrifice some historical returns for consistency. Don't run out and buy a fund that just hit a home run; it might strike out the year after you buy it. Better to seek funds that consistently hit singles and doubles. If you get consistent above-average returns, you'll get superior results over the long haul.

- **Management.** Make sure that the same team has been managing the fund for at least the last five years. When a fund changes managers, you simply don't know whether the new management will do better or worse. You also may not be able to find out the track record of the new manager.

- **Size.** With index funds, go for the largest size fund because it would (or should) have the lowest expenses. But with actively managed funds, avoid unproven funds of small size, as well as very large, ponderous funds that may lack the flexibility to move from stock to stock or industry to industry as conditions warrant. We have arbitrarily selected equity funds with a minimum asset size of $1 billion and a maximum of $10 billion. The largest size (two funds) turned out to be $6.2 billion. For bond funds, we established a minimum asset size of $2 billion. As it turned out, without setting an upside limit for bond funds, only one (Vanguard GNMA) exceeded $7 billion.

- **No Load:** You know our feelings on this. We want to start with $1 working for us, not 95¢.

♦ **Expense Ratios.** We expect the administrator and the investment advisor for the fund to make a profit. But we don't want that green monster called greed to rear its ugly head. We think you should stick with equity funds where the expense ratios are less than 0.50 percent for large cap, 1.25 percent for mid cap, and 1.50 percent for small cap. For bond funds, our ceiling is 0.50 percent.

(We went online to Morningstar at www.morningstar.com and used their Premium Fund Screener software to find mutual funds that met the above criteria.[1] All funds listed below meet the pre-stated criteria for performance, management tenure, no load, and retail customer availability.

Incidentally, all but four of our selected funds have a four-star or five-star rating from Morningstar (those four have three stars). The Morningstar Rating System (with 5 being the highest and 1 the lowest) is a quantitative assessment of a fund's past performance—both return and risk.

We have included the telephone number so you can contact the fund directly for literature. We have excluded short-term bond funds, along with emerging country funds (which should only be purchased in closed-end format, as discussed previously). Finally, we have eliminated any funds that you, as a retail investor, would not be eligible to purchase.

♦ **Large-Cap Growth: Asset size $1billion+ and an expense ratio max of 0.75%.**

Elfun Trusts, 1-800-242-0134

♦ **Large Blend: Asset size $1 billion+, expense ratio max 0.75%**

GE S&S Program Mutual, 1-800-242-0134

Schwab Total Stock Market, 1-800-435-4000

State Farm Growth, 1-800-447-0740

♦ **Large Value: Asset size $1 billion+, expense ratio max 0.75%**

Columbia Large Cap Value Z, 1-800-422-373

Hartford Dividend & Growth HLS, 1-800-862-6668

- **Mid-Cap Growth: Asset size $1billion+, expense ratio max 1.25%**

  Artisan Mid Cap Inv, 1-800-344-1770

  Meridian Growth, 1-800-446-6662

  Waddell & Reed Adv New Concept, 1-888-923-3355

- **Mid-Cap Blend: Asset size $1 billion+, expense ratio max 1.25%**

  Columbia Mid Cap Index Z, 1-800-422-3737

- **Mid-Cap Value: Asset size $1 billion+, expense ratio max 1.25%**

  Artisan Mid Cap Value, 1-800-344-1770

- **Small Growth: Asset size $1 billion+, expense ratio max 1.50%**

  Royce Value Plus Svc, 1-800-221-4268

- **Small Blend: Asset size $1 billion+, expense ratio max 1.50%**

  Columbia Small Cap Index Z, 1-800-422-3737

  Royce Value Svc, 1-800-221-4268

  Gabelli Small Cap Growth AAA, 1-800-422-3554

- **Small Value: Asset size $1 billion+, expense ratio max 1.50%**

  Royce Total Return Invt, 1-800-221-4268

- **International Stock: Asset size $1 billion+, expense ratio max 0.75%**

  American Beacon Intl Equity AMR, 1-800-967-9009

  Hartford International Opp HLS, 1-888-843-7824

- **Long Government: Asset size $2 billion+, expense ratio max 0.50%**

  Vanguard Long-Term U.S. Treasury, 1-800-662-7447

- **Intermediate Government: Asset size $2 billion+, expense ratio max 0.50%**

  Vanguard GNMA, 1-800-662-7447

  Vanguard Interm-Term Treasury, 1-800-662-7447

- **Long-Term Bond: Asset size $2 billion+, expense ratio max 0.50%**

  Vanguard Long-Term Bond Index, 1-800-662-7447

- ◆ **Intermediate-Term Bond: Asset size $2 billion+, expense ratio max 0.50%**

  Hartford Total return Bond HLS, 1-888-843-7824

- ◆ **Muni National Long-Term: Asset size $2 billion+, expense ratio max 0.50%**

  DWS Managed Municipal Bonds, 1-800-621-1048

  Fidelity Municipal Income, 1-800-544-8888

- ◆ **Muni National Intermediate: Asset size $2 billion, expense ratio max 0.50%**

  Vanguard High-Yield Tax-Exempt, 1-800-662-7447

In reviewing the above list, please remember that we like mutual funds for equities, but recommend that you buy individual government securities (or municipals) for the bond portion of your portfolio. There are two problems with bond funds:

1. Much of the yield is eaten up by management fees.

2. When you buy into a bond fund, you can't stagger interest income to meet your individual income needs the way you can when you buy individual bonds and you know their maturity dates. We really like the idea of buying bonds of different maturities so that after you retire, you have interest income coming in every month that matches up with your monthly expenses, as well as annual bond maturities to reinvest as you see fit.

At the end of each quarter, newspapers such as *The New York Times* and *The Wall Street Journal* publish special supplements on mutual funds. These provide a wealth of information on many funds. Use these supplements to do your own screening! Or better still, do as we did, and go online to Morningstar (www.morningstar.com) and use their Premium Fund Selector. The service is free for the first two weeks (as of this writing), and $16.95 per month thereafter. It may be especially helpful to screen for state-specific muni bond funds, which we did not have the space to list in their entirety. You can also call Morningstar at 1-800-735-0700. Give it a try. What have you got to lose?

Money Market Funds

With respect to both taxable and tax-free money market funds, we used a much simpler screening process. We began with a working list of the 15 to 20 funds in each category with the highest seven-day yields as of September 23, 2008, as tabulated by iMoneynet, Inc. We further narrowed the list to include only larger funds, which we defined as those with at least $1 billion in assets. Finally, we eliminated those funds with an initial investment requirement greater than $3,000. Each list begins with the qualifying fund having the highest yield.

U. S. Government Retail Money Funds (data as of 9/23/08)

Fund Name	Assests ($ millions)	Investment $ Minimum	Telephone Number
Fidelity U.S. Govt Reserves	4,335.4	2,500	1-800-544-6666
Morgan Stanley U.S. Govt MMT	1,841.7	1,000	1-800-869-6397
Vanguard Federal MMF	9,136.6	3,000	1-800-662-7447
SSgA US Govt MMF/ Cl.A	2,459.1	1,000	1-800-647-7327
J.P. Morgan US Govt MMF/Morgan	3,416.4	1,000	1-800-766-7722
Wells Fargo Adv Govt MMF/Cl A	1,348.9	1,000	1-800-253-6584

U.S. Prime Retail Money Funds (data as of 9/23/08)

Fund Name	Assests ($ millions)	Investment $ Minimum	Telephone Number
USAA Money Market Fund	5,772.7	3,000	1-800-531-8448
Fidelity Select Money Market	7,451.8	2,500	1-800-544-6666

continues

U.S. Prime Retail Money Funds (data as of 9/23/08)   (continued)

Fund Name	Assests ($ millions)	Investment $ Minimum	Telephone Number
Oppenheimer MMF/ Cl A	2,238.8	1,000	1-800-525-7048
T. Rowe Price Prime Reserve	6,369.4	2,500	1-800-638-5660
TCW Money Market Fund	1,370.5	2,000	1-800-386-3829
Marshall Prime MMF/ Investor Class	2,436.2	1,000	1-800-236-3863
Fidelity Cash Reserves	127,892.2	2,500	1-800-544-6666

U.S. Tax-Free National Retail Money Funds (data as of 9/23/08)

Fund Name	Assests ($ millions)	Investment $ Minimum	Telephone Number
USAA Tax-Exempt MMF	3,361.7	3,000	1-800-531-8448
Vanguard Tax-Exempt MMF	23,386.9	3,000	1-800-662-7447

(Source: iMoneyNet, Inc./imoneynet.com/508-616-6600)

Space does not permit us to list state-specific funds, which may well be the first choice for those in higher tax brackets and high-tax states. But the list at least provides a starting point. Should you wish to relax or tighten our criteria, and/or should you wish to pursue state-specific funds, call iMoneyNet at (508) 616-6600, or better still visit www.imoneynet.com.

Lifestyle and Tax-Efficient Funds

Two other new types of funds deserve mention. One is the so-called lifestyle fund. This fund allows you to set a target retirement date, and, as you approach that date, the asset allocation automatically shifts to less equity exposure. Be aware that a generic stock/bond ratio might not be appropriate for most investors because the ratio makes assumptions that might not apply to your age or risk tolerance. Nevertheless, the automatic asset allocation rebalancing concept is appealing. Vanguard seems to be the leader at this point.

We are wholeheartedly enthusiastic about a new concept that we discussed earlier for individual investing: so-called tax-efficient (or tax-managed, tax-preferred, and so on) funds. The concept is only several years old, with no more than 40 funds available at present. Once again, Vanguard appears to be the leader.

In years when actively managed equity funds are recording large realized gains, tax-managed funds could be a good choice for your taxable investments. Vanguard currently offers the Tax-Managed Growth and Income Fund, the Tax-Managed Capital Appreciation Fund, the T.M. Balanced Fund, the T.M. Small-Cap Fund, and the T.M International Fund

Pick a Date to Rebalance Your Mutual Fund Holdings Annually

Well, by now you know what date that is. That's right, your birthday (unless it falls in January or near a big holiday). But what are you going to rebalance, and which portfolio(s)?

For your tax-deferred accounts (IRAs, 401[k]s, etc.), any actions you take will not trigger a tax bite. So if you are in equity mutual funds, rebalance them back to your original targets or your revised targets. This should only be necessary if the stock market has gone up or down significantly in the previous 12 months. Of course, if you have hit one of those rebalancing years and it's time to reduce your equity exposure, make the move irrespective of what the market has done.

If you have just one equity mutual fund, this is a fairly simple procedure: sell some of your equity fund and use the proceeds to buy Treasury notes or bonds or shares in a bond fund. But what if you have more than one equity fund? Then you have to rebalance these funds within the equity portion. Let's say your portfolio of equity mutual funds looks like this:

	Initial Target	Current
Large-Cap Growth	30%	33%
Large-Cap Value	30	33
Mid-Cap Growth	10	10
Mid-Cap Value	5	5
Small-Cap Growth	5	4
Small-Cap Value	5	4
International	10	8
Emerging Markets	5	3
Total	100	100

First and foremost, figure out how much the equity segment of your portfolio is worth in dollars, then rebalance the individual equity funds so the percentage invested in each corresponds to your original target.

With taxable accounts, the goal is to generate as few capital gains as possible. That's why we recommend passive equity holdings and/or index funds, which minimize taxes—if nothing's being sold, no capital gains are being generated. You don't want to sell equities in a taxable account unless you are at a milestone year (you might be approaching first-year college expenses, for example). If the equities in your taxable accounts have declined significantly, however, you do want to rebalance upward. Use the proceeds from bond or bond fund sales, which should generate minimal capital gains. That's all there is to it!

The Least You Need to Know

- Low-cost index funds can be an excellent choice for building a diversified portfolio.
- Look for open-end funds that keep expenses low and don't charge load or 12b-1 fees.
- Mutual funds are great for the equity portion of your portfolio, but for the fixed-income component, skip bond funds and buy individual securities.
- Keep an eye out for developments in lifestyle and tax-efficient funds; these could be good buys.

Chapter 15

Investing in Real Estate: Pros and Cons

In This Chapter

♦ Bad reasons to invest in real estate

♦ REITs—great "hands-off" real estate investments

♦ How rental income hits your tax return

♦ What to look for in a location

♦ Calculating funds from operations

Everyone needs a place to live, and in Chapter 8, we talked about how to put a roof over your head and finance it, too. In this chapter, we take a look at real estate as an investment, not just shelter.

Why Own Real Estate?

Investors are attracted to real estate for many of the same reasons they own common stocks and bonds. Most of the reasons investors cite for wanting to include real estate in their portfolios, however, are not all that strong.

Let's take a look:

1. **Income.** Real estate can generate income (rent!). With real estate, the income you earn from the investment is the difference between the rental income you receive and your operating expenses. Bonds and most stocks also generate income, however, and it's typically more reliable and secure than the income coming from a rental property. This is especially true of U.S. Government securities and high-quality, above-average-growth common stocks.

2. **Appreciation.** Real estate's value can increase over time, although as we've seen recently, it can decrease, too. Stocks and, to a limited degree, bonds can also appreciate over time.

3. **Leverage.** Real estate can be bought on *leverage*. You might, for example, put $20,000 down to buy a $100,000 property. If the property's value increases 10 percent in two years, or $10,000, you've made a 50 percent return on your $20,000 investment. Of course, if the property's value declines 10 percent, you lose 50 percent! If the leverage game appeals to you (it doesn't to us), you can satisfy it with less hassle using options or futures.

def•i•ni•tion

To buy something on **leverage** means to finance its purchase with debt. When you take a mortgage on a real estate property, you are borrowing money from a bank to buy the property. Leverage is measured by the debt-to-equity ratio:

Debt ÷ Equity = debt-to-equity ratio

As you pay off the mortgage, your debt-to-equity ratio changes because the debt gets smaller and equity (ownership) gets bigger.

Advantages of Investing Through REITs

We hate to break it to you if you had visions of becoming the next Donald Trump, but there's another reason real estate may not be a great investment for taxable accounts—gains on real estate are taxed as ordinary income! You don't get that nice capital gains tax break you get when you hold stocks or bonds for over one year.

When you own shares in an ordinary corporation, you are taxed twice; once when the company pays its tax bill, and then again when the after-tax profits are paid out to you in the form of a cash dividend. In 1960, Congress created real estate investment trusts, or REITs; a special type of corporation not subject to this double-taxation.

REITs are exempt from taxes as long as they distribute at least 95 percent of their operating income to the shareholders and as long as they invest primarily in real estate. All the larger REITs are listed on either the New York or American stock exchanges.

Why would the folks on Capitol Hill take such action? To encourage individual investors to pool their assets together for property investment, providing the economies of scale that were previously available only to the wealthy.

Types of REITs

There are three categories of REITs:

- **Equity REITs.** These enterprises acquire, manage, renovate, build, and sell real estate. Equity REITs are often focused in a specific type of operation such as retail, apartment complexes, industrial, hotel and resort, and self-storage.

- **Mortgage REITs.** These entities invest primarily in real estate mortgages. We recommend that you exclude mortgage REITs and concentrate on equity and hybrid REITs because the former, for all intents and purposes, serves as a fixed-income security. You'd be better off investing in Treasuries.

- **Hybrid REITs.** A blend between equity and mortgage REITs, the hybrid can be an attractive option for your portfolio.

Super Strategies

We recommend that you exclude mortgage REITs and concentrate on equity and hybrid REITs. Mortgage REITs fill basically the same purpose in your portfolio as fixed-income securities, and, as we've discussed throughout this book, Treasuries are your best bet there. If you insist on a mortgage-based product, focus on three U.S. government-created agencies discussed previously: Federal National Mortgage Association, Federal Home Loan Mortgage Corporation, and the Government National Mortgage Association. Their short names are Fannie Mae, Freddie Mac, and Ginnie Mae, respectively.

REITs respond to two different investment stimuli: the bond market and the real estate market. They are considered conservative investments and tend to mimic the bond market. On the other hand, they are sensitive to trends in their particular real estate market (apartments, commercial or shopping centers, and industrial structures/ parks). They are especially sensitive to trends in property values and rental rates. As a result, prices of REITs often run counter to the general stock market.

Super Strategies

Perhaps the single most important determinant of a REIT's success is the quality of management. Always evaluate the past track record of a management team before committing your capital. Your portfolio will thank you.

REIT Funds Offer Better Quality and Safety

If you want to pursue REITs for 5 to 10 percent of your equity portfolio, we strongly suggest that you emphasize quality and safety.

Perhaps the only group challenging financial stocks on the downside in the current bear market at the time of this writing are the REITs. And unlike the financials, REITs are not getting a financial bailout from the Feds. Without question, the weakest of the weak have been those REITs that own and operate retail malls (where it seems "going out of business" sales are the new norm).

Given the above, the reader can understand why we *strongly* urge that any REIT fix be satisfied by purchasing REIT funds. Our old friend Vanguard has both a REIT Index fund and a REIT ETF (exchange-traded fund).

Still want to tiptoe through the minefield? Okay, here's a short list screened by S&P Star Rating[1] (4 or higher, 5 being the highest or strongest Buy) and Debt to Equity Ratio (2 or lower; 0 = no debt, 3+ is highest debt ratio).

Company Name	Symbol	S&P Star Rating	Sub-industry	Debt to Equity Ratio
Alexandria R.E. Equities	ARE	4	Office REITs	2.00
American Campus Communities	ACC	4	Residential REITs	1.54

[1] *Standard & Poor's (1-800-852-1641) via Charles Schwab & Co. Stock Screener.*

Company Name	Symbol	S&P Star Rating	Sub-industry	Debt to Equity Ratio
Mack-Cali Realty	CLI	4	Office REITs	1.42
Plum Creek Timber	PCL	4	Specialized REITs	1.33
Regency Centers	REG	4	Retail REITs	1.37

Not All REITs Are Alike

To increase performance, REITs tend to focus on one or two areas of core competence. Some specialize in building residential real estate; some in corporate parks.

Regardless of the specialty in which you invest, there are a few standard questions you should ask yourself when acquiring a REIT.

- ◆ What type of property does the REIT own—low, middle, or high income?

- ◆ In which geographic markets does the company operate?

- ◆ Are there high barriers to entry that could make it more difficult for competitors to open new units and compete effectively?

- ◆ Are any of those markets currently experiencing a pricing bubble or depression?

- ◆ Will expected changes in interest rates materially affect the results of the business?

Probably the most familiar and easily understood REITs are those that focus on residential properties such as apartment communities. The most potent danger for companies operating in this market is the potential for overcapacity. Often, during cyclical booms, the number of available units in a given geographic area will increase. As long as economic conditions permit, all players profit. At some point, however, the excess supply will necessitate a lowering of average rental rates in order to maintain high occupancy rates.

REIT Resources

To help you further your REIT education, here are some additional resources that can provide valuable insights into accounting, tax, and other considerations.

♦ **Green Street Advisors (www.greenstreetadvisors.com).** This institutional research firm is the preeminent authority on REITs and other publicly traded real estate securities. Check out the sample reports on the company's site.

♦ **Invest in REITs (www.investinreits.com).** Free guide to REIT investing, glossary of terms, charts, tables, and other great resources are available from this site.

♦ *Investing in REITs* **by Ralph Block (Book).** If you own or are considering investing in REITs, you need to read this book! The author systematically explains how to spot excellent REITs, build a diversified portfolio, and factor economic vulnerabilities and accounting considerations into your analysis.

♦ **National Association of Real Estate Investment Trusts.** NAREIT is a great source of cold, hard statistical data on the industry. (www.nareit.com)

Four Types of Real Estate Ownership

A REIT is as far removed from the day-to-day management as you can get and still retain the basic benefits of real estate investing. More hands-on types of investment in real estate include:

1. **Single ownership:** you and you alone.

2. **Partnership:** a way to finance the purchase of larger, more expensive buildings. Partnerships don't always go smoothly, so be sure you have the right or option to buy a controlling interest.

3. **Corporation:** not a good move for the individual investor because you will end up paying taxes at both corporate and individual levels. Also, you lose the tax shelter benefit of deducting any depreciation on your property from your personal income.

4. **Limited Partnership:** We delve into this type of ownership in greater detail in Chapter 24. But, basically, a limited partnership comprises a general partner and a number of limited partners (including you). This form was popular in the

1980s but has dropped in popularity because investors have realized how hard it can be to sell your share in the partnership and get your money back. Liquidity and marketability are drawbacks of limited partnerships. Limited partnerships are also used for energy (oil and gas) investments.

Eight Basic Forms of Real Estate

If we haven't talked you out of investing in real estate yet, here are the eight basic forms of real estate you can explore:

1. Duplex. Typically, you live in one half and rent out the other half.

2. Apartment Building. Here again, you could live "on site," or retain a resident manager to live on site and perform necessary odd jobs. Depending on the size and age of the building, you might need a property manager. The property manager would be responsible for collecting rents, paying bills, maintaining the grounds, contracting for repairs, etc. This could run you up to 10 percent of your gross rental income from the building.

3. Hotels/Motels. Years ago, "Ma and Pa" motels were fairly common, but the chains have turned this into a tough business. The "bed and breakfast" business, though a charming fantasy for many beleaguered urban couples, is even tougher. Sure, that cozy inn in Vermont looked good on Bob Newhart's show, but bear in mind that to run a bed and breakfast you've got to be on call 24 hours a day as chef, handyman, and concierge.

4. Office Buildings. Unlike singles, duplexes, and apartment buildings, office buildings rent on a per-square-foot basis. Leases are usually longer for offices—five years with additional option years, for example, compared to one/two year rentals for residential property.

5. Shopping Centers. Mini-malls, medium-size malls (with one major or anchor tenant plus local tenants), larger malls (two anchors, one on each end plus local stores in between), and super regional malls, like the Mall of America—this country loves malls. But unless you're very wealthy, you probably wouldn't be invited to invest in the partnerships and corporations that own most malls. If you invest in REITs, though, you'll end up with a piece of the action, as most REITs eventually own the best shopping centers.

6. Warehouses and Industrial Buildings.

7. Mobile Home Parks.

8. Land.

Land is the most speculative real estate investment because there is no depreciation to help cut your taxes and no rental income. You could sell cutting rights to a logger or grazing/planting rights to ranchers/farmers, but that's about it. You could get lucky and sell out for big bucks to a developer. But while you're waiting, you'll be paying taxes and loan payments (if you borrowed to purchase the land). We maintain that the only really good reason to buy land is if you intend to build a home for yourself on it. Then again, there is only a fixed amount of land. In the spirit of Will Rogers: "Buy land, they ain't makin' any more of it."

How do we deal with the *depreciation* of the land portion of your real estate investment? Your tax bill should be broken down into an appraised value of the land and an appraised value for "improvements" (or your "structure" or "building"). Take the land dollar sum and divide it into total appraised value to get a percent (e.g., $20,000 ÷ $100,000 = .20, or 20 percent). Multiply your current professionally appraised market value by this percent and deduct it. This is your depreciable value (e.g., $150,000 × .20 = $30,000; less from $150,000 = $120,000 depreciable base).

Fiscal Facts _____

In real estate, **depreciation** is defined in terms of the minimum useful life of the property. For residential property, the useful life is defined as 27.5 years (or 3.64 percent per year); for all other real estate, the useful life is 39 years (2.56 percent per year). How do we get these numbers? One hundred percent divided by 27.5 = 3.64 percent. And remember, you cannot depreciate the land upon which your residence is built.

Purchase and Rental of Homes and Apartment Buildings

First and foremost, be financially prepared and market-wise. "Financially prepared" means, ideally, to have your down payment set aside. Having to rustle up the down payment by selling assets for cash or borrowing (mortgaging your future) is not smart. Also, you should already have spoken to a mortgage banker to ensure that you will qualify for the mortgage. In fact, if you can be pre-approved, it adds to your attraction as a prospective buyer. Check with a realtor or mortgage banker about what you need to do to be pre-approved.

"Market-wise" means you know what's available in the area where you would like to own and have researched the prices of the types of properties you want to own. Market-wise also means you've regularly taken the market's pulse for at least a year. You can tell when it's rising sharply, flat, or declining—and you can spot a buying opportunity.

Many newspapers include information on recent home/condo sales to assist you. Brokers will also give you data on recent sales and trends.

Location, Location, Location

Location, location, location: the three rules of real estate investing! But what's "location"? Let's define it this way (you want as many of the following as possible):

1. **Good Schools.** Good schools act like a magnet (who doesn't want their kids to go to a good school?). They are the first thing many potential buyers or renters look for when planning a move into the area.

2. **Low Taxes.** You can avoid high property taxes, in part, by avoiding smaller municipalities where the school, police, and fire costs are spread over a smaller taxable populace. But high taxes are only one issue; the other is the rate of increase in taxes. Rapidly growing townships often mean rapidly increasing costs and, for you, higher tax bills. So look for areas that are already largely built up.

3. **Convenience.** Buy property with easy access to main roads or arteries as well as convenient public transportation to shops, entertainment, and places of worship.

How Rental Income Hits Your Tax Return

Let's say you're about to make your first foray into real estate investment by renting out a home that you own. How does the rental income hit your income tax statement? See the following page for an example of what Schedule E (Supplemental Income and Loss) of Form 1040 would look like, assuming that the rental contract begins July 1.

Because it's a July 1 rental, you are going to record $5/12$ of your annual income and expenses. And in this case, the tenant is paying (or reimbursing) you for telephone, heat, and electricity, but not cable TV (which is the $137 next to Line 18). Now, let's go over this form blow by blow:

♦ Under Line 1 you would put "residential property" and the specific address.

♦ Line 2 is primarily for people who rent out a second or vacation home. You are entitled to up to 14 days for your personal use. If you use the home for more than 14 days, your tax situation gets more complicated, and you should work with an accountant.

◆ Line 3 is actual rents received. $10,000 is equivalent to a monthly rent of $2,000 (times 5 months).

◆ Line 8 is the broker's commission of 10 percent.

◆ Line 9 is homeowner's insurance, again apportioned.

◆ Line 12 is mortgage interest (but not any portion allocable to principal pay-down).

◆ Line 16 is real estate taxes.

◆ Line 18 is the aforementioned cable bills.

◆ Line 19 is the subtotal of expenses.

◆ Line 20 is depreciation.

◆ Line 21 is total expenses after depreciation.

◆ Line 22 is a loss, but one that we cannot use unless we have a gain in other "passive" (e.g., real estate) income.

Note that even though we can't use the tax loss, we still have a "profit" of $1,422 (Line 3 less Line 19) on which we have no tax due. Pretty snazzy.

The Least You Need to Know

◆ Most of the goals investors cite for wanting to include real estate in their portfolios would be better met by investments in stocks and bonds.

◆ The 1986 Tax Reform Act ruled that real estate losses can be used only to offset real estate income, thus ending one of the best reasons for individual investors to own real estate—the tax break.

◆ Gains on real estate are taxed at income tax rates, not at (typically lower) capital gains rates.

◆ Real Estate Investment Trusts (REITs) are an opportunity to rake in some of the benefits of investing in real estate while avoiding the potential tax hit.

◆ If you still want to buy real estate, become market-wise and location-savvy.

Part 4

Rolling with Life's Changes

In investing money, the amount of interest you want should depend on whether you want to eat well or sleep well.

—J. Kenfield Morley

Life is full of transitions, shocks, and assorted doozies. Our happiness has little to do with avoiding life's changes and everything to do with being prepared to roll with them.

Properly managed investments can make transitions like buying a home or retiring a lot smoother. Knowing how to handle exciting developments that affect your investments, such as changing jobs or inheriting money, can ease the stress that even the most positive events can cause. It's also crucial to know how to protect your assets from potentially devastating events.

This part is a primer on how to cover your assets through life's biggest challenges: marriage, divorce, inheriting money, changing jobs, and even that final transition we'd all rather pretend is never going to happen. At least not to us.

Chapter 16

Work Smart, Not Just Hard: Getting the Max from Your Job

In This Chapter

- ◆ Five vital questions for a new employer
- ◆ When your Social Security benefits can be taxed
- ◆ The changing retirement age
- ◆ How Medicare works

Are you one of those people who ignore every memo and form about complicated-sounding things like 401(k)s and vesting that come across your desk? Do you figure that if you ignore them, maybe they'll go away? Well, what's going away is your opportunity to squeeze the most dollars possible out of your job.

Now that we've got your attention ... think of this chapter as your personal machete. Use it to cut through the thickets of paper and nonsense that many corporate human resource departments love to erect between you and simple answers about how to best handle the retirement benefits offered by your employer. And, if you're self-employed or thinking about becoming self-employed, we'll show you how to set up your own retirement account and get a major tax break in the process.

What to Ask a New Employer

There are five topics you must discuss with personnel immediately when you start a job at a new company. Make an appointment ASAP with a human resources person. You'll shock and amaze him or her if you walk in there with these questions under your hat:

1. "Do you have a pension plan, and, if so, when am I eligible to participate?"

   Typically, each credited year requires 1,000 hours of work. If you start work before June 30, therefore, you will probably be eligible that year. If your hire date is much later than that, you will probably not be eligible until the following year. Find out if you will qualify in year one of your employment. How long will you have to work at the company until you are fully vested? Five years is typical.

2. "Can I transfer the money in my existing 401(k) plan to your 401(k) plan? How exactly do I do that? When can I start to participate in your plan? What are the investment choices offered by your 401(k) plan? Does the employer contribute and to what degree?"

   Get very specific answers here so you don't risk leaving the assets in your current 401(k) plan unsheltered. You typically only have 60 days to get this together before the IRS can swoop in. You usually will be able to participate in your new employer's 401(k) plan after you've been there one year.

3. "Is there a bonus or incentive plan? How general or specific is it? Is it tied to my job performance or the performance of the company or my department as a whole? When will I be informed of the amount? When is it paid to me? Do I have to be a full-time employee when the checks are passed out?"

   It's better to have a bonus that's tied directly to your own performance, not to the performance of others. That way you control your own destiny. Bear in mind, also, that you don't want to screw yourself out of a big bonus or incentive check at your current job by leaving to take a new one. Before you leave, check out any pertinent dates. If waiting a few weeks to start your new job will keep you from losing money, you could either arrange that or negotiate a sign-on bonus with your new employer.

4. "Are there stock options? Am I eligible for them?"

   If the answer to both questions is yes, get the details. Normally, if you are eligible, stock options would have already been dangled as incentive to get you on board in the first place and would have been included in your hiring agreement.

5. "Does the company have a health plan? When do I and my family become eligible? Is there a choice of plans, or just one?"

   You want to know what kind of choice you have. There may be just one HMO, several alternative HMOs, or a traditional plan. There may be some variation that allows you to opt in or out of your HMO. Typically, you are eligible on the first of each month.

Super Strategies

When you start a new job, meet with your human resources contact right away to ask about the company's …

   ◆ Pension plan.
   ◆ 401(k) plan and whether you can transfer money from your existing 401(k) into it.
   ◆ Bonus or incentive plans.
   ◆ Stock options.
   ◆ Health plan.

Also check with HR at your old job to make sure that you aren't forfeiting a bonus or incentive check by leaving. Sometimes just postponing your departure a few weeks can make a big difference.

Transferring Retirement Accounts

You have three options with your 401(k) plan when you change jobs:

1. Keep it with your previous employer, if it will allow you to do so (and many do).

2. Transfer it to your new employer, provided that it is willing to take your assets (almost all will).

3. Create an IRA rollover with a bank or broker.

If you choose option #2 or #3, remember that you have only 60 days to get this done; otherwise, the Feds will assume you are taking a distribution and hit you with taxes and, potentially, penalties. Given the choice, most people are most comfortable with option #2; when people leave a firm, they like it to be a clean break. Option #3 is really for those who can't do #2 or #1.

So You're Your Own Boss

If you are self-employed, you have to provide for yourself benefits that employers normally provide, such as retirement planning and health insurance. You should also carefully research all aspects of working from home. You'll want to maximize your business tax deductions to offset the fringe benefits lost when you leave an employer to set up your own business, such as health insurance, pension plan, sick leave, and vacations.

Setting Up Your Own Retirement Plan

One great way to both reduce your taxes and provide an important employment benefit for yourself is to set up your own retirement plan. You can choose from the following plans:

- SIMPLE-IRA—these seem to be taking the place of SEP-IRAs for most people

- Keogh (which will probably be referred to by your banker simply as a defined contribution plan, or D.C.)

- Owner-only 401(k)

Fiscal Facts _____

When you work for a company that provides health insurance, retirement plans, and other benefits, these fringe benefits are typically worth between 25 percent to 50 percent of your salary. If your salary is $60,000, for example, your benefits are worth between $15,000 and $30,000.

(Source: Paul and Sarah Edwards, authors of *Working from Home*, G.P. Putnam's Sons, 1994)

Any bank, mutual fund or brokerage firm, or insurance company will be delighted to provide you with the forms you need to open these plans—especially if you are thinking of keeping your assets with their institution. SIMPLEs are very easy to open yourself, but you'll need help with the rather complicated paperwork required to set up a

Keogh. For the owner-only 401(k) plans, contact Pioneer or Bank of America and ask about their Uni-K plans.

If you've been self-employed for a while but haven't gotten around to setting up your retirement plan, boy, have you been missing out on a major deduction on your federal income tax!

Let's look at each of these plans individually.

SIMPLE-IRAs are for self-employed people, small business owners, and their employees. The maximum contribution you can make for yourself to a SIMPLE-IRA in 2009 is $11,500 if you are below 50, and $14,000 if you are older than 50.

For Keoghs, for self-employed people, the contribution limit is $49,000 for 2009.

For 401(k) plans, used by corporate employees; 403(b) plans, used by employees working for nonprofits and educational institutions; and 457 plans, used by state and local government employees, the deferral limit for 2008 was $15,500 and the limit for 2009 is $16,500. There is no distinction based on age regarding how much you can contribute.

The owner-only 401(k) is, as the name implies, ideal for the sole owner/employee of a business and his/her spouse. Like regular 401(k)s, it has two pieces: the employee contribution and the employer contribution, only in this case the employee and the employer are the same person! The maximum contribution for 2009 from the employee would be $16,500. The total sum, of course, is tax-deductible. It's a good deal for toiling entrepreneurs.

We believe the Uni-K Plan to be the superior owner-only 401(k) plan presently available. Pioneer Investment Management USA Inc. is the trustee. Pioneer is an old-line firm, founded in Boston in 1928 at the birth of the mutual fund concept. If you are a sole proprietor interested in this plan, you can contact Pioneer directly but must work with a financial advisor.

Mutual funds are the only products you can select for your Uni-K plan and they can be chosen individually from a selection of Pioneer, AIM, Oppenhemier, and Alliance funds, or via portfolio groups (e.g., Aggressive Growth, Growth, Income, and so on).

People who hit the magic age 70½ trigger for required IRA distribution used to often be confused by the IRS distribution tables. Starting January 31, 2002, however, financial institutions were required to report to you exactly how much, at minimum, you must withdraw each year.

def•i•ni•tion

Net earnings from self-employment are the amount of income on which you pay self-employment tax, minus the tax itself. Self-employment tax is what self-employed people have to pay into Social Security because they don't have an employer contributing on their behalf.

Let's say your *net earnings* on self-employment—after you deduct business and home-office deductions and the self-employment tax—are $25,000 and your federal income tax rate is 27 percent. Your federal income tax will be $25,000 × .27, or $6,750.

Now, what if you invest 15 percent of that $25,000 in a SEP-IRA? You would invest $25,000 × .15, or $3,750. And you can deduct that $3,750 from the $25,000 you earned, so now you owe federal income tax on just $21,250. Your tax rate just dropped from 27 percent to 15 percent because that deduction dropped you into a lower tax bracket. Now the amount of federal income tax you owe is only $21,250 × .15, or $3,187.50. That's a lot easier to fork over to Uncle Sam than $6,750, plus you've tucked away $3,750 to grow tax-deferred until you retire.

Super Strategies

If you are self-employed and haven't opened a SIMPLE-IRA account yet, get thee to a bank immediately! You are missing out on a huge opportunity to shelter your hard-earned bucks from Uncle Sam. If you invest the maximum allowable percentage of your earnings, for example, you can deduct your entire investment from your income. This swift move will slice your income tax, plus that precious money is now sheltered under an IRA where it can grow peacefully tax-deferred until you retire.

Retirement ... at Last!

Whether you work for a big corporation or yourself, if you're doing well, you may be tempted to consider retiring early. Should you retire early? It sounds great, but remember:

1. Your benefits from Social Security and your employer's retirement plan will be reduced or even become nonexistent, depending on when you decide to retire. This means your own retirement portfolio will have to be that much larger.

2. Retiring early means your retirement dollars will have to last longer. Again, this means you'll need to accumulate more assets that will generate retirement income.

Fiscal Facts _____

Where do your Social Security tax dollars go? Out of every $1 …

- ◆ 70¢ goes to a trust fund to pay retirees
- ◆ 19¢ goes to a trust fund to pay Medicare beneficiaries
- ◆ 11¢ goes to a trust fund to pay benefits to qualified disabled people

How the Retirement Age You Choose Affects Social Security

Let's look specifically at Social Security. You can retire at any time between age 62 and full retirement age. Your full (or "normal") retirement age depends on when you were born. Social Security Online provides a chart here www.socialsecurity.gov/retire2/ agereduction.htm that you can use to find your full retirement age and by how much your benefits would be reduced if you were to retire early. At age 62, you will only receive about 80 percent of what you would have received had you waited until age 65 to retire.

Starting in 2003, the full retirement age was increased in steps until it reaches age 67. Those born in 1937 or earlier were not affected by the increase in the full retirement age.

Those born in 1938 will have full retirement age defined as 65 years and 2 months. Add two months for each year after 1938 that you were born. For those born in 1960 and later, 67 will be the full retirement age. If you were born in 1960 and want to take early retirement at age 62, your benefit will only be 70 percent of the age 67 full benefit. Find yourself on the table below, compliments of the Social Security Administration:

Age to Receive Full Social Security Benefits

Year of Birth	Full Retirement Age
1937 or earlier	65
1938	65 and 2 months
1939	65 and 4 months
1940	65 and 6 months

continues

Age to Receive Full Social Security Benefits   (continued)

Year of Birth	Full Retirement Age
1941	65 and 8 months
1942	65 and 10 months
1943–1954	66
1955	66 and 2 months
1956	66 and 4 months
1957	66 and 6 months
1958	66 and 8 months
1959	66 and 10 months
1960 and later	67

Pay Tax on Social Security Benefits? Sad, but True

Are your Social Security benefits taxable? In some cases they are. Here's the gist of it:

If you file your federal tax return as an individual and your combined income is between $25,000 and $34,000, you may have to pay taxes on 50 percent of your Social Security benefits. If your *combined income* is above $34,000, up to 85 percent of your Social Security benefits are subject to tax. If you file a joint return, the numbers are between $32,000 and $44,000 (up to 50 percent) and over $44,000 (up to 85 percent).

About 20 percent of the people receiving Social Security pay taxes on their benefits. Each year recipients receive a Social Security Benefit Statement (Form SSA-1099). Use this form when filling out your federal income tax to determine if any of your benefits are subject to tax.

def•i•ni•tion

Combined income is adjusted gross income (remember that?) plus nontaxable interest (interest on municipal bonds, for example) plus half of your Social Security benefits. It's just another way to hit up the fat cats!

Can You Work and Still Collect Social Security?

Can you work and still get all your Social Security benefits? It depends on your age and the amount. If you are under 65, the earnings limit is $11,280. And "earnings" are limited to wages and self-employment income. Income from investments and other sources is excluded.

What happens if you earn more than that? Your Social Security check will be cut by one dollar for every two dollars you earn over the limit. Another reason to think twice about retiring early! For those who have attained full retirement age (FRA), there is no retirement earnings test, thanks to the Senior Citizens' Freedom to Work Act of 2000! This means that your Social Security check amount is not reduced. You may still have to pay taxes, however, on the amount.

Advantages to Delaying Retirement

What if you choose to delay retirement? There are some advantages. Depending on when you were born, your eventual annual Social Security benefits will be increased from 5 percent (for those born before 1933) to 8 percent (for those born in 1943 or later). But if you do decide to retire after age 65, please sign up for Medicare anyway at age 65; otherwise, your medical insurance could cost more.

Your spouse is also eligible to receive benefits at his or her full retirement age, which is currently 65. How much? Either 50 percent of your benefits or his or her actual earned benefits, whichever is higher. Your spouse can begin collecting benefits as early as age 62, but they will be reduced roughly 4 percent per year before full retirement age.

When and How to Apply for Your S.S. Benefits

Apply for Social Security benefits three months before the date you want the benefits to start. The Social Security Administration recommends that you discuss your plans with one of their representatives the year before you plan to retire.

Remember, the rules are not simple or straightforward, and are subject to change. What do you need to apply for benefits? Plan on having to present the following:

◆ Your Social Security number

◆ Your birth certificate (original or certified copy)

- Your latest W-2 or self-employment tax return

- Your military discharge papers

- Your bank name and account number (if you want to arrange direct deposit of your benefits)

How Does Medicare Work?

We've mentioned Medicare a few times. What's that all about? Medicare is a federal health insurance plan for people 65 and older (plus people qualified as being disabled, regardless of age). Medicare is divided into two parts: Part A and Part B. Part A is hospital insurance and Part B is for medical insurance—it covers doctor visits and other nonhospital expenses.

Part A and a Hospital Stay

Part A is what a portion of the Social Security deductions from your paycheck were going to for all those years. So you have already paid for it. However, "it" does not cover all of your hospital room and board charge. The difference is covered by co-insurance payments that either you or your insurance company must pay. You will also have to cover an annual deductible. If you arrange for your Social Security benefits to begin at age 65, you are automatically enrolled in Medicare Part A. If you choose to retire after your 65th birthday, be sure to sign up for Medicare at age 65; otherwise you won't be enrolled in Medicare Part A.

How to Pay for the Expenses Medicare Doesn't Cover

Part B of Medicare is optional. "Optional" is a misleading word, however, because you will be automatically enrolled—and the premium deducted from your monthly Social Security benefit check—unless you proactively opt out. If you opt in, the premium will not cover all your expenses. What's missing?

First there is an annual deductible. Second, in many instances, there is an 80/20 split: Medicare pays 80 percent, and you (or your insurance company) pay the remaining 20 percent. The question becomes this: Do you want to pay for the necessary coinsurance, or do you want to select one of the 10 existing Medicare supplement policies? If you choose one of the latter, they basically cover your coinsurance for both parts A and B, but charge you a premium. But wait, there's a third option: you can go the

HMO route. The HMOs are cheaper but restrict you to specific doctors and procedures.

If you want more information on Medicare, visit www.medicare.gov, where you will find information explaining the latest Medicare drug, hospital, and medical insurance plans.

Crash Alert

Retiree health insurance offered by your employer may be another option you can use to cover the gap in Medicare coverage. Carefully check to make sure, however, that your employer's retiree health insurance being offered will provide the same benefits and roughly the same coverage you enjoy now. If not, you could end up in a pickle, looking for insurance at age 70 to 75 with possible pre-existing conditions. This client profile does not appeal to insurance companies.

What About Lump-Sum Retirement Benefits?

When you do announce your retirement, your employer may very well offer you the option of receiving your defined benefit annuity in a single lump-sum payment. Essentially, your employer will take an interest rate provided by the federal government and apply it to your monthly benefit. You can either reject the option, or take the lump sum and turn it over to an insurance company, or invest it yourself. Just remember to confirm that your monthly income is going to be noticeably increased by going the lump-sum route. If that's not the case, sit back, relax, and enjoy the monthly checks from your employer's plan administrator.

Much has been written about a strategy where a bank or mortgage company buys your home (freeing up capital for you), and you pay the equivalent of a lease or rental fee. In other words, you would free up equity in your home while still enjoying living there. Although this is a reasonable option, we think you should give at least equal weight to the idea of selling your home and "downsizing" into a residence that is less expensive to own and maintain. Check with your local realtor to see whether either of these options—or just staying put—makes the most sense (and dollars) to you.

The Least You Need to Know

♦ When you start a new job, ask right away about the company's pension and 401(k) plans, incentive plans, stock options, and health plans.

♦ If you're self-employed, any bank, mutual fund firm, brokerage, or insurance company will be happy to help you set up your own retirement plan.

♦ Retiring early reduces your Social Security benefits.

♦ You will need some form of health insurance after retirement to cover expenses not paid by Medicare.

17

The Ramifications of Romance

In This Chapter

- Using a pre-nup to avoid financial disaster
- Should you keep bank accounts and investments separate?
- The marriage tax
- Untangling assets after divorce

It's hard to think about money and love at the same time—but both have the ability to make us either turn green and act nuts or feel very secure and happy. Money and love are inescapably intertwined once two people marry. Every financial move you make is affected by your marital status, from how you choose to bank and invest, to how you protect your assets and the amount of tax you pay. In this chapter, we will go over the financial ramifications of romance.

When You Need a Pre-Nup

We've all been bombarded with tabloid tales about this or that wealthy celebrity who invokes a pre-nuptial agreement when the wedding of the year turns into the divorce of the decade. What is a pre-nup, exactly? A *pre-nuptial agreement* is a legal document, signed by both parties, stating "that is yours and this is mine." With roughly half of all marriages ending in divorce, and with roughly half of the assets usually going to each party, you can understand why a wealthy spouse whose mate is not exactly flush would demand a pre-nup.

def•i•ni•tion

A **pre-nuptial agreement** is a legally binding document signed by two people before they get married. Most pre-nuptial agreements simply spell out who owns what and who will get what in the event the marriage ends in a divorce. A few pre-nuptial agreements that have made the news lately go into great detail, even specifying how often the couple will have sex or see their in-laws!

But what about you? You're going to tell us you're not wealthy, but are you bringing something into the marriage that could eventually represent substantial wealth? A patented idea? Shares in your business—which could grow to become a regional or national chain? The great American novel in your desk drawer that finally finds its way to a supportive publisher? And what about those personal items handed down from generation to generation in your family? Or how about stock options that have no particular value at the time of marriage but will be worth a great deal some years hence?

Without a pre-nuptial agreement, you and your spouse will be subject to the property-settlement laws of the state in which you reside. In nine "community property" states (Arizona, California, Idaho, Louisiana, Nevada, New Mexico, Texas, Washington, Wisconsin) all assets ruled to be marital property by the court will be split 50/50—even if one partner earned all the money. Alaska is an opt-in community property state; property is separate property unless both parties agree to make it community property through a community property agreement or a community property trust.

"Community property" typically includes:

◆ All physical property, from real estate to cars, and from appliances to furniture

◆ All money made during the marriage

- Any money deposited in 401(k), savings, or retirement accounts

- Any collections (art, stamp, otherwise)

- Any businesses begun during the marriage

- Any gifts received by either spouse unless solely inherited and not commingled with household funds

- Any money in bank accounts, regardless of whose name is on the account

- Any electronics equipment

- Potentially, future earnings from things made during the marriage may be community property. For instance, if you sell a book during a marriage, and it takes off as a best-seller after a divorce, an ex-spouse might be entitled to half the profits.

In the other states, marital property division is up to the judge. And, surprisingly, even assets acquired before the marriage, such as a house, stock, or even a business, are thrown into the pot. In some states, even a professional degree earned during a marriage is included. If you become a doctor, lawyer, or accountant during the marriage, for example, your spouse might be able to claim half your earnings stemming from that degree.

We are not suggesting you turn to your spouse and say, "Honey, we need a pre-nup." That's a hard sell, and frankly, after you're married it's too late. It's even too late if you wait until just before the wedding. Many courts will throw out a pre-nup that one party can prove he or she was pressured to sign because the wedding was already planned.

But before your marriage, be it your first, third, or fifth, we suggest you talk seriously with your lawyer about a pre-nuptial agreement. This applies to women as well as men; if you and/or your soon-to-be spouse have or expect to earn a lot of money, hammer out a pre-nup before you say "I do." It could save a lot of pain and anguish later on.

The Marriage Tax Becomes the Marriage Bonus

The tax code was drawn up back in the day when one spouse worked and the other (guess which one?) stayed home and took care of the kids. So marriage got a favorable treatment under the tax code. The numbers looked roughly like this:

Status	Taxable Income	Tax Due
Single	$50,000	$10,880
Married, Filing Jointly	$50,000	$8,787

The marriage tax break persisted for years, but it only worked for families with one breadwinner. Working couples who got married got slammed. Below take a look at how two people, both with taxable income of $50,000, were affected if they got married and both continued to work.

Status	Income Total	Income/Income Tax
Two Single People Married, Filing Jointly	$50,000 + $50,000 = $100,000 =	$100,000/$20,752 $100,000/$21,864
Married, Filing Separately	$50,000 + $50,000 =	$100,000/$21,864

A couple was penalized $1,112 if they got married! The Economic Growth & Tax Reconciliation Act of 2001 was touted as offering some relief from the "marriage penalty" by increasing the standard deduction for married filers and increasing the 15 percent tax bracket to include more married filers' income. These changes were phased in slowly until 2005, and the rest of the change hit in 2008. The top of the 10 percent and 15 percent brackets on joint returns are now exactly twice as high as the ceilings on single returns (they used to be less than double). Today most married couples get a marriage bonus: they pay less income tax than they would if each partner were single. The more unequal the spouses' income, the more likely that combining them on a joint return will pull some of the higher earner's income into a lower bracket. You get less of a break if both spouses earn comparable incomes.

Joint Bank Accounts

What about combining bank accounts? Unless one of you is living a secret life or the two of you have trouble communicating, there is no reason to keep separate checking accounts.

The main advantage of one versus several checking accounts is the savings on monthly service charges and fees. In addition, if you have the type of account that pays a minimum interest rate for minimum balances, it's obviously easier to meet the minimum balance requirement when you combine assets in one account. An exception needs to be made if you are a principal or sole proprietor of a business; in that case, a separate business checking account is a must.

Crash Alert

If you and your spouse decide to share a checking account, we can't stress enough the importance of communication. Make it a habit to go over checks written and deposits/withdrawals made on a daily basis to avoid messy and expensive overdraft charges. And if your marriage should fall on the rocks and you separate, immediately dissolve any joint checking accounts.

Should You Keep Separate Investment Portfolios?

Whether you keep separate or joint investment portfolios depends on the type of account. Some accounts, like IRAs, must be legally kept separate. The same applies to any 401(k) or 403(b) retirement plan, or a defined benefit (pension) plan: the employee is the sole legal owner.

For taxable accounts, however, a joint name is preferable, for three reasons.

1. Most investment advisors and planners charge a fee based on a percentage of your assets, and the greater the assets the lower the fee. An advisor may charge 2 percent to manage $500,000, and only 1 percent on $1 million, for example. Also, most, if not all, financial planners charge a minimum dollar fee, and you wouldn't want to pay two minimum fees.

2. Even if you don't use an investment advisor or counselor, it's still easier to balance and manage a single portfolio, rather than two or more. We strongly suggest you stick with one broker for the same reason. Less confusing!

3. One spouse is usually going to be less investment-savvy than the other. The spouse who takes less naturally to investing is always going to be tempted to say, "Oh, I let Fred/Mary take care of that." But what happens to that spouse if financially astute Fred or Mary is no longer around? Far too many elderly widows have found themselves in exactly this vulnerable position, easy prey to the con artists who unfortunately exist in the investment business. Joint ownership confers upon the other party both the right and the obligation to know what is going on with their investments.

Untangling Your Assets During Divorce

Suppose you have moved, gradually or precipitously, from blissful wedlock to separate padlocks. Who gets what and how? Generally, you (and your lawyer) will look to the laws of the state in which you plan to file for divorce. As we mentioned, nine states split all marital assets 50/50. Some states will favor the wife, especially if she is non-working and a mother.

Handling the House

How easy or difficult the division of property will be depends upon the complexity of the assets and the attitudes of the individuals getting divorced. But, as a general rule, estimate the value of each asset and assume that each party will get half.

For many couples, their home is their biggest asset. To divide this asset or give it to one party, you'll need to have it appraised. One of the first calls you should make, therefore, is to your Realtor. And don't even bother with secrecy; everyone probably knows what's happened.

Divvying Up Other Assets

The most difficult types of assets to deal with are family heirlooms and compensation-related issues like stock options and family businesses.

- First, you should each make a list of your individual assets and place a fair market value on each (to the best of your ability).

- Next, you and your lawyer should sit down with your soon-to-be ex-spouse and his or her lawyer to reconcile any differences.

Family heirlooms that have been in your family will generally go to you; but you may or may not have to give up something in return. A lot depends on your spouse's attitude.

Stock options are a bear: What were they worth at the time of the marriage? What are they worth now? What could they be worth? Just give your lawyer the facts and let him or her deal with the issue. If it can be negotiated, great; if not, you may have to litigate. State laws vary on this specific asset, but best to assume that stock options are one of the marital assets subject to distribution in a divorce. If it turns out otherwise, lucky you.

Provide your lawyer with the date and amount of options granted, and the date and price at which they can be exercised. You'll also need to obtain, in writing, a statement from your employer regarding whether the options are a basic part of your compensation package, or an incentive for future efforts.

QDROs—How to Split Retirement Assets When You Split

QDRO stands for Qualified Domestic Relations Order, and it spells out how the assets held in pension and 401(k), 403(b), and 457 plans will be split in a divorce. They do not cover IRAs.

If you and your soon-to-be-ex can agree on how to split retirement assets (in a dollar or percent split), check with your plan administrator to obtain the necessary forms. Once completed, these become an official part of the divorce agreement (so be sure the divorce judge gets a copy). QDROs were created by the Employment Retirement Income Security Act of 1974—that means they are federal law and trump any IRS ruling, any pre-nup, and even any local judicial ruling.

You don't have to resort to QDROs if you can come up with other means of fairly dividing assets (e.g., "You keep the house; I'll keep the pension"). But that's not always possible, and a QDRO is a smart alternative. In a simple, straightforward fashion, a QDRO directs the plan administrator to distribute X dollars or Y percent to the other spouse. Ideally it would be used to create or add to an IRA Rollover Account. Without it the recipient of funds from a split of retirement plan assets would be subject to federal taxes and in some cases even an early withdrawal penalty. Forewarned is forearmed!

Negotiate with Your Head, Not Your Spleen

If you've seen the movie *The War of the Roses*, you have some inkling of the dark side of divorce. Sometimes two people can be zipping through an amicable divorce until she decides she wants half of the Simon and Garfunkel collection and he insists on keeping the dog—with no visitation rights. And then comes that killer statement: "Well, if you're going to be that way …," and everything unravels.

The chances that you and your lawyer are going to pull the wool over the eyes of your spouse and his or her lawyer are pretty small. So be reasonable and fair. Where there is an asset or issue that you feel quite strongly about, be firm but convey the firmness via your lawyer. The more obstreperous things become, the longer the process takes, and lawyers charge by the hour. It's your money.

Unless you have a very amicable divorce pending (whatever that is), move out of the house immediately. You can arrange to come back and do your inventory and obtain necessary clothing at a mutually agreed-upon time and date. It's a good idea to agree on that time and date before leaving.

Super Strategies

Divorce between two working spouses without children is (or should be) straightforward. Add a child or children and emotional pain enters the equation. Change one spouse to nonworking, add children and a long marriage, and you have a really difficult situation. But our advice is the same in every divorce situation: keep your cool, be fair, be firm when you feel strongly about an issue or asset, and keep it lawyer to lawyer.

Other Divorce Options

Before you go the divorce route, please try a separation (legal or informal). With a little time and a little space, along with a fuller understanding of the dollar and emotional costs involved, many marriages can be repaired. Joint therapy and/or marriage counseling can also help repair the torn fabric of a marriage.

If divorce is inevitable and feelings are amicable, think about "no-fault" divorce. The two of you simply go before the judge and say it was no one's fault that the marriage failed. This can save a lot in legal fees, and you'll be unhitched that much faster.

The Least You Need to Know

◆ You need a pre-nuptial agreement if you are bringing anything into a marriage that could eventually represent substantial wealth.

◆ If you don't have a pre-nup, you will be subject to the property settlement laws of your state if you get divorced.

◆ In 2008, the "marriage tax" turned into a marriage bonus.

◆ Married couples should keep their tax-deferred retirement accounts separate but share taxable investment accounts jointly.

◆ QDRO stands for Qualified Domestic Relations Order, and it spells out how the assets held in pension and 401(k), 403(b), and 457 plans will be split in a divorce.

18

Cutting Expenses *Is* Investing

In This Chapter

- ◆ Getting a grip on your spending
- ◆ Figuring your marginal tax rate
- ◆ Fresh ideas on how to cut expenses
- ◆ Little things that add up

Believe it or not, it's a lot easier to spend $1 less than to earn $1 more. How so? Well, to earn more, you either have to work longer hours or take greater risks with your investments. What's more, you pay taxes on each additional dollar you earn on your job—but saving is free!

Someone once said that the best exercise for losing weight is to push yourself away from the table. The same is true of savings: just push yourself away from that sales counter! Spending can be addictive for many people, but learning to "just say no" is one of the best things you can do for your financial security.

Become a Hunter/Gatherer

In Chapter 5, we provided two real-life illustrations of personal balance sheets and income statements. One set was for Fred, a young man who, if you recall, was not in great financial shape. The other was for Bill and Mary, a happy couple on the right track. One set of financial statements took about 20 minutes to compile, while it took over a day to sort out the expense side for the other set. Can you guess which set took longer to compile? (Hint: Who was in the bigger mess?)

> **Super Strategies**
>
> Learn to buy off-season. For instance, purchase your holiday cards in January or a winter coat in April. Because no one else is thinking about purchasing these items during the off-season, the demand is low and the price is right!

You can't save if you don't know what you have, and the only way to figure it out is to gather information on your spending habits. So be a gatherer! Get a notebook and create a page for each spending category (clothing, groceries, and so on), and total them up each month. Use the personal income statement we provided in Chapter 5 to make a monthly income statement for yourself. After 12 months, you'll see some patterns emerging. Was the August clothing bill higher because you took advantage of summer markdowns, or because of heavy back-to-school purchases? Did you notice your entertainment costs rising with the barometer in the summer because it was too hot to put on the stove and you ate out a lot? How about the holidays? Did your credit card bills double because you made all of your purchases in November and December?

Pay close attention to these patterns. Once you start getting a grip on your spending, you will become addicted to saving because it gives you both dollars and personal satisfaction. It all begins with the monthly drill of accumulating and tabulating your expenses. It's your money, and you work hard for it. Why not work just a little harder to hold on to it?

Your Tax Bracket Is Higher Than You Think

Saving becomes even more attractive when you realize that because income tax is graduated, you pay more tax on the last few dollars you earn than you do on the bulk of your income. For example, if you earn $35,000 a year and pay $3,500 in federal income tax, that doesn't mean you are in the 10 percent tax bracket. It means you pay an average of 10 percent in taxes on your income. But in reality, you pay no income tax on the first few thousand and probably closer to 35 percent on the last few. Now, if you were given a raise of $2,000, you'd pay nearly $500 of it for federal income tax and $153 to Social Security. That's $653 in federal tax on $2,000. That's a tax bracket of around 33 percent! So for every additional dollar you earn, you have to pay at least *a third* in taxes. Ouch! This tax rate is called your *marginal tax rate*.

def•i•ni•tion

Our income tax is progressive (as opposed to flat), meaning the more money you make, the more tax you pay per dollar. You pay no tax, in fact, on the first few dollars you earn and progressively more tax as you earn more. The rate you pay on the last few dollars you earn is your **marginal tax rate**.

A penny saved is more than just a penny earned. It could be up to two pennies earned! Maybe you don't need to earn more; after all, every new dollar you earn is subject to that hefty marginal tax rate. Maybe you can pile up a nest egg to invest by saving, instead of by moonlighting as a security guard.

Crash Alert

Federal (and state) tax withholding represents another area of potential savings. Many people over-withhold so they get a nice refund check after the tax year is over. But this lets the government, rather than you, earn interest on that money. Consider a $1,200 tax refund. If you had saved the $100 per month at 5 percent interest, instead of letting the government hold on to it, you'd be $30 ahead, because you'd get to use the money for about six months.

Risk-Free Saving Where You Least Expect It

Saving is actually one of the best investments around! The coolest thing about saving is that it's the one investment activity that breaks the rule about high returns requiring you to take on greater risk. Let's say you have a newborn and you run through five packs of diapers a week. Buying them individually, each pack costs $5, so you spend $25 a week on diapers. Zowie, that's $100 a month on diapers. Turns out, the store sells a case of diapers, which is one month's worth, at a 20 percent discount. On $100 worth of diapers, that discount is $20. The case of diapers costs $80. Hmmm … let's figure out your return on this investment.

Before, you paid $25 a week for diapers. Now, you're putting out $80 for a month's worth. Your discount on every pack of diapers is $1 ($5 – $4 = $1). Over a year, that will add up to a savings of $260 (i.e., $1 × 5 packs = $5 × 52 weeks = $260). So, for investing a measly $80 in discount diapers each month, you earn a return of $260. That's a return on investment of more than 20 percent!

$1,040 (actual annual expense) – $1,300 (annual full price) ÷ $1,300 × 100 = 20 percent

And the only risk is that your baby will become miraculously toilet trained before you get a chance to use up that case of diapers (you wish!). Even better, the government doesn't get its hands on that $260. It's tax-free and it's yours, all yours. If you really want to feel like a hotshot, figure that if your marginal tax rate is around 30 percent, you would have had to earn $260 plus $78 to cover the taxes to come up with $260. Saving money wherever you can is definitely the road to riches. The rest of this chapter should give you some fresh ideas on how to cut expenses on things like …

◆ Shopping.

◆ Car expenses.

◆ Banking.

◆ Life insurance.

◆ Real estate taxes.

◆ Credit card fees.

Let the saving begin ….

Buying Bulk Is a Great Investment

Buying in bulk, as in the example above, is a great way to save, provided that you keep it in perspective. Do you have to pile towels on the floor because the linen closet is filled with bargain toilet paper? Do you have to park your car outside because the garage is filled with discount tires? Don't laugh; we've seen it all! Just keep a couple of simple rules in mind and you'll be fine.

1. Are you taking advantage of a special sale at your local supermarket, or driving across town to a warehouse place like Sam's Club? If it's the latter, is there

a membership fee, and how much? Remember, you have to mentally *amortize* (write off) the fee against your savings. Be sure to do this. As an example, the Sam's membership fee is $40 per year. Are you saving enough by making purchases there to make the $40 fee worthwhile? The fee may well be worth it for you, but be aware of it.

2. Try to limit your purchases to around a three-month supply as opposed to a year supply—unless you're planning on converting your home into a mini-supermarket, that is. And remember, prices can go down as well as up. So if you buy a one-year supply of choco-late chip cookies after a long period of price increases, you may have bought at the "top," with little or no savings to show.

def•i•ni•tion

To **amortize** means to write off a debt or fee over time. If you pay a fee of $240 a year to join a gym, for example, you might want to amortize that fee over the year by including $20 a month on your monthly income statement as your gym fee.

3. Factor in transportation costs. We know people in New York City who drive to Vermont and Maine to shop at factory outlet stores, only they forget to factor in the cost of the gas they use, not to mention their time. And sometimes the prices aren't much better than they are locally.

Your Car: Leasing vs. Ownership

There are two ways to look at this issue: first, from an aesthetic point of view, and second, from a financial point of view. If you simply like to drive around in a new car every two to three years, either because it makes you feel good or because you feel it is important for your business image, then lease. If, on the other hand, you want the least-expensive alternative, then buy (or take out a loan).

Advantages of Leasing

What are the advantages of leasing? Well, there's that thrill of driving a new car every two or three years. In addition, because the monthly payments are less, you are able to drive a more expensive car. Why are the payments less? Because you are not buying the car, you are simply paying for the *depreciation*, or the wear and tear, on the vehicle. When the lease is up, the dealer retains title to the car.

def•i•ni•tion

Depreciation is the loss in value of an item over time due to wear and tear. Like amortization, the financial reflection of depreciation can be spread out over time. If you own a computer and use it in your home business, for example, the IRS allows you to deduct part of the computer's value each year as a depreciation expense.

You also have a little more flexibility: At the end of the lease, you can either walk away or purchase the car. Why is this important? If you use the car in your business, you can deduct the rental payments on your business tax return.

Disadvantages of Leasing

Leasing sounds pretty good so far, right? Let's look at the negatives and how to reduce some of them.

1. **Capitalized Cost Deduction.** This is the leasing equivalent of a down payment. The larger this figure, the lower your monthly payments. You can usually negotiate this figure lower, sometimes a lot lower. Just make sure you do so without budging on the monthly payment.

2. **Disposition Fee.** This is a fee charged if you do not buy the car. Tell the dealer you don't want to pay this fee (or have the dealer deduct this cost from some other category).

3. **Excess Wear and Tear.** This is subjective and determined by each individual dealer at his or her discretion. What about parking lot "dingers," or a broken outside mirror or antenna? Are these excess or normal? Have the dealer define excess wear and tear for you—in writing.

4. **Annual Mileage Allowance.** This usually runs 10,000 to 15,000 miles per year. You get no credit if you use less than the allowance and you pay a penalty (e.g., 20¢ per mile) if you run over the allowance. Be sure to determine your projected miles before making the lease decision. If you know your mileage will be greater than the allowance, you can usually "buy" additional miles (e.g., 10¢ per mile), but excess mileage can be an expensive proposition. Here's an extreme example: Jack's contract reads 10,000 miles per year on a 36-month lease, with excess

miles charged at 20¢ per mile. His actual mileage turns out to be 60,000 (20,000 per year). His charge for excess miles of 30,000 (60,000 actual − 30,000 contractual) is $6,000 (30,000 × 20¢)! Ouch! Even if he'd bought an extra 10,000 miles per year for 10¢ per mile, he's still out $3,000! Moral of the story: If you are going to put a lot of miles on your car, don't lease.

The Bottom Line on Leasing

Every situation is different, but in general:

♦ The economics favor leasing if you plan to keep the car for less than two years.

♦ It's a toss-up for years three and four.

♦ The economics favor buying if you plan to keep your car for more than four years. Why? Because when you buy, you are financing something that will have some value when you stop making payments. All you are financing with a lease is depreciation. At the end of a lease period you have nothing. The costs of actually buying a car are simple and few in number: rate (in percent) and monthly financing charge, plus any paperwork fee. And, of course, how much you want, or have, to put down (down payment).

If you do go for the lease option, try to limit your search to cars on a lease "special." These are deals made when the manufacturer and/or dealer absorbs some of your cost and gives up some of their profit to promote a particular model. Why? Well, perhaps they have an excess inventory. For example, assume a Honda Civic is priced at $30,000 and the dealers are offering a "special" 36-month lease (no money down) of $325 per month. The upgraded S version, meanwhile, might be priced at $36,000, or 20 percent more. However, there is no special lease, and the best you can do is $475 per month for 36 months, or 46 percent more.

So if you plan to put low mileage on your car and trade it in frequently, it pays for you to use a lease—but only go for cars on a special lease package. Otherwise, buy your car and bargain down everything and anything you can. It's your money! If you want additional information on leasing, check out www.leasesource.com, which has an online worksheet to determine leasing pluses and minuses.

For more general information on car pricing and leasing, visit *Consumer Reports* at www.consumerreports.org.

Other great sources of info:

◆ *Edmund's Automobile Buyer's Guide*: www.edmund.com

◆ *Kelley Blue Book* (indispensable if you are going to sell your current car or trade it in on a new one): www.kbb.com

If You Buy a Car

If you can own your car for at least eight years, you will have maximized your investment. Before buying, don't forget to check online for the lowest prices and read magazines like *Consumer Reports* for helpful tips. Above all, shop around for your financing; don't just accept the dealer's rate. Here again, the Internet can be a great source of helpful information, as can local banks.

Finally, if you live in an urban area, make sure you really need a car. If you do, don't forget to factor in the cost of parking. Good public transportation can be a great alternative, supplemented by rentals when you need a vehicle for vacations or specific trips. The savings can be substantial.

Choosing a Bank

Banks make money by taking in deposits from customers and lending it out to other customers. That's why banks pay you less interest on your savings account than they charge you when you want a loan. The difference is the bank's profit. If a bank pays you 4 percent on your savings account and lends money to a company for 12 percent, the bank has made 8 percent. Different banks pay different savings account and CD rates, however, so shop around before you choose a bank. Many local newspapers carry various bank-account fees in table format once a week; check in the financial section of yours.

If convenience is important to you, make a short list of banks near your home or workplace. Think about the types of bank accounts you want, and then comparison shop via telephone. Before you do, estimate roughly how many checks you write per month. Different banks have different fees and requirements. Some banks will require a minimum balance, but will waive check-writing fees if you keep that balance. Others allow you, say, five free checks a month. Others charge you for each check you write, no matter what. Some banks will allow you to combine balances from savings accounts, CDs, and checking accounts to meet a minimum balance. Then there are ATM fees to contend with. Some banks won't charge you if you use their machine, but will charge you $1 or more for using a machine at another banking institution. Some banks charge you no matter whose ATM you use. These fees may not sound like much, but they really add up.

Another option is to forego a bank checking account altogether and use one that draws from your money market fund.

It's a good idea to choose a bank that offers overdraft protection as well. An overdraft is a bounced check. These can easily cost you $30 per pop and are usually the result of carelessness (when you don't keep your check register up-to-date) or poor communication (when you and your spouse don't update your individual entries in the joint checking account).

Knocking Down Real Estate Taxes

Real estate taxes are established by a local board of assessors or a town assessor who estimates how much your home is worth. Basically, your home is assessed a certain value, and that value is multiplied by the property tax rate, for every $1,000 of value in your home. Schools are typically the highest consumer of tax dollars (up to around 70 percent or more), followed by municipal services, such as police and fire departments.

If your home is assessed at $245,000 and your tax rate for your town is $5 per $1,000, your tax bill is $245 × $5, or $1,225. It's always possible that your house has been over-valued by the assessor. Check to see if your home has been assessed in line with your neighbors' houses, making allowance for number of bedrooms and other features, such as a deck or pool. Also compare your house with similar homes in other parts of town. The town office or assessor's office will make this information available to you.

If you feel your assessment is too high, check with the assessor's office for the proper procedure. Nothing ventured, nothing gained. Be careful, however, not to start the process without a good case—assessments can be raised as well as lowered.

Credit Cards

Credit cards are a very expensive debt if you don't pay off the balance in full each month. Annual rates of 20 percent or more are increasingly common, plus many cards charge a membership fee. Look at it this way: let's say you're carrying around a $2,000 balance on a credit card that has an 18 percent annual interest rate. Each month you pay them the minimum amount, which we'll say is $20. The yearly interest on that

$2,000 balance ($2,000 x.18) is $360. Your minimum $20 a month payment you've been making adds up to $240 for a year. *You're not even paying off the interest!* A bad investment. Very bad.

If you're doing everything "right" financially and are earning a solid return on some solid investments, what's the point if you're paying out tons of interest on your credit cards? You may be earning 15 percent on $5,000 in a great stock mutual fund, but if you're paying 18 percent on $5,000 on a maxed-out credit card, well, you're not getting ahead, are you?

First, if you have more than one credit card, ditch the rest and get down to one. No one needs more than one credit card. Now, which one should you carry? If you have trouble paying off your balance in full each month, think about switching to a *charge card*, as opposed to a *credit card*, such as the American Express card. In other words, you are required to pay the balance off in full each month, so you won't be tempted to carry it (and you'll think twice about what you charge on it!).

def•i•ni•tion

The difference between a **credit card** and a **charge card** is that a credit card enables you to carry a debt indefinitely, as long as you pay interest. Any debt put on a charge card, in contrast, has to be paid for within a specified period, typically 30 days. If you don't pay off your charge card account during that period, you will have to pay penalties and interest.

If you do have the discipline to pay off your card every month, why not get one that works for you? If you travel frequently by air, think about a card that offers free mileage. If you drive, how about a card that earns free gas or dollars toward the purchase of a new car? Once you have your monthly balance under control, you'd be amazed at how many transactions (supermarkets, doctor/dentist bills, and so on) you can put on your card and how the bonuses pile up.

The Least You Need to Know

◆ You pay taxes on each additional dollar you earn on your job, but saving is free, so it's a lot easier to get ahead by saving than by working more.

◆ Get in the habit of preparing monthly income statements to keep track of your spending.

◆ You can earn a higher rate of return from buying in bulk than from many investments.

◆ If you plan to own a car for under two years, leasing may be a better deal than buying.

◆ Choose a bank that offers overdraft protection, as well as the convenience you need and the best rates in your area.

Chapter

19

Covering Your Assets

In This Chapter

- Determining your insurance needs
- Life insurance simplified
- Insuring your home and other assets

You might not think of insurance as related to investment, but a single uninsured catastrophe can wipe out years of gains in your portfolio. Making sure you have adequate medical, home, auto, and life insurance is an important piece of your life as a savvy investor. You don't want to ever have to sell off great-performing stocks, or worse, dip into your retirement accounts to cover a hospital bill or buy a new car because you didn't have your assets covered.

There are basically three types of insurance everyone needs to carry:

- Life insurance, which provides income for your family in the event of your death.
- Health insurance, including disability income insurance. Disability insurance should cover 50 to 75 percent of your salary. Make sure it's noncancelable and guaranteed renewable.

◆ Liability insurance, which covers you if anyone sues because they are injured on your property or by your car. You'll save a bundle in premiums if you look to cover only major losses, not minor ones.

Don't Insure What You Can Afford to Replace

If you think of insurance as an offset to a catastrophe, you will save a lot in insurance premiums. Take your car as an example (before we get to your life). Most insurers offer you a deductible on collision insurance ranging from $250 to $1,000. In other words, you pay out of your own pocket for the first $250 or the first $1,000 of damage, depending on what deductible you choose.

If your snazzy new auto is worth $30,000, what will your premiums be? Well, depending upon the insurer and the state in which you live, the $250 deductible policy will cost you around $1,600, and the $1,000 deductible policy will cost you $660. You save roughly $1,000 per annum. In the first year, the extra cost of a collision (which is the difference in deductibles) is almost exactly offset by the lower premium!

You know we've got a rule of thumb for you, and here it is: Take the difference between the collision premiums for the minimum and the maximum deductible, and divide it by the difference in deductibles.

Premium for max. deductible – premium for min. deductible
÷ maximum deductible – minimum deductible

If the resulting ratio is one-third or higher, opt for the maximum deductible.

Super Strategies
Once you realize that you should carry coverage for catastrophes but not for every conceivable expense, you can save or reinvest the premium dollars saved. "Ah," you say, "but what if I have a catastrophe? How do I deal with a $1,000 out-of-pocket expense?" Well, remember the emergency fund? That, in part, is what it's for. Emergencies.

Life Insurance Simplified

Life insurance has one purpose: to provide for your family in the event of your demise. Your beneficiary can use the proceeds of your life insurance policy to cover your funeral expenses, pay your estate taxes, and raise your children.

Determining Your Insurance Needs

Far too many people carry far too much life insurance, giving rise to the popular expression "insurance poor." There are two ways to estimate how much life insurance you really need.

1. Make a list of expenses your family will need to cover if you die.

2. Figure out how much of your salary your family would need to replace if you die.

Here's an example of an expenses list.

Funeral expenses: $20,000

Outstanding debts: $5,000

Remaining mortgage: $100,000

College costs for children: $60,000

Annual minimum: ($50,000 ÷ .06 or 6%) $833,000 to $1,018,000

Less: Stocks, bonds, insurance, etc.: $300,000 to $718,000

Less: Social Security & other retirement benefits (if operable): $50,000

Net New Insurance Needs: $668,000

The "annual minimum" of $833,000 is the sum that will generate $50,000 a year in income for the family to live on if it's invested at 6 percent. This family will need life insurance coverage for $668,000 should the breadwinner(s) die.

To determine how much life insurance you need to replace your salary, simply multiply your present salary times the number of years your family will need it. If your family will need your $75,000-a-year salary for 15 more years, for example, you'll need $1,125,000 in life insurance. We don't necessarily endorse either method of estimating your life insurance needs. But at least they will get you thinking.

The Five Basic Types of Life Insurance

There are as many different types of life insurance policies as there are days in the year. And insurance agents sell them all, using every sales technique in the book. For the sake of simplicity (and your sanity), we are going to boil these down to five broad choices. It won't be easy going, but if you get through this next section, you'll be a lot more clued in than most people when you sit down with your insurance agent.

1. **Term Life.** The cheapest life insurance policies guarantee benefits only if you die before a specified term. They are called term life insurance policies. You pay X dollars in premiums and are insured for Y amount for Z years. If you die within the Z period, your beneficiaries get the Y amount. If you die after Z years, they get zip. The idea is to set Z years for a period after your kids are grown and able to take care of themselves.

   If this appeals to you, ask your insurance agent about declining term insurance. With this policy, the amount of protection decreases each year (just as your need does). Declining term insurance should be your cheapest option.

2. **Whole Life.** Whole life insurance is much more expensive than term insurance, but accumulates more value. A portion of your monthly premium goes to the insurer, who invests it on your behalf. Over time, compounding does its magic and the cash value of your policy grows exponentially. Upon your death, your family gets a death benefit plus the money that has accumulated in the policy.

3. **Joint Life and Survivorship.** Two popular variations used by two-worker families and business partnerships are joint life and survivorship. With joint life, two or more people are insured, and the face amount is paid upon the death of the first individual to the second individual. Survivorship policies are also called "second-to-die" insurance. With second-to-die, no payment from the insurance company is made until the second insured dies. Premiums are payable until the second death. If you die, your assets are sheltered by the marital deduction, but your surviving spouse's are not. The second-to-die policy can pay the taxes resulting from your spouse's death. This policy is also very popular with business partnerships.

4. **Universal Life.** This is a life insurance contract that, like whole life insurance, accumulates cash value. It is more flexible, however. The death benefit may be increased or decreased, and the premium changes to reflect that increase or decrease. A back-end load of around 7 percent is typically charged when you make any changes in your policy.

5. **Variable Life.** Variable life is a securities-based, whole life product. The insurance company sets up a separate account to hold the assets, which come from your premium payments, and invests them in common stocks, bonds, and/or money market securities. Because the value of the securities changes daily, so

does your potential death benefit. The change is always on the upside, however. You are guaranteed the face amount of the policy. Premiums are fixed.

5A. **Variable Universal Life Policy.** This is like a Cadillac with all the options. It includes flexible premium payments, an adjustable death benefit, and two cash benefit options. The cash values are held in a separate account (as with a variable life policy), and the investment performance can affect the amount of the death benefit.

The policy holder may pay premiums in any amount and with whatever frequency (monthly, quarterly, etc.) he or she finds convenient. Loads are deducted from the premiums to cover sales and administrative expenses; and they can be either "front-end" or "back-end."

However—and it's a big "however"—there are monthly deductions from these separate accounts to pay for the insurance coverage provided by your policy. And if there is an insufficient sum in the accounts, the policy holder must deposit additional dollars to keep the policy in force.

What do all these options cost? That's not easy to answer, but here's as good a comparison as you will find. For 10-year term life, we selected John Hancock. They are not the lowest in terms of annual premiums, but they enjoy one of the highest ratings (AM BEST A++, S&P AAA). We felt this was important, if not critical, given the fact that even some major insurance companies went under during the credit crisis of 2008. For Universal Life and Whole Life, we opted to go with a very solid company: Northwestern Mutual. Incidentally, the "health class" in each category is what's known as "preferred nontobacco." And yes, ladies, we are aware that you enjoy lower rates across-the-board compared to your male counterparts! Incidentally, in the whole life and universal life categories, survivorship is often referred to as second-to-die.

Annual Rate Examples for $1,000,000 Policy

	10-Year Term	Universal Life	Whole Life	Universal Life Survivorship	Whole Life Survivorship
Age 45—male	$870	$8,380	$22,070	$4,566	$12,240
Age 45—Female	$740	$6,795	$18,460	$4,566	$12,240

continues

Annual Rate Examples for $1,000,000 Policy   (continued)

	10-Year Term	Universal Life	Whole Life	Universal Life Survivorship	Whole Life Survivorship
Age 65— male	$6,170	$20,210	$61,770	$11,800	$32,170
Age 65— female	$3,650	$15,929	$48,100	$11,800	$32,170

All Universal Life and Whole Life are full pay.

* After 10 years, client needs to requalify. Premiums increase substantially e.g. a male age 55 would be looking at a premium of e.g. $2,150.

Source: Daniel L. Gerding, CLU, Harris Bancorp Insurance Services, Inc. 847-441-4874

Are you totally confused? Maybe this will help:

Comparison Data

Features	Type of Policy Term	Permanent	Universal	Variable
Death Benefit	Fixed, level	Fixed, level	Adjustable, level or increase	Depends upon performance; guaranteed minimum
Premiums	Fixed schedule, increasing	Fixed schedule, fixed amount	Flexible schedule, flexible amount	Fixed schedule, fixed amount
Cash Values	None	Fixed and guaranteed	Current interest plus guaranteed minimum	Depends upon performance

Term Life Insurance

If you have straight or ordinary life insurance, look into term insurance. Term insurance covers you for a specific term—say, 20 years—instead of your entire life. You can obtain the same dollar amount of insurance for much lower premiums with term life insurance. Many people set the term to cover them until the year their last child is expected to graduate from college. Also check with your employer to see if you are eligible for a group insurance rate.

> **Super Strategies**
>
> How much should you pay in insurance premiums? Some experts recommend 10 percent of your income, while others say whatever it takes to provide half your current income. Let a good agent help you assess your situation. How do you find a good agent? Ask friends and family for recommendations. That's your best bet.

Annuities

Insurance companies also sell annuities, which are regular payments for the length of the life of the person who owns the annuity contract. Like life insurance, an annuity is a contract between the insurance company and the purchaser (you). This person is called the "annuitant." Typically, you would designate yourself the annuitant and name a beneficiary, who will receive whatever value is left over in the annuity when you die.

 Crash Alert

Life insurance is a commodity, so shop accordingly. You do want to be sure that the insurance carrier will be able to pay your death benefits, so always check into the financial capabilities of your insurer. A good way to start is to call your state insurance commissioner and see if any complaints or charges are outstanding.

Here's the interesting difference between life insurance and annuities. With life insurance, the insurer is hoping that you will live long enough to pay enough premiums to more than cover the death benefit. The longer you live, the better for the insurance company. With an annuity, on the other hand, the payments stop rather than start at death, so the shorter your life, the happier the insurance company. Kinda ghoulish, eh?

Importantly, for both fixed and variable annuities, your death benefit will at least equal the amount you paid for the contract. This is one of the features that insurers use to trumpet variable annuities over mutual funds. Your mutual funds, after all, could theoretically decline in value below what you put into them. A variable annuity, as we mentioned in Chapter 12, is basically a mutual fund with an insurance contract wrapped around it. You get to invest in the possibilities of growth with the underlying mutual fund, plus you are assured a defined death benefit. However, we think you're better off buying mutual funds for your portfolio and separate term life insurance.

Your Kids Don't Need Life Insurance

Insurance agents will use three reasons to sell you life insurance for your kids:

1. Premiums are low because of their young age.

2. It guarantees their insurability in the event of major health problems.

3. The cash value can be used for the child's education.

Okay, these are all valid reasons, but we just don't buy it. And we don't think you should. There are better ways to finance a child's education, as we discussed in Chapter 16. And if your child has major health problems, group health insurance, not life insurance, seems the more appropriate course.

Disability insurance, on the other hand, is a must—for you, not your kids. Disability insurance replaces your income if you are disabled and can't work. Short-term (e.g., three months) disability is usually a part of your group health plan, but you'll need to buy long-term disability insurance (LTD) to cover you should a disability prevent you from working for a long time. Some employers offer this insurance to employees; if yours doesn't, contact your insurance agent.

Plan on paying about $50 to $100 per month for disability insurance. It's a small price to pay for a lot of peace of mind. LTD will serve as a salary substitute if you are ever disabled.

Insuring Your Home and Other Assets

Finally, be sure to discuss homeowner's insurance with your agent. Your mortgage bank will require you to carry insurance at least equal to the outstanding mortgage. Your main concern should be coverage for fire, flood, and wind damage.

Flood insurance, if you live in a flood plain, can be purchased most cheaply from the federal government. You may have seen articles about Topsail Island, one of the barrier islands off North Carolina. That's Hurricane Alley, and the people living there are in a continuing build/destroy/rebuild cycle. We can't imagine what they would do without flood insurance.

If you're not in a flood plain and the worse floods you face are one inch of water in the basement every 10 years, you don't need flood coverage. Fire will be your main concern. Be sure your coverage is for 100 percent of the current replacement value of your home.

If you own any important works of art or antiques, take out a fine arts policy. This insurance is not cheap, but it's the only protection available for such precious items.

> **Super Strategies**
>
> When you insure the contents of your home, be sure to go from room to room with a camera to prove what you have and what it looks like. Store the photos on an external hard drive or CD and keep it in your safe-deposit box, not in your home.

If you own expensive jewelry, you may wish to take out a personal articles policy. Premiums vary by value, location, and deductible, so check with your insurance agent. As a property owner, you should also seriously consider taking out liability insurance. This is insurance that will protect you from being wiped out by any lawsuits brought by someone who slips on your sidewalk or is otherwise injured on your premises. An "umbrella" policy providing a million dollars of coverage for various liability issues will cost from about $150 to $300 a year. It's well worth it for the peace of mind, which, after all, is what covering your assets is all about.

The Least You Need to Know

- Don't insure what you can afford to replace.

- Life insurance has one purpose: to provide for your family in the event of your death.

- There are five basic types of life insurance: term, whole, joint, universal, and variable.

- Your kids don't need life insurance.

- Besides life and health insurance, you need disability and auto insurance. If you're a homeowner, you will need homeowner's and liability insurance.

Part  Advanced Investing Strategies

Money is better than poverty, if only for financial reasons.

—Woody Allen

By now you've developed your own investment I.Q., and it's pretty darn high. You're capable of understanding some fairly complex investments and can decide whether or not to include them in your portfolio.

Most of us will never trade pork bellies or gold, but we can use the same tools that commodities traders use—such as options and futures contracts—to strengthen our own portfolios and protect them from volatile market swings. This part builds on everything you've learned so far and shows you how to apply advanced plays to your investments.

Take a look at the offerings in this part. It'll feel good to have a clue when you hear about hedge funds or private equity funds at a party or on the news. You may even find that not only do you understand these investments, but they may also help you meet your goals.

Chapter 20

Keeping Uncle Sam's Mitts off Your Assets

In This Chapter

- ◆ Probate-proofing your will
- ◆ Saving on estate taxes
- ◆ Cons of passing everything onto your spouse
- ◆ Trusts and gifts

Most people react to estate planning the same way they do to pre-nuptial agreements: "That's just for the wealthy." But it's definitely not. Don't assume, for example, that if you were to die, your spouse would automatically inherit your assets. Without a will, that's not guaranteed. And, without careful estate planning, the government—not your heirs or spouse—is likely to end up with at least half of your hard-earned assets.

There are two main definitions of the word "estate":

1. A sizable piece of land with a large house. This is what most people associate with the word "estate."

2. All of one's possessions. This is what you should associate with the word "estate."

Do you care what happens to your estate—who gets what, and when? If you pay an accountant to make sure you pay the lowest possible income tax, does it not make sense to pay a tax/trust attorney to ensure that your estate will not take an unnecessary hit from estate taxes? Now, have we got your attention?

Why You Don't Want to Die Without a Will

Let's start with the most basic estate-planning strategy: the will. A *will* is a legal document, signed by you and witnessed, that gives explicit directions as to who or what is to get whatever specific assets of yours you choose to list. If you have children under the age of 18, you would specify in your will a guardian whom you want to take care of them upon your death.

Technically, you don't need a lawyer to draw up a will, but we strongly recommend that you use one. If you die without a will, it is referred to as dying "intestate." That means the state (and even potentially an ex-spouse), rather than you, decides how and to whom your assets will be distributed.

"The state," in this case, is that part of the judicial system known as probate court. Without a will, the state may give some of your assets to heirs who do not need them, while others who do need them get less or none. Even scarier, if you are a single surviving spouse with children and you die without a will, the court, not you, will appoint a guardian for your children. Finally, dying intestate delays the distribution of your assets and adds to the expense. None of these scenarios sound too hot, do they?

We feel very strongly that everyone with assets needs to have a will. It should be reviewed every year to reflect any changes in your personal, legal, or financial situation. And you know when, don't you? That's right, on your birthday. Except, from now on, we are no longer referring to it as your birthday. After all, we all reach a point in our adult life when we don't want to acknowledge the date of our birth anymore. So henceforth, we will refer to your birthday as your *review day*. Okay? Reviewing your will each Review Day will literally take five minutes. And changing your will, for whatever reason, is a simple matter requiring a phone call to your attorney. It's also a good idea for both you and your spouse to make out your wills at the same time, so you can make sure you're not expressing conflicting wishes—regarding your children, for example, which could cause problems if you both die at or near the same time.

One final matter you should address with your will is the naming of an executor. Your *executor* will distribute your assets as you have set forth in the will. Although you can name anyone, we suggest appointing a professional, such as your attorney or someone from your bank trust department, and a close family member (spouse or sibling) as co-executors. Believe us, this is not an honorary position!

def•i•ni•tion

A **will** keeps your assets out of probate court, or probate. With a will, you legally designate who will get your assets and your **executor** (i.e., a person you appoint to carry out the provisions and directions of your will) makes sure that happens after you die. If you die without a will, or if your will is contested, your estate can end up in your state's probate court, to be fought over by anyone who can demonstrate a claim to your assets.

Probate: The Process of Administering Your Will

The next step in the estate planning process is coming up with ways to make sure your will doesn't end up in probate court. Probate is the process of administering your will (or divvying up your assets if you die intestate). Probating takes time, costs money, and allows the public to view your personal assets (and you thought you had heard the last of your ex!). Fortunately, there are several ways to avoid probate court.

Living Trust

Perhaps the best-known way to avoid probate court is the *living trust.*

A living trust is a legal document that allows you to designate someone to manage your assets if you die or are incapacitated. The trust is typically managed by a trustee for you and for whomever else (your spouse, usually) you wish to include. This document is especially important if you have health concerns that could leave you incapacitated, and it is important for most people to have these days because of medical advances that have resulted in more people "living" in incapacitated states.

Often you serve as trustee for yourself with provisions for someone else (a professional) to serve in the event of your death or incapacitation. You can also name a friend or relative as trustee/co-trustee. Because you

def•i•ni•tion

One way to keep your estate out of probate court is to use a **living trust**, which names someone to actually manage your assets if you die or are incapacitated. The technical name for this trust is inter vivos—feel free to impress friends and neighbors with this phrase!

created the living trust, you can change it whenever you wish, just as you can modify your will. A will and living trust are often created and modified at the same time, and drawn up by the same estate-planning attorney.

Crash Alert _____

> If you create a living trust and choose to exclude specific assets for any reason, you can include or add them to the trust per the terms of your will. This is referred to as a "pour over" provision in your will. However, you will still need to have these specific assets probated since they were technically not in your living trust at your death.

Joint Ownership

A simpler and less expensive way of avoiding probate is to keep some assets (home, securities, etc.) in joint ownership. Joint ownership does preclude several terrific estate-planning techniques that will reduce or eliminate state taxes. (We'll discuss those shortly.) Joint ownership is worth considering as an alternative to a living trust, however. Either joint ownership or the living trust is a good first step in the estate-planning process.

Before we leave probate, let's mention one class of assets that are automatically excluded: beneficiary-designated accounts. When you designate a beneficiary for your

- Retirement accounts (IRAs, pensions, 401[k]s, etc.)
- Life insurance policies
- Qualified tuition programs (529s)

the assets in these accounts bypass probate and go directly to your designated beneficiary: spouse, child, etc. These sums are still included in your taxable estate, however.

Estate Tax Repealed in 2010!

Now that we've taken care of the probate issue, let's proceed to estate taxes. These taxes were among the most onerous in the U.S. tax system, starting at 37 percent and running up as high as 55 percent. It was a bummer to think that you might have a million dollars to leave to your kids, but the government could take half of it before the money even got to them.

On June 7, 2001, President George W. Bush fulfilled his campaign promise to reduce taxes by signing a $1.35 trillion tax cut package known as the Economic Growth and Tax Relief Reconciliation Act of 2001. A key section of the Tax Relief Act of 2001 created a significant increase in the estate tax exemption, with a full repeal slated for 2010.

On January 1, 2010, there will be a full repeal of all estate taxes. That's the good news. Now for the bad: The repeal will expire on December 31, 2010, and the law in effect prior to June 7, 2001 will be revived. That means the maximum estate tax exemption will return to $1 million, and the highest rate will jump back up to 55 percent. This so-called "sunset provision," which we are betting the Feds will invoke, citing "budgetary safeguards," has given rise to a rather sick joke among legal eagles:

Lawyer to aging client: "Try very hard to expire in 2010."

Only in America! Well, enjoy the respite while it lasts.

The sunset provision will keep the debate on the estate tax brewing for the next decade.

They Can Tax *That?!*

Maybe you think you don't have to worry about estate planning because your estate isn't worth over $1 million. But take a close look at what's included in the definition of "estate." It adds up fast. Let's make a partial list:

- ◆ Taxable investments (stocks, bonds, mutual funds, CDs, money market accounts, etc.)

- ◆ Employer-sponsored retirement plan benefits

- ◆ All IRAs

- ◆ Personal residences less their mortgages

- ◆ Business/partnership interests

- ◆ Life insurance proceeds (at time of death)

- ◆ Automobiles, boats (less loans)

- ◆ Jewelry and collectibles (antique furniture, paintings, coins, stamps, etc.)

Fiscal Facts

Federal Estate Tax Return Form 706 must generally be filed and taxes paid by the estate within nine months following the estate owner's death.

- Other items of value (clothing, furniture, etc.)
- Taxable lifetime gifts

Does any of this look familiar? It should mimic what's on your personal balance sheet.

Super Strategies

As you get older, the value of your estate is going to continue to increase. You may not be a millionaire now, but you may be in 2016 or 2026. Start protecting your estate now. First, carefully estimate the value of your estate. Have jewelry, collectibles, and other property appraised. Think about what gifts you want to make to charities and to family members. In short, use this chapter as inspiration to get organized—then, see your attorney!

Are there any deductions? Precious few. We've indicated some in our partial list (mortgages and car loans). Others include funeral expenses, transfers to charities of your choice, and the cost of administering your estate (trust bank fees and the like).

Cons of Passing Everything on to Your Spouse

There is one big deduction you can take on your estate: the unlimited marital deduction. The tax code says that you may deduct from your estate the value of all assets that are transferred from you to your spouse, either directly (via a will) or in a trust. In that case, there would be no tax on your estate: zero, zip, nada.

But yes, Virginia, there is a catch.

If you pass away, your assets (and your share of any joint assets) pass to your spouse and there is no estate tax on your estate. But what happens when your spouse dies? Your spouse's estate won't be able to use the unlimited marital deduction because you're dust.

What if your spouse dies first? Then you get the unlimited marital deduction benefit on his or her estate—and your own estate loses that benefit. Yes, as the surviving spouse you still get the unified credit exclusion ($1.46 million in 2009), but it has to apply to the total of both your and your deceased spouse's estate.

Are there any better options? Yes, and we will briefly outline a few of them for you in a minute, but first, let's bring up one more issue to make sure you are totally confused: The Generation Skipping Transfer Tax (GST).

Watch That Generation Gap

The GST tax was intended to prevent Rockefeller-rich families from preserving their wealth by giving to grandchildren instead of to children and thereby skipping an entire generation of tax.

It was an unbelievable 55 percent, tacked on top of other estate and gift taxes. If your total gifts (directly or via trust accounts) exceeds $2 million (or $4 million if the total is joint with your spouse), you're taxed at 50 percent on the excess. And you can't get around the GST tax by setting up a trust for your child that passes to your grand-child at the time of the child's death, although your child could set up the trust. The tax law changes reduce the GST amount and tax rate in lockstep with the estate tax exemptions and rates, with the tax repealed in 2010 but set to zoom back up to pre-Tax Relief Act levels as of January 1, 2011. All the new developments in tax law are another good reason to consult with an estate-planning attorney.

Tax-Saving Alternatives

There are some trusts you can set up to reduce your estate tax bill.

Credit Shelter Trust

A smarter way to use the unlimited marital deduction is to divide your assets in half and will only half to your spouse. Use the other half to set up a credit shelter trust (CST). Your spouse gets all the income generated by the trust's investments during his or her lifetime. The principal goes to your children when your spouse dies. Ideally, the assets used to set up the CST will be no more than the exclusion amount ($2 million in 2009) in the year of your death. At the time of your death, assets equal to the exclusion amount for that year go to create the CST, and the balance goes directly to your spouse via the unlimited marital deduction. At the time of your spouse's death, the CST is excluded from his or her estate. Voilà! You've cut your and your spouse's estate tax bill in half.

QTIP: No, Not the Kind You Stick in Your Ear

In addition to the CST, you can also set up, via your will, a second trust that qualifies for the marital deduction. What kind of trust qualifies? The most popular choice is called the Qualified Terminable Interest Property Trust, or "QTIP" for short.

With a QTIP, your spouse receives the income during his/her lifetime. At the time of your spouse's death, the assets pass on to whomever you've named in your will. The assets are still included in your spouse's estate, but you retain control of the assets "from the grave." The QTIP is great for a second marriage, for example, because you can make sure some of your assets reach the children of your first marriage after your second spouse dies.

Charitable Trusts

There are two kinds of charitable trusts:

1. Charitable Remainder Trusts (CRTs)

2. Charitable Lead Trusts (CLTs)

With the CRT, you set up a trust for the charity of your choice, but you retain all rights to the income generated by the trust until you and/or your spouse dies. At that time, the assets go to the charity. You get a charitable gift deduction (Schedule A on IRS Form 1040) and the assets in the trust are excluded from your estate.

CRTs take one of two forms: either a Charitable Remainder Annuity Trust or a Charitable Remainder Unitrust. The former pays a fixed dollar sum to you each year; the latter pays you a fixed percentage of the assets.

Alternatively, the Charitable Lead Trust provides all income to the charity of your choice for a set period—20 years, for example. At the end of that period, the assets revert to whomever (son, granddaughters, etc.) you initially named as the remainder beneficiary.

You can establish a CRT or CLT:

◆ At the time of your death, via your will, protecting some of your estate from taxation.

◆ During your lifetime, improving both your income tax and estate tax situations.

Other Ways to Reduce Estate Taxes

There are several other ways to cut estate taxes and make sure more of your hard-earned money goes to the people you love, not to the IRS. Again, we recommend that you consult an attorney, but at least if you read this chapter, you'll walk into the law office reasonably well informed (always a plus, especially if you're paying by the hour). Consulting a licensed CPA wouldn't hurt, either.

Life (Saver!) Insurance

Life insurance can be used to pay any estate taxes, thereby nullifying the need for your heirs to sell estate assets to raise the cash for the tax bill. You can also create a life insurance trust to hold or purchase life insurance. At your death, the trustee would collect the proceeds and invest them for the benefit of whomever you named as beneficiaries. The proceeds won't be included in your estate as long as the policies are purchased at least three years before your death or transferred to the trust three years before death.

The Gift That Keeps on Giving

Gifting is another nifty way to lessen the burden of your pesky Uncle Sam. In 2009, you can give $13,000 per person per year ($26,000 if you're making a joint gift with your spouse). This is an excellent way to reduce your estate, and thereby reduce your potential estate tax. Giving appreciated or potentially appreciating assets such as stock or real estate is a particularly good idea.

If you make medical or educational payments on behalf of your heirs, these payments are excluded from your estate—provided you make payments directly to the source. Education is limited to tuition, and you must pay the college directly. Medical payments must be paid directly to the hospital, doctor, or clinic, or to the insurance company, if you are paying for medical insurance. These exclusions only apply when you make payment on behalf of others, not for yourself.

Just a Little Token—Gifts to Minors' Trusts

You can also set up a trust for a child or grandchild and appoint a trustee (a parent, usually) to oversee the use of the funds in the trust. The trustee can pay out necessary sums for the minor's needs—college tuition, for example. At age 21 the child or grandchild has full access to the trust, however.

Personal Residence Trust

You might also talk to your attorney about transferring your home to a trust, while retaining the right to use the home for a specified number of years.

Super Strategies

If it makes you nervous that your child or grandchild can get into a trust at age 21, you can set up a Crummy Powers trust. A Crummy Powers trust gives the child or grandchild access to the trust for only a few days each year to make withdrawals. Technically, the child or grandchild has access to the principal, but for a very limited number of days each year. How much damage can they do?

For a personal residence trust, you make a member of your family the beneficiary. If you die before the specified number of years is up, the residence stays in your estate (and you have lost nothing). If you live beyond the specified time, you get an exclusion for one of the biggest assets in your estate. The downside to this arrangement, of course, is that ownership reverts to the named beneficiary. If you want to continue to live in the residence, you must pay this named beneficiary a "competitive" rent. Let's hope you are on good terms with him or her at that time!

This is but a short list of some of the more popular measures to save on estate taxes. We urge you to seek professional assistance if you wish to pursue any of these options; individual state laws differ, federal law is subject to annual change and interpretation, and we can't possibly cover all of the nuances for each of these alternatives. Above all, don't put off estate planning. As we've said throughout this book: it's your money!

What If You Inherit Money?

All this complicated talk about estate planning has probably got you wondering what to do should Uncle Fritz kick the bucket and leave you half of the $20,000 stuffed under his mattress.

When you inherit money, you will have two questions:

1. How much do I get?
2. How much do I owe?

What to Do When Your Ship Comes In

The first question, if it involves financial assets, is easy to answer, as nearly all securities have public market values.

The second question is a little more complex. In most cases, the cost of securities you inherit will be marked up to "date of death" (DOD). This is good news. It means that if you sell them shortly after receiving them, you will owe little or no capital gains taxes.

Although DOD minimizes your potential taxes, it maximizes the deceased's estate value. Depending on the final sum and the manner in which the assets were set up, therefore, you may owe estate tax after the estate is settled.

When an estate is being settled, the executor is concerned with determining the value of each asset as quickly as possible, and distributing these assets as soon as possible. Normally, marketable financial assets are sold, so the executor is distributing cash to the heirs. However, the heirs may jointly request that some or all of the securities be distributed "in kind." This means that if the estate holds 400 shares of General Electric and there are four heirs, each heir will receive 100 shares of General Electric.

Beyond Cash: Property, Businesses, and Valuables

Although most estates are valued on a date-of-death basis, the federal tax code also provides for an alternate valuation date: six months after the decedent's death. What's this alternate date for? Typically, the date is used if an estate is dominated by real estate or privately held businesses. The six-month leeway gives the executor time to hire an appraiser to estimate the "fair and sound value" of the estate. If the executor is able to "distribute, sell, exchange, or otherwise dispose" of the property within six months, it will be valued as of "date-of-death," not six months hence.

Household and personal items, such as watches, rings, antiques, paintings, etc., are considered what you probably consider them already: valuables. Their worth is esti-mated by the IRS's "willing buyer/willing seller" rule, which reads: "The price at which the property would change hands between a willing buyer and a willing seller, neither being under any compulsion to buy or to sell and both having reasonable knowledge of relevant facts."

If you didn't catch that, it just means the price is whatever the market will bear for the item(s) at the time, regardless of the circumstances under which they're being sold (i.e., the death of your great Aunt Tilly). The executor will most likely hire an appraiser to do an item-by-item, room-by-room appraisal. The appraisal will help you determine which items, if any, hold more than sentimental value. For those items, ask your insurance agent for a "fine arts" insurance policy.

What to Do with the Dough

After the first two questions have been answered, you will have a third: "What should I do with the dough?" In order of priority, until the money runs out, do the following:

1. Pay off "bad" debt: credit cards, auto loans, etc.

2. Pay off student loans, if you have any.

3. Replenish emergency funds.

4. Bring retirement plan assets up to the level you've determined (using our handy guide, of course) they need to be to reach your retirement savings target.

5. Put the balance in educational funds, if you have children.

6. Pay down your mortgage with any remaining proceeds.

Please, do not do the following:

1. Buy a bigger house.

2. Buy that new luxury car.

3. Buy a boat, snowmobile, or any other large, expensive piece of recreational equipment.

If you want a treat, take a nice vacation. It's a lot less expensive and won't stick around to haunt you.

The Least You Need to Know

◆ A will is a legal document, signed by you and witnessed, that gives explicit directions as to who or what is to get your assets.

◆ A living trust is a document that allows you to choose someone to manage your assets should you die or become incapacitated.

◆ Estate taxes are among the most onerous in the U.S. tax system; use a good attorney to help you protect your estate.

◆ You can reduce your estate (and therefore your estate taxes) by giving $13,000 per person per year while you're still living.

◆ When you inherit money, use it to strengthen your finances by paying off "bad" debt and replenishing emergency funds.

Hedging Your Options

In This Chapter

♦ All about options

♦ Protecting your portfolio with puts and calls

♦ Selling short versus trading options

♦ Protecting stock positions

♦ Advanced hedging strategies

Well, we promised that at the end of this book we would get into some advanced investment plays, and here we are—about to tackle options. Can you believe you even know enough to get into this topic? But if you've been with us so far, you definitely do!

Weighing Your Options

Options are contracts that give you the option, but not the obligation, to buy or sell a specified quantity of a financial instrument such as common stock. Options have two purposes:

♦ To act as insurance for those who believe prices are going to fall and want to protect their portfolio.

♦ To enable you to profit from rises in stock prices.

Both options and futures contracts, which we discuss in the next chapter, are called *hedges*. You've no doubt heard the phrase, "He's hedging his bets." Options and futures contracts can be used to hedge your bets on the stock market. A caveat: the strategies we'll be discussing in this and the next few chapters are quite sophisticated and should not be undertaken without careful research and the support of a trusted financial advisor or broker.

def•i•ni•tion

An **option** is a contract that is listed on an exchange just like a stock. The contract states what is to be delivered for what price and during what time period. At the end of the designated time period, the option loses all its value.

Our goal is simply to give you enough background so you can ask that trusted pro intelligent questions. Toward that end, we've gone a bit deep on some topics; if you can get through it, great, but if you can't, don't sweat it now. Just keep us around as your personal reference. Should you find yourself considering any of these investments in the near future, we'll still be right here on your shelf.

Puts and Calls

There are two kinds of options contracts: *puts* and *calls*. When you buy a call option, you are buying the right to purchase a stock at a set price, called the *strike price*, for a specified period of time—usually a few months.

def•i•ni•tion

The **strike price**, also called the exercise price, is the price at which the holder of an options contract can buy (**call**) or sell (**put**) the underlying security. For example, a Computer-Nerd, Inc., 50-call option means you can buy 100 shares of ComputerNerd, Inc., at $50 per share. A ComputerNerd, Inc., 50-put option means you can sell 100 shares of ComputerNerd, Inc., at $50 per share.

Here's a very simple example of how a call options contract works. Let's say you're thinking about buying 100 shares of ComputerNerd, Inc., stock, which is currently selling for $40 a share. You've heard that the company's coming out with an awesome new spreadsheet program and the stock price could rise sharply as a result. Hmmm ... what to do?

You could lay out the $4,000 now for the 100 shares and hold them, praying nightly that you were right about that software and looking forward to selling your stock for $6,000 when the share price rises to $60 for a tidy $2,000 profit. But what if ComputerNerd doesn't release the software on schedule due to an unanticipated glitch, causing the stock price to sink to $20? Oy! This could make for some very restless nights.

Hedge Your Bet with a Call

This is where an option comes in very handy. Instead of laying out $4,000 for 100 shares of ComputerNerd, Inc., contact your broker and buy a three-month call option on 100 shares of Computer Nerd stock at a strike price of $40. The option will only cost you, say, $400. Now, if the stock does rise to $60 before your three months are up, you have a contract entitling you to buy the stock for only $40. You'd pay only $4,000 for $6,000 worth of stock. You could turn around and sell the stock right away for a $2,000 profit. Pretty nifty!

If the stock price falls below $40, simply don't exercise the call option. Sure, you're out the $400 you spent on the options contract, but that's a lot easier to swallow than having spent $4,000 on the stock and watching its value shrink to $3,000 or $2,000 or less. With the call option, you've hedged your bet.

A put option is the opposite of a call option. A *put* is a contract that gives you the option to sell a security at a specified price until the contract's expiration date. With a call, you are hoping for the price of the security to rise, but with a put, you are protecting against a decline.

Prevent Portfolio Wipeout with a Put

Let's say you're bearish on ComputerNerd, Inc. You're convinced the company's spreadsheet software, which everyone else thinks is going to turn the industry on its ear, is destined for failure. Unfortunately, your spouse thinks differently and insists on buying 100 shares of ComputerNerd at $40 a share. How do you protect yourself from disaster?

Fiscal Facts

Options trade in "round lot equivalents" of 100 shares. Each options contract covers 100 shares of the underlying security. Options are quoted in dollar terms, with the 100 shares underneath each option implied; a $2 option, for example, really costs $200—$2 for each share.

Go to your online brokerage or call your broker and buy a three-month put option with a strike price of $36. This contract guarantees that for three months you can dump those 100 shares of ComputerNerd for at least $36 per share. If the stock tanks within the next three months, you can get out at $36, even if the share price drops to, say, $18. Instead of watching helplessly as your $4,000 stake in ComputerNerd drops to $1,800, you can exercise your option and get out with $3,600 intact. Because you've hedged your spouse's bet, you lose only $400, plus whatever you spent on the put options contract.

How Did This Get Started?

Options trading has been around about as long as securities trading, but until the 1970s, options traded in an informal, unregulated manner. Brokerage houses specializing in "puts and calls" would advertise their specials of the day in publications such as *The Wall Street Journal*. There was no regulated market.

After the 1973–1974 bear market for stocks took prices of popular indices like the Dow Jones and the S&P 500 down some 40 percent, it became clear that options could play an important role in stabilizing the market and protecting investors from severe drops. The government got involved in standardizing options trading. This led to the creation of the Chicago Board Options Exchange (CBOE). With the creation of the CBOE and its sister institution, the Options Clearing Corporation (OCC), trading in options grew phenomenally.

Risk-Loving Speculator Seeks Cautious Hedgehog

Options can be viewed in two ways: as rank speculation ("I bet you $200 that ComputerNerd, Inc., stock will go up 20 points in 90 days") or as a hedge ("I can protect myself against my ComputerNerd stock going down by buying put options with a $40 strike price for three months"). When you think about it, it takes both a speculator and a hedger to complete a contract.

An option's price is called a premium. The premium is the price the options buyer pays and the options writer receives for the option. The premium is like a commission, except that the premium diminishes in value steadily until the contract expires.

A three-month contract offered June 1, 2009, to buy a ComputerNerd, Inc., 50-call option might sell for $3, for example, when it's first offered. The price will decline, however, over the course of the three months. Why? Because as time passes, the option is protecting the buyer for less and less time.

The option's price, or premium, is the maximum loss that the buyer of the contract can experience. An option for 200 shares at $3 costs $600. That's the premium. If the price of the stock doesn't go your way and you never exercise the option, you lose the $600. But that's all.

In the Money

Options are referred to as either:

- "In the money"
- "Out of the money"
- "At the money"

This swinging lingo simply defines the difference between the option strike price and the current price of the underlying stock.

If the strike price is less than the current market price, for example, a call option would be described as "in the money." You are already ahead by the difference (or spread) between the strike price and market price.

This same situation would be described as "out of the money" for a put option, however. Why? Because, you are behind by the same amount for the put. You are betting the stock will go down, but, darn, it's going the other way.

 Fiscal Facts

As the expiration date for an option approaches, the premium gets smaller.

"At the money" means the stock price and strike price are equal.

Reading an Options Table

Let's take a look at a sample options table for the Coca-Cola Company. Let's look at the first contract on the third line. This is a Coca-Cola $42.50 call option; you see it has its own ticker symbol (KOKV). The buyer of the contract has the right—but not the obligation—to purchase 100 shares of Coca-Cola at $42.50 per share, which is $1.77 less than the closing price of the common stock ($44.27) on May 11 (you'd need to look up the stock price). This is an example of a call option that is "in the money," because the buyer has the right to purchase the stock for a lower price than it is selling for on the open market.

The contract, like all of those in the table, expires on November 19. Recall that all contracts expire on the Saturday following the third Friday in the month. The volume was 19, or 19 contracts. Because each contract equals 100 shares, the Coca-Cola November 42.50 call options traded an equivalent of 1,900 shares of the underlying common stock.

The last (or closing) premium of $3.20 means that it would cost you $3.20 times 100 (everything being expressed in 100-share terms), or $320, to purchase this call options contract. And notice that your break-even point (strike price + premium – closing price of the underlying common stock) is $42.50 + $5.10 – $44.27, or $3.33. If the stock price goes up more than $3.33 the next trading day, you are ahead of the game. Of course, the stock price and the premium are subject to constant fluctuation (but that's the exciting part, right?).

Now, check out the put. Notice that there is a put option for the same $42.50 strike price. Here, the purchaser is wagering that the share price will decline. Because the strike price is less than the closing price, the put options contract is presently out of the money. The stock would have to decline by more than the difference, or more than $1.77, to be in the money. Notice that the break-even point is different: first, you have to get to at the money, which is the $42.50 strike price; then, you have to recover your premium, or $1.20, for a total stock price decline of $2.97.

	Calls						Puts			
Symbol	Open Interest	Net Volume	Strike Change	Net Last	Open Price	Last	Change	Volume	Interest	Symbol
KOKU	499	0	0.00	7.60	37.5	.25	-.05	50	1,352	KOWU
KOKH	1,055	0	0.00	5.10	40.0	.55	-.05	10	1,934	KOWH
KOKV	4,538	19	0.10	3.20	42.5	1.20	0.00	0	4,056	KOWV
KOKH	1,055	0	0.00	5.10	40.0	0.55	-0.05	10	1,934	KOWH
KOKV	4,538	19	0.10	3.20	42.5	1.20	0.00	0	4,056	KOWV

	Calls				Puts					
Symbol	Open Interest	Net Volume	Strike Change	Net Last	Open Price	Last	Change	Volume	Interest	Symbol
KOKI	10,758	660	-0.05	1.50	45.0	2.20	0.00	5	902	KOWI
KOKW	3,894	215	0.05	0.65	47.5	4.00	0.00	0	268	KOWW
KOKJ	475	160	0.00	0.25	50.0	6.10	0.00	0	200	KOWJ
KOKK	0	0	0.00	0.00	55.0	10.90	0.00	0	52	KOWK

Options Galore

Financial newspapers like *The Wall Street Journal* used to carry extensive statistics for options and other financial instruments; however, most newspapers have cut back their statistical offerings quite a bit. Thanks to the Internet, however, you can quickly look up quotes for countless options. One newspaper that does still carry extensive statistics is *Investor's Business Daily* (IBD), specifically The Monday Special Edition. For a free trial subscription, call 1-800-831-2525. As Bluto said in the movie *Animal House:* "… it don't cost nothin'."

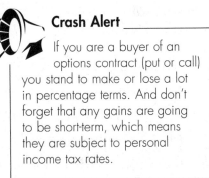

Crash Alert

If you are a buyer of an options contract (put or call) you stand to make or lose a lot in percentage terms. And don't forget that any gains are going to be short-term, which means they are subject to personal income tax rates.

Puts and options can help to hedge your investments, but they can also be risky. Here's an example of a put contract that could take a bite out of your portfolio:

Option/Strike	Vol.	Exch	Last	Net Chg	Close
CISCO Aug 12.50 P	20,350	XC	0.35	–0.80	12.99

The P stands for Put; since August 7 was an "up" day in the market, the contracts with the biggest losses were put contracts. XC stands for the Exchange Composite. The net change of –0.80 means that the premium declined 0.80 from the August 6 close 1.15! In other words, had you purchased the put option (CISCO Aug 12.50) at the close on August 6 and sold it at the close on August 7, you would have lost 69.6 percent for the day (–0.80 ÷ 1.15 = –69.60 percent)! In dollar terms, if you spent $115, you received $35, for a loss of $80.

> ### Super Strategies
>
> A variation of the covered call strategy is called a "buy-write" program, where you simultaneously buy, let's say, 100 shares of AT&T and write a call option on them. Some professional firms hire individuals specifically for their buy-write expertise to add value to the retirement accounts under their management.

Selling Short vs. Trading Options

Before the options market developed, speculators who wanted to bet that a stock's price was going to fall had only one play—to "short" the stock. When you short a stock, you don't actually buy the shares—you borrow them from a broker. You take the stock you've borrowed and sell it. Then you pray (fervently!) that the price of the stock will fall before you have to give the shares back to the broker.

What are you going to use to buy the shares to give back to the broker? That's right, the money you made selling the borrowed stock. What if you don't make any money selling the borrowed stock? You're in big trouble.

Let's say you borrowed 100 shares of ComputerNerd, Inc., agreeing to return them the next day. You go out and sell the 100 shares for $40 per share and make $4,000. If the stock price falls to $32, you'll only need to use $3,200 to buy the 100 shares to return to the broker. You can pocket $800 profit. Pretty nifty.

But what if the stock price shoots up to $50 per share? Uh oh, you're gonna need $5,000 to purchase those 100 shares. Well, you've got $4,000 from selling short. That other $1,000 is going to have to come out of your pocket. Big bummer.

Now you understand why the vast majority of options contracts are not exercised: the buyer of the put or call option is interested in trading the contract, not the underlying stock. The potential for profit is so much greater with options contracts.

Risky Business

Throughout this book, we've harped on the relationship between risk and return—and options are no exception. The very fact that you can reap such high returns with options should tip you off that they are extremely risky.

The day someone lost 69.6 percent on Cisco August 12.50 put contracts, for example, someone else could have made a bundle on Cisco October 15 call contracts. The contract closed at 0.65, up 0.10 for a day gain of 18.2 percent (+0.10/0.55)! The underlying common stock of Cisco gained only 7.6 percent that day. The option provided a much higher return.

Sellers of options contracts take on even more risk. As we said before, the buyer's maximum loss per contract is the amount of the premium. If, on May 12, you sold a call option for Coca-Cola November 19 with a $42.50 strike price, you would receive a premium of $320. But if Coke stock rose to $50 per share, you would have to spend $5,000 to be in a position to deliver if, by some chance, your contract was exercised. So, worst-case scenario, you could suffer out-of-pocket costs of $4,680 ($5,000 − $320). Oh, the pain.

Option Strategies That Protect Your Stock Positions

In the previous example, we assumed that you, as the options writer, did not actually own the stock and would have to go buy it if the option you sold was exercised.

def•i•ni•tion

An option expires—becomes worthless—on its expiration date. Options expire on the Saturday following the third Friday of the month in which they can be exercised. For example, ComputerNerd, Inc., December 50 options expire on December 16, 2009. Nine months is typically the maximum expiration date on an option.

An **options writer** (or "seller" or "issuer") creates the options contract, and must stand ready to honor the terms of the contract. The **options buyer** (or "holder") pays the options writer a premium for the right to buy the shares of ComputerNerd, Inc., in a call option or sell the shares of ComputerNerd, Inc., in a put option.

But suppose you did own the stock. You could write (sell) an options contract on the stock. This is called "covered call writing." When you own the underlying stock, writing a call is a conservative course of action. When you do so, you earn additional income minus the premium the options buyer pays you—which can help offset any minor price weakness in your stock. If the stock moves up in price, and for some reason the option is exercised, you already own the stock, so you won't take a hit on the price. Pretty much a win-win deal.

An even more conservative step is to purchase a put option for a stock you already own. This gives you downside protection for simply the cost of the put. And, of course, you would fully benefit if the price of the stock went up.

You get unlimited upside, as well as protection on the downside, because the value of the put increases as the price of the stock decreases. This works especially well if the strike price is at or close to the market price, and you purchase the longest put contract, which has the lowest premium and provides more time for the strategy to pay off. This strategy works best if you are concerned about a significant correction in the stock market or your particular stock.

Again, remember that all these strategies involving put and call options trigger income tax events for taxable accounts. Repeat after us: "I will visit my trusted professional should I become intrigued."

Stock Index Options

Unlike individual stock options, stock index options give you a chance to hedge your entire equity portfolio—assuming it is diversified.

Stock index options dominate the options scene due to the broad acceptance of the product by money managers. These include well-known broad indices, such as the Dow Jones Industrials, S&P 500, S&P 100, NASDAQ 100, Russell 2000, sector or industry indices, and indices for foreign stock markets.

S&P Index Options

You can find quotes for various stock index options at www.moneycentral.msn.com. Let's take a look at the options contracts for two indices: the S&P 100 and the S&P 500 on December 5, 2008.

If we look under the 20 Most Active Index Options table in IBD, and scan down to Dec 875 call and Dec 875 Put, we see the following:

	Index Price	Option Price	Option Change	Volume
DEC 875 CALL	876.07	37.00	+10.70	6,768
DEC 875 PUT	876.07	36.90	−21.10	6,628

Source: Investor's Business Daily December 8, 2008, 1-800-831-2525

We selected these two contracts because they are the closest to the current price (876.07). The value of the contract, the total exercise price, and the premium are each derived by multiplying by 100:

$100 \times \$876.07 = \$87,607$ = contract price
$100 \times \$875C = \$87500$ = total exercise price
$100 \times \$37 = \$3,700$ = cost to purchase option

Unlike individual stock options, index option contracts are settled with cash, not with the security.

You can exercise the contract on any day, just like with individual stock options; however, the contract is settled with cash, not with the security.

The S&P 500 follows the same format and procedure as the S&P 100, with one important difference: S&P 500 Index Options (SPX) may *only* be exercised on the last business day before expiration. This is referred to as a European-style option. American-style options can be exercised on any given day.

Hedge Strategies for Index Options

Hedge strategies for index options are similar to those for individual stock options. Suppose you wanted to hedge your diversified stock portfolio by purchasing the correct number of put contracts. By "correct number" we mean that you would buy put contracts with values that approximate the decline in your equity portfolio that you are worried about experiencing.

Similar to purchasing insurance—which, in effect, this is—your premium is your maximum cost. Let's assume your equity portfolio is presently worth $1 million and is invested similarly to the S&P 100. Multiply $100 times the current value of the S&P 100 ($555.21) and you'll get $55,521. Divide this into $1 million and you'll get $18.01 (round down to 18). To hedge your portfolio, you'll need to buy 18 put contracts.

Pick the put contract closest to the current index price, or 560p, for the month you want. The premium for August 550 put options, for example, is $15.20. What's the maximum cost to you? $15.20 times $100 is the cost per contract, and you need 18 contracts. Your cost is $27,360, or 2.736 percent of your equity portfolio. As you can see, this is not cheap insurance. Equity index hedging is not for amateurs.

The Braveheart of Wall Street

Still with us? Good! If you're hankering for more, we've got two more aggressive strategies for you:

- **Straddles**. These are the simultaneous purchase of a put and call for the same stock or index at the same strike price and expiration date. The straddle buyer makes money if the price of the stock moves significantly up or down. The straddle writer makes money even if there is little or no stock price movement by capturing two premiums. This is a very hot strategy among professionals.

- **The spread**. This is the purchase and sale of options on the same stock, only the options have either a different strike price with same expiration date or the same strike price and different expiration dates.

  A bull spread involves purchasing an option with a lower strike price (i.e., "in the money") and the sale of an option at a higher strike price (i.e., "out of the money").

  With a bear spread, you sell the option at a lower strike price and purchase the option at a higher strike price.

These strategies can get quite esoteric and should not be tried in the comfort of your own home. And remember, again, that any success translates into short-term gains, which means you'll be paying income tax on them.

LEAPS

Finally, we have LEAPS, which stands for Long-Term Equity Anticipation Security. These are long-term options contracts that are very popular with individual investors. There are two main differences between LEAPS and regular options:

- LEAPS can be written for up to a three-year expiration date vs. a maximum of nine months for traditional options. If you are really convinced that the market is going to move strongly in a certain direction, LEAPS give you more time than a traditional option to wait for that move to happen. All LEAPS expire in December on the Saturday following the third Friday.

- The price of LEAPS is one tenth the price and size of a traditional option. This is much more manageable for individual investors than having to buy 100 round lots every time you want to buy a regular option.

The combination of a longer term and lower contract size (one tenth the size of standard contracts) make LEAPS attractive to individual investors. Just be sure you look before you leap—all the strategies in this chapter are from a very volatile and sophisticated game best left to experts.

The Least You Need to Know

- Options are contracts that give you the option, but not the obligation, to buy or sell a specified quantity of stocks or bonds.

- Options and futures contracts are called "hedges."

- When you purchase a "put," you acquire the right to sell a security at a predetermined price. When you purchase a "call," you acquire the right to buy a security at a predetermined price.

- You can use options to protect your portfolio from stock market moves.

- Enlist the aid of an experienced broker if you want to get involved with options.

Chapter 22

Fancy Futures

In This Chapter

- How a future differs from an option
- Butter to zinc—the seven main types of commodities
- Buying on margin
- Using futures to offset uncertainty

Looking for a bright future? Well then, you've come to the right chapter. A futures contract is a legal agreement between two parties. One agrees to purchase from the other a specified asset at a specified price at a specified time in the future. Futures contracts are made on everything from commodities, like pork bellies or sugar, to stocks and indices.

There are also options on futures. Now, don't let this confuse you. Just remember that the purpose of these "advanced play" chapters is simply to give you some background in these complicated investments.

Both options and futures are called *derivatives* because they "derive" their value from the underlying security, index, or commodity they represent. Derivatives tend to be short-term "plays" dominated by large institutions. You participate at your own peril. If you do decide to play the game, be sure you work with a very experienced full-service broker specializing in options/futures.

What Is a Commodity?

A *commodity* is a basic food or raw material. If you turn once again to our old friend *The Wall Street Journal,* you will see toward the back of Section C a subheading titled Cash Prices. Listed here are cash prices for seven broad commodity categories, plus the London Metal Exchange Prices. The seven categories are:

♦ Grains and Feeds (barley, bran, corn, cottonseed meal, hominy, bonemeal, oats, sorghum, soybean meal, and wheat)

♦ Foods (beef carcass, broilers, butter, cheddar cheese, cocoa, coffee, eggs, flour, hams, hogs, pork bellies and loins, steers, and sugar)

♦ Fats and Oils (coconut oil, corn oil, grease, lard, palm oil, soybean oil, and tallow)

♦ Fibers and Textiles (burlap, cotton, and wool)

♦ Metals (aluminum, antimony, copper, lead, steel scrap, tin, and zinc)

♦ Miscellaneous (rubber and steer hides)

♦ Precious Metals (gold, platinum, and silver)

def•i•ni•tion

A **commodity** is a basic food or raw material, such as cotton, gold, or pork bellies. There are seven main categories of commodities that trade on specialized exchanges.

Fiscal Facts

Futures trading is regulated by a federal agency, the Commodity Futures Trading Commission (CFTC). The CFTC, in turn, oversees the National Futures Association (NFA), which is the industry's self-regulating body.

For each of these items, the *Journal* reports the previous day's closing price. *The Journal* might report, for example, that Top Quality Minneapolis Barley was priced at $2.45 per bushel. (Note: "Minneapolis" here refers to the exchange on which the barley is traded, not a type of barley.) The London Metal Exchange reports prices per metric ton for aluminum, tin, copper, lead, nickel, and zinc.

It All Began with Farmers

The first commodity exchange in the United States, and currently the largest futures exchange, is the Chicago Board of Trade (CBOT). The CBOT was formed some 150 years ago to serve as a medium of exchange for cash crops such as wheat and corn.

Futures trading began shortly after the end of the Civil War. Today, futures contracts are made not only for commodities but also for:

- Interest rates on all kinds of notes and bonds, including Treasury bills, notes, and bonds

- Indices like the Dow Jones Industrials, the S&P 500, and the NASDAQ 100

- Currency, from the Japanese yen to the Euro

How a Future Differs from an Option

An option is a right, but not an obligation, to buy or sell something at a specified price within a specified time. A *futures contract*, in contrast, is an obligation accepted by both the buyer and seller to make a specific trade at a specified time and price. Where an option buyer pays a premium, both parties in a futures contract put down a deposit, which is called a *margin*.

The buyer of a future is "long" or has a "long position." A seller is "short" or has a "short position." Futures orders are entered with a broker just like stock orders.

def•i•ni•tion

A **future,** or **futures contract,** is an agreement between a buyer and seller to make a specific trade at a specified future date and price. Both parties put down a deposit, called a **margin.**

Buying or selling futures is like trading stocks. "Long" means you own "it" (a stock, a bushel of wheat, whatever) and are betting that "it" will rise in price. "Short" means you do not intend to buy it and are betting that it will decline in price (and if it declines enough, you'll buy it then).

- "Market" means at the market price

- "Limit" means at or below the limit price to buy, at or above the limit price to sell

- "Stop loss" means execute the order if the contract declines to a predetermined price, at which point the order is executed on a "best price" basis

In the old days, a futures contract could literally result in 5,000 bushels of wheat being dumped on your front lawn! Today, few contracts go to the delivery date, and when they do, delivery is acknowledged by warehouse receipts. The reason delivery rarely takes place is because the buyer doesn't really want the commodity; he or she simply wants to make money by trading it. So at some point before delivery date, the buyer will sell, and the seller will buy, canceling the contract.

Fiscal Facts _____

In the stock market, the Federal Reserve has ultimate authority over extension of credit by brokers to their customers (i.e., margin requirements) via "Regulation T." This power was given to the institution as a tool to implement fiscal policy.

Crash Alert _____

If your maintenance margin falls below the level required by your brokerage firm, you will receive a "margin call" warning you to put up sufficient cash to return your balance to the original margin level. If you fail to respond, your broker will liquidate your position by selling securities in your account. Maybe even the ones Grandma gave you. Yes, it's a cold, cruel world.

It's like a stock trade: if you buy 100 shares of General Electric at 10 A.M. and sell those 100 GE shares at noon, you no longer have a position in the stock. You probably bought the stock because you thought the price was going to go up and you could sell it for more than you paid for it. Once you've sold the stock, you have what we in the biz call "no position."

How Margins Work

When you buy a futures asset, you need to put down that deposit, called a margin. Before you can buy a future, your broker needs to be sure that you have sufficient money in your account to cover the margin.

Margin takes two forms:

♦ Initial or original—what you have to have in your account to initiate the purchase of the futures contract

♦ Maintenance—what you have to have in your account to maintain (keep) the futures contract

The initial margin is set by the exchange that trades the futures contract you are interested in purchasing. This amount will vary, depending on market conditions, but is usually around 10 percent. Your brokerage firm, however, may require a higher margin. Its decision is binding (unless you choose to take your business elsewhere).

The maintenance margin is also determined by the exchange. Typically, the maintenance margin is 75 percent of the initial margin.

Here's an example: let's say you buy a $10,000 futures contract with an initial margin of $1,000. If the contract value declines to $9,750, your margin will drop, as a result, to the maintenance level, which is $750 (75 percent of $1,000).

Why? Well, your initial margin was $1,000, but the contract's value has since declined by $250 ($10,000 – $9,750 = $250). That decline comes out of your margin, reducing it from $1,000 to $750 ($1,000 – $250 = $750). At this point, you're still okay, because your margin hasn't fallen below the maintenance level. If the contract drops further, though—to $9,500, for example—your margin is cut to $500. You will be informed that you must deposit an additional $500 to bring your account back up to the initial margin of $1,000.

This simple example shows just how risky futures contracts can be. A small move in the price of the underlying commodity translates to a large dollar gain or loss for the contract holder.

Using Futures to Offset Uncertainty

Why do people mess with these risky investments? Because, just as with options, there are hedgers and there are speculators. Speculators are in the market to "make a killing" (or get killed). Hedgers are trying to offset a future unknown. Let's look at a couple of examples of how ordinary people use futures contracts as hedges against risk and uncertainty.

Suppose you're a cotton farmer. The current price of 40¢ per pound would provide you with a decent profit, but your crop won't be ready to go on the market for another six months. What if the price of cotton declines to 30¢ per pound by then? You could be wiped out. So you sell (go short) March 2009 cotton futures. If cotton does drop to 30¢, you make money on your short—the premium for which you sold it. This money offsets the loss on your "cash" crop. If cotton stays at 40¢, you can cover your short position by purchasing a contract at 40¢. Now you have a loss, but you can offset it with the profitable sale of your cash crop.

Here's another example. Suppose you are a home builder about to open up a new development. You accept contracts for completion of new homes six to nine months from now. You've agreed to sell each house at a fixed price—but what if lumber prices go through the roof in the next six months and eat up all your profit?

Well, you could buy lumber futures at $288.70 per 1,000 board feet. If the price of lumber goes up, you have two choices:

♦ You could pay the higher price for the lumber and offset it by selling your lumber futures contract for a profit. Remember, if the price of lumber has gone up past $288.70 per 1,000 board feet, somebody out there will be happy to buy your contract.

♦ You could accept delivery of the lumber from your futures contract.

What if the price of lumber goes down? Well, the loss on the contract is offset with the lower price you actually pay for your lumber. Either way, you've hedged very nicely. This is a form of insurance, and that's what a hedger is looking for.

Financial Futures

Financial futures currently dominate the futures market. How would an investor use financial futures to hedge? Suppose you are the proud owner of a $1 million equity portfolio (taxable). You have a feeling that stock prices are going to start falling, but you're not absolutely sure; if you sell some of your existing stock positions and the share prices subsequently rises, you've lost an opportunity and incurred capital gains taxes. You look in *The Wall Street Journal* on December 5, 2008, and under the Future Prices heading you see the following:

DJ Industrial Average (CBT) – $10 D Index

	Open	High	Low	Settle	Change	Open Interest
Futures	8560	8635	8265	8402	−177	31,628
Actual DJ	8591	8632	8259	8376		

These are futures contracts on the Dow Jones Industrial Average. *Open, high, low,* and *settle* are the prices for the previous day. *Chg* is the change in price for that day's trading. Here, it's –177 points. Open interest is the number of outstanding contracts.

If your portfolio is fairly similar to the Dow Jones Industrials, you could use these futures contracts to neutralize the negative effect a market decline would have on the value of your portfolio.

The March 2009 contract, for example, is valued at $8,379 × $10 = $83,790. Your $1 million equity portfolio divided by $83,790 per contract would require 11.9346 contracts to neutralize a market decline. You could buy 12 contracts and plan to sell them later in 2009. If the market declines, your profit on the sale of the contract offsets your "paper" (unrealized) loss on your equity portfolio. If the market goes up, your equity portfolio appreciation offsets the loss on your contract.

Note, however, that if the market declines and you close out your contracts at a profit, that profit will be taxed at ordinary income tax rates (you have to hold an investment for at least a year to get the lower capital gains tax rate). Hence, this hedging works much better for tax-advantaged accounts. The taxable investor fearing a market decline has three options:

♦ Use futures contracts, accepting the margin costs and tax consequences

♦ Sell stocks, incurring capital gains and commission dollar consequences

♦ Do nothing and ride out the potential storm

As we've noted throughout this book, over time the stock market has consistently recovered from even the most wrenching declines. Individual investors do best when they choose option three, and just ride it out. But we thought you should know a little about financial futures anyway, if only to impress somebody.

Options on Futures—Oy!

Options on futures contracts are about as risky as you can get. Like regular options, options on futures are a right, not an obligation, to buy or sell. As with regular options, you can either buy calls or puts. Interest rate options on futures, especially on Treasury bonds, are extra hot right now.

Fiscal Facts _____

Whether gold will ever regain even a vestige of its former allure is open to question. "Gold bugs" argue vociferously that the only long-term financial discipline for individual nations in a global economy is direct linkage of local currencies to gold. Fortunately or unfortunately (depending on your views), national leaders don't want to have their economic policies limited by a fixed amount of currency in circulation.

In *The Wall Street Journal*, under "Futures Options Prices," you will find "Interest Rate," and under that subheading the following:

T-Bonds (CBT)

$100,000; points and 64ths of 100 percent

Super Strategies

How to hold gold (and other precious metals): you can buy and store gold bars or coins, but these provide no income return, and storage—even in a safe deposit box—costs money. A better strategy is to hold shares of precious metals companies or precious metals mutual funds.

If you wanted to purchase September call options with a strike price of 106, your premium would be 1-61. Because the option is quoted in 64ths, 1-61 means $1^{61}\!/_{64}$ $^{161}\!/$, or 1.953125. Each premium point amounts to $1,000, so the premium would cost you 1.953125 times $1,000, or $1,953.13. You can also buy puts/calls on stock index futures.

The contracts are for specific months and can extend out to two years.

Spread Strategies for Speculators

Speculators toy with all these different futures contracts. Spreads are one of the more famous commodity futures strategies used by speculators. Typically, the speculator is looking for the price differential to widen or narrow between two different crops, like wheat and oats. He buys a futures contract on the commodity he expects to go up more in price, and sells a contract on the other. What happens to the spread in price between the two commodities is critical; not whether one or both increase or decrease.

If you expect oats to increase in price versus wheat, for example, you would buy an oats contract and sell a wheat contract. If you're right, you can make a lot of money. If you're wrong, you can lose a bundle. That's why it's called speculation.

"Program trading" is an expression you've probably heard on the news to describe why the stock market fluctuated sharply in the last hour or so of a trading day. Program traders work for large institutions and set up automated hedges that are triggered when the market hits certain key prices. In effect, they establish a spread—between the S&P 500 Index and a future contract on the index, for example.

When the spread widens because the future price rises, program traders automatically sell futures and buy the index. If the spread narrows via a lower futures price, they sell the index and buy the futures contract. Because the process tends to be highly automated, several institutions buying or selling large sums at any given time can have a dramatic impact on the stock market. In fact, program trading was blamed for the market crash of October 1987.

Gold Nuggets

Earlier in this chapter, just for fun, we showed you where to find prices for all kinds of commodities in *The Wall Street Journal*. Unless you're a farmer or bridge builder, these markets should not concern you, with one possible exception: precious metals.

For centuries, the civilized (and sometimes not-so-civilized) world measured wealth in gold. Paper currencies were backed by it, dreams were spun from it, and wars were fought for it. It was, without exception, the one insurance policy against the ravages of inflation. In this country, President Richard Nixon severed the last direct tie between our currency and gold in 1971, freeing the dollar to seek its ultimate value. With the quadrupling of oil prices and double-digit inflation during Nixon's term, gold had soared from around $30 per ounce to over $800 per ounce. As a result of the severance of gold's link with the dollar, investors no longer view gold as a monetary asset, but rather as a commodity.

The question for you, the investor, is whether you should own some or no gold. The answer depends entirely on how you feel about inflation and the dollar. Near the end of 2008, when the dollar was under pressure due to the financial crisis in the United States, gold was selling at $763.80 per troy ounce (December 4, 2008, price).There is compelling evidence that, in an inflationary environment, you would be better off investing in income-producing assets that can raise prices at a rate equal to or in excess of the inflation rate. This would include farmland, which could be leased out to tenant farmers, or an operating business such as Coca-Cola that can raise prices with little reduction in demand.

Because we're your pals, here's a list in alphabetical order of 5 precious metal companies, along with exchange list/ticker symbols:

- Barrick Gold Corp. NYSE [ABX]

- Coeur D'Alene Mines Corp. NYSE [CDE]

- Hecla Mining Co. NYSE [HL]

◆ Newmont Mining Corp. NYSE [NEM]

◆ Placer Dome Inc. NYSE [PDG]

If you prefer the diversification of mutual funds (and, as you know by now, we do), here are some of the largest no-load precious metal funds, listed alphabetically:

◆ American Century Global Gold, www.americancentury.com, 1-800-345-2021

◆ Midas Funds www.midasfunds.com, 1-800-400-6432

◆ DWS-Scudder Gold and Precious Metals Fund, www.dws-investments.com, 1-800-621-1048

The Least You Need to Know

◆ A futures contract is a binding agreement between two parties. One agrees to purchase from the other a specified asset at a specified price at a specified time in the future.

◆ A commodity is a basic food or raw material.

◆ When you buy a futures asset, you need to put down a 10 percent deposit, called a margin.

◆ Futures can be used to hedge against anticipated changes in prices.

◆ If you want some precious metal in your portfolio, consider shares of mining companies or precious metal mutual funds.

Chapter 23

Alternative Investments

In This Chapter

◆ Investments once available only to the rich

◆ Exploring hedge, venture capital, and LBO funds

◆ Investing in business dealings via private equity funds and limited partnerships

"We're so glad we've had this time together …." Sorry, got caught up in a Carol Burnett moment. But seriously, we hope you've enjoyed this book. If you've read all (okay, most) of the chapters, you now have a solid grounding in investment basics that will help you sail through your financial life. You've also explored some fun stuff, like options, futures, and precious metals. In this, our final chapter, we'll zip through a few of the "alternative investments" that used to be discussed only in exclusive country clubs among millionaires but have become available to the average investor.

How Regular Folk Discovered Alternative Investments

"Alternative investments" are equity products like *hedge funds* or venture capital funds that used to strictly be the province of very wealthy investors, large public and private retirement plans, or universities with huge endowments like Harvard or Yale. These funds used to require $10 to $20 million minimum investments, so they were only reasonable for people or institutions that had at least 10 times that much in their portfolios.

def•i•ni•tion

A **hedge fund** is an unregistered investment fund whose managers can pretty much do whatever they want—invest in currencies or commodities, go short or long, use options and futures, etc. Some funds are very conservative, whereas others are quite aggressive and make all kinds of risky currency and interest rate plays.

A few years back, however, two events occurred that introduced alternative investments to the rest of us. One was a best-selling book, *Barbarians at the Gate: The Fall of RJR Nabisco*, by Bryan Burrough and John Helyar. The book depicted, in an entertaining way, the efforts of firms like Kohlberg Kravis Roberts (KKR) to take over R. J. Reynolds via a "leveraged buyout."

In a leveraged buyout (LBO), one firm will offer to buy up any and all stock of another company at a price significantly higher than the current trading price of the stock. The idea is that the stockholders will be so excited by this higher price that they will sell all their stock to the takeover company. Once KKR owns all of R. J. Reynolds stock, for example, it owns R. J. Reynolds and can do with it what it will. And what it will do is send in a team to pare down debt and cut costs (meaning fire lots of people), making the revamped R. J. Reynolds lean and mean and very attractive to new potential stockholders. Then it will take the firm public again, selling its stock and making a fortune on the sale.

The second event was the media spotlight turned on investors like George Soros, whose hedge funds were blamed by several national leaders for adversely affecting and artificially manipulating currency values around the world. In the wake of the financial crisis of 2008, we do expect to see hedge funds faced with greater regulation.

Hedge Funds

Historically, hedge funds had limited the number of investors to fewer than 100 participants, which meant that they didn't have to register under the Investment Company Act of 1940 ("The '40 Act"). Due to the fact that they are unregistered, hedge funds can invest in currencies, commodities, public stocks and bonds, or whatever they like; they can do so by going long (buying), going short (selling borrowed shares), or using options and futures.

Venture Capital and LBO Funds

While hedge funds move in and out of markets quickly, basically speculating with options and futures and the like, other funds invest for the long haul in new or recently created businesses. These "private equity" funds are more like partnerships than traditional mutual funds. With a straightforward mutual fund, you own shares in whatever publicly traded stocks the mutual fund managers buy. Private equity funds invest in privately owned businesses that do not have stock trading in a public market.

 Fiscal Facts _____

Unlike publicly traded funds, which are corporate entities owned by shareholders, private equity funds are partnerships. More specifically, there is a general partner who creates the fund, and limited partners who provide the capital. Typically, the general partner (GP) receives a 1 to 2 percent annual fee for managing the fund, and 20 percent of the profits realized. The limited partners (LP) receive the remaining 80 percent of the profits (after the return of their capital).

Venture capital funds, for instance, provide the capital for start-up businesses. Investors in a venture capital fund are limited partners. The manager of the fund is the general partner.

Leveraged buyout funds are also proliferating. LBOs use primarily, if not entirely, borrowed money to purchase the outstanding stock of a publicly traded company by offering to purchase it from stockholders at a premium. This turns that company from a public to a private company, owned by the LBO's investors. Then the LBO team rigorously reduces the company's costs, pays down its debt, and takes it public once again—kind of like taking a race car with a blown engine off the track, rebuilding the engine, and putting it back on the track.

def•i•ni•tion

A **venture capital fund** invests in new businesses by providing start-up capital. The investors in a venture capital fund are limited partners in the businesses in which the fund invests and are entitled to a share of its profits. A **leveraged buyout fund,** on the other hand, borrows money to buy a company, revamp it, and take it public. Investors profit from what the LBO fund makes when it resells the company's stock.

The rewards? Industry data is hard to come by because there are no reporting requirements for these funds, but they seek to do at least 150 percent better than the Standard & Poor's 500 Index.

The Private Equity Fund of Funds

Historically, as we said, investment in hedge funds and private equity funds was limited to large institutional investors and wealthy individuals. In effect, Wall Street was servicing Park Avenue. In part, because of the voracious appetite for new capital, Wall Street, along with some major trust banks, has introduced a new concept: the private equity fund of funds. This doesn't mean Wall Street is serving Main Street USA, but it is a step in that direction.

A private equity fund of funds also has a general partner (GP) and investors who are limited partners (LPs). The GP receives typically a 1 to 2 percent annual fee, and a 5 percent share of the profits. What does the GP do? The GP selects other private equity funds (typically 10 to 15) in which to invest.

If you are a limited partner in a private equity fund of funds, you become, essentially, a limited partner in whatever funds your GP chooses to buy.

What You Need to Qualify for a Fund of Funds

How do you get to be an LP in a private equity fund of funds? Let's start with financial requirements. A limited partnership interest typically requires a minimum commitment of $500,000. This doesn't mean you write out a check for $500,000 and sit back to wait for the profits to roll in. (For one, who has an extra $500,000 just lying around?) It means that over the next three to six years you will receive "calls" to kick in as much as $500,000, typically in 5 percent pieces ($25,000), with the first 5 percent due when you sign the partnership papers. Obviously, this is a much easier check to write!

Because the partnership interests are not registered as securities under the Securities Act of 1933, you also have to qualify as an "accredited investor." This is defined as someone with more than $1 million of net worth or more than $200,000 ($300,000 if filed/filing a joint return) of adjusted gross income for the previous two years and expected for the current year.

On top of that, you are required to affirm that you are acquiring your LP interest as an investment and not for resale or distribution, and that you will not assign or transfer your interest without the consent of the GP. Got that? Now you can dazzle the cocktail crowd!

But wait, there's more! Congress also stated in a follow-up bill passed in 1940 that to participate in a limited partnership you must also be a "qualified purchaser." Today that's typically defined as meaning that you must have more than $5 million in investments (stocks, bonds, real estate held for investment purposes, commodities, and cash all qualify). How did Congress know back in 1933 and 1940 what current dollar worth would qualify someone as an "accredited investor" and a "qualified purchaser"? They

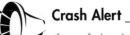 **Crash Alert**

If you fail to honor a capital call from a limited partnership within 20 days you could face interest charges, and possibly even run the risk of having your interest sold for as little as 50 percent of book value. You definitely don't want to miss a call!

didn't. What they did do was entrust the Securities and Exchange Commission (SEC) to establish and revise, from time to time, the definitions of an "accredited investor" and a "qualified purchaser." The general partner (GP) of a limited partnership knows that if any of his limited partners is not qualified, the GP could lose his or her exclusion from the 1933 Act and 1940 Act. Therefore, the GP takes on the responsibility and ultimate authority to approve your application to be a limited partner.

How Limited Partnership Works

Assuming you are approved to invest as a limited partner in a fund of funds, what is the sequence of events?

1. You will honor the first capital call, which is 5 percent of your total commitment at the closing. So if you have agreed to a total commitment of $500,000, you will write out a check for $25,000 at the closing.

2. You will receive additional capital calls of, say, 5 percent over the first six years or so.

3. You may begin to receive distributions (moolah!) from the fund as early as the third year.

4. As a limited partner, you are entitled to a return of your "invested" capital, plus a pre-determined return (called the "preferred return").

5. After the LPs receive back their invested capital and the preferred return, the GP is entitled to a "carried interest amount" equal to 5 percent of the "carried interest account." The carried interest account is the difference between the aggregate portfolio distributions and the invested capital—in other words, 5 percent of the gain. This is called a "catch-up distribution."

6. After #4 and #5 have been honored, subsequent distributions are split (e.g., 5 percent GP, 95 percent LPs).

7. The fund will last for the number of years in the contract or until all assets are distributed, whichever occurs last.

Pros and Cons of LP Investments

There are several points to consider before getting involved with a fund of funds:

◆ You will receive an IRS Form K-1 to use to report partnership income each year. These are not usually available to meet the April 15 tax deadline, however. You can choose to either file an amended return or pay 110 percent of the previous year's taxes. We recommend that you choose the latter option.

◆ Because your fund has multiple fund holdings and multiple investment holdings in each fund, you will probably face state tax returns in at least several states other than your own.

◆ A fund of funds results in an additional layer of fees that makes it more difficult for you to beat the benchmarks on a long-term basis.

So if you are able to invest and decide that investing in an LP is for you, keep in mind the following advantages …

◆ Potentially superior returns to the public equity market

◆ A diversified portfolio of private equity investments

◆ An opportunity to participate in an equity class traditionally reserved for very wealthy individuals

… and disadvantages:

◆ These are risky and illiquid investments

◆ You have to make a very long-term commitment to the fund

◆ The tax filing requirements are a pain in the neck

The Least You Need to Know

◆ "Alternative investments" are equity products like hedge funds or venture capital funds that used to be strictly the province of very wealthy investors.

◆ A hedge fund is an unregistered investment fund whose managers can pretty much do whatever they want—invest in currencies or commodities, go short or long, use options and futures, and so on.

◆ Private equity funds invest in privately owned businesses that do not have stock trading on the stock market.

◆ Venture capital funds provide the capital for start-up businesses.

Glossary

12b-1   Servicing fee charged on mutual fund.

401(k)   Retirement savings plan that allows employees who are eligible to choose how much of their pay is to be deducted for investment purposes and how the dollars are to be invested.

403(b)   A version of the 401(k) used by public employers, such as schools, hospitals, and other not-for-profit organizations.

adjustable-rate mortgage (ARM)   A mortgage with an interest rate priced off the yield for the 10-year Treasury note. Since the yield on the note changes every six months, so will the interest rate on the ARM.

adjusted gross income (AGI)   AGI is gross income from your W-2 form, plus interest income, rents, royalties, etc., minus medical account deductions, alimony payments, and other adjustments.

alternative investment   An equity-based investment, such as a hedge fund or venture capital fund. Alternative investments used to be available only to very wealthy investors.

amortize   To write off a debt or fee over time.

annual report   Report, prepared by a corporation, that includes full disclosure of its financial statements.

annuity   An investment that yields fixed payments during the investment holder's lifetime or for a stated number of years.

ask price   The lowest price that a seller of a security is willing to accept for it in the market.

assets   Any item of value—from baseball cards to stocks—that you own.

back-end load   Fee charged when you redeem (sell) your shares in a mutual fund. Also referred to as "back-end," "back-door load," or "deferred sales charges."

balance sheet   A financial statement that shows what you own (your assets) and what you owe (your liabilities) at a given point in time.

bid price   The maximum price a buyer is willing to pay for a security in the market.

bill   An IOU that the U.S. government issues when it wants to borrow money for one year or less. The government agrees to pay back the lender at a specified maturity date, with interest.

bond   An IOU that a corporation or government agency issues when it wants to borrow money for more than 10 years. The issuer agrees to pay back the lender at a specified maturity date, with interest.

broker   A generic name for middlemen who facilitate trades between buyers and sellers.

business plan   Document prepared by entrepreneurs to show exactly how a new business will be operated; includes projections for sales and profits.

call option   Contract giving the contract holder the right to purchase a stock at a set price, called the strike price, for a specified period of time, usually a few months.

capital   A fancy word for money that is used for business purposes. Corporations issue stock to raise capital, for example.

capital gain   Profit arising from the appreciation of a security.

cash equivalent   Investment that possesses little or no risk and can be converted into cash within 90 days.

certificates of deposit   Money market instruments typically sold by banks in three-month, six-month, or one-year maturities. CDs are very safe investments because they are fully insured by the FDIC, up to $100,000.

collateral   Something you own that can be pledged against a loan.

commission   A percentage fee paid to a broker for executing a trade.

commodity   Any product sold in the financial markets that can actually be weighed, such as gold, silver, pork bellies, sugar, or grain.

compound interest   The money you earn on interest (or dividends or capital gains) that you earned in a previous period. Compound interest enables your money to grow exponentially.

corporation   A legal entity that is separate from the owners of the business. This provides limited liability for the stockholders, ensuring they will not be personally sued for the conduct of the business.

credit card   An account that enables you to carry a debt indefinitely, as long as you pay interest.

credit report   Report created by a private credit reporting agency (CRA) that is based on what creditors have said about you.

current ratio   A test of liquidity. Calculated by dividing current assets by current liabilities.

debit card   Card that enables you to make purchases with a direct deduction from your checking account.

deductible   The amount of expense you agree to cover before your insurance kicks in.

defined benefit plan   An employer-financed retirement plan that pays you an annual sum upon retirement.

depreciation   The loss in value of an item over time, due to wear and tear.

discount   The amount a bond is trading below par (100).

discount broker   Broker who simply executes trades, for a lower commission and without the additional services provided by a full-service broker.

diversification   A method of decreasing risk by increasing the variety of assets in a portfolio. If you own lots of different stocks, for example, your whole portfolio won't tank if one company goes bankrupt.

dividend   A cash distribution to the shareholders of a corporation that represents the owner's pro-rated portion of the profits.

Dow Jones Industrial Average (DJIA)   An average of 30 well-known companies, such as AT&T and McDonald's, chosen by the editors of *The Wall Street Journal* to represent trends in the stock market.

Education IRA   Introduced in 1998, and now called "Coverdell ESA," this is an IRA to which you can make tax-deferred contributions of up to $2,000 per year, per beneficiary, until your kids are 18. Withdrawals for qualified educational purposes are tax-free.

equity   Ownership of property, such as stock or a house.

executor   Person who makes sure that the provisions of a will are carried out.

expiration date   Date by which an options contract must be exercised or lose its value.

fiduciary   A person or entity responsible for investing money on behalf of another person or entity.

fixed annuity   An annuity that promises to provide a fixed (predetermined) sum in an annual or other regular (e.g., monthly) interval.

fixed-income   Investment that provides income that remains constant and doesn't fluctuate (like stock prices do, for example). Bonds are fixed-income investments because when you buy a bond you are promised regular, steady interest payments.

front-end load   Sales charge deducted from the principal invested in a mutual fund.

future or **futures contract**   An agreement between a buyer and seller to make a specific trade at a specified future date and price.

general obligation bond   A bond backed by the tax-raising ability of the issuing state or municipality.

hedge fund   An unregistered investment fund whose managers can pretty much do whatever they want—invest in currencies or commodities, go short or long, use options and futures, etc.

income statement   A financial statement that delineates income and expenses.

index fund   A mutual fund designed to mimic the performance of an established benchmark such as the S&P 500.

inflation   A general rise in prices.

initial public offering (IPO)   A corporation's first stock sale.

institutional investor   A corporation, hospital, city government, or other large entity that has a portfolio.

interest   Payment you receive for lending someone your money. Interest is also the fee you pay when you borrow money.

IRA   An Individual Retirement Account, which is basically a shell that protects money you put in it from taxation until you start to take money out.

Keogh   Pension plan that allows business owners to shelter more income than SEPs or SIMPLEs do and to create vesting schedules for employees.

leveraged buyout fund   Fund that borrows money to buy a company, revamp it, and take it public. Investors profit from what the LBO fund makes when it resells the company's stock.

liability   A debt you owe. The opposite of an asset, which is something you own.

lien   A legal right to take someone's property and hold it until the owner pays a debt.

liquidity   The ease with which an investment can be converted to cash.

living trust   Legal document that names someone to manage your assets if you die or are incapacitated.

load   Sales fees and commissions charged to investors in a mutual fund.

long bond   The 30-year Treasury bond.

Long-Term Equity Anticipation Security (LEAPS)   Long-term options contracts that are very popular with individual investors.

lump sum   The entire value of an investment taken in cash at once.

margin   Deposit put down by both parties in a futures contract.

marginal tax rate   The tax rate you pay on the last few dollars you earn.

money market   Highly liquid financial instruments with rates that vary from day to day, week to week, or month to month.

municipal bond   A bond issued by a municipality like your city, town, or county. The interest paid by municipal bonds is, with a few exceptions, not taxed by the federal government.

mutual fund   A company that collects money from investors and invests on their behalf, usually in diversified securities.

net asset value (NAV)   The dollar value of all the marketable securities (stocks, for example) owned by a mutual fund, less expenses and divided by the number of the fund's shares outstanding.

net earnings from self-employment   The amount of income on which you pay self-employment tax, minus the tax itself.

note   An IOU that a corporation or government agency issues when it wants to borrow money for between 1 and 10 years. The issuer agrees to pay back the lender at a specified maturity date, with interest.

option   A contract that states what is to be delivered for what price and what time period. The option is a right, but not an obligation, to exercise the rights stated in the options contract. At the end of the designated time period, the option loses all its value.

options buyer or **"holder"**   Pays an options writer a premium for the right to exercise the options contract created by the options writer.

options writer or **"seller"** or **"issuer"**   Creates an options contract, and must stand ready to honor the terms of the contract.

par   The original price of a bond, note, or bill. It is also the amount that the security will pay back at maturity and is referred to as *100*.

penny stock   Stock trading at a low price, usually a few dollars.

pension   A regular payment made to you (or your family, if you pass away) by your employer that reflects how much you earned and how many years you worked at your job.

portfolio   A collection of assets such as stocks, bonds, mutual funds, real estate, fine arts, baseball cards, and so on.

premium   The amount that a bond is trading above par (over 100).

pre-tax   Describes dollars that are deducted from your pay before taxes are applied. Pre-tax contributions to a 401(k) or 403(b), for example, are deducted from your pay before it is taxed.

principal   The original dollar amount of a fixed-income investment; the amount received upon maturity.

probate   State court that decides how an estate will be distributed when the deceased person's will is nonexistent or unclear.

prospectus   A legal document prepared by a mutual fund and sent out to potential investors that describes the fund and its operations.

put option   A contract that gives you the option to sell a security at a specified price until the contract's expiration date.

quick ratio   A measure of liquidity. Calculated by dividing current assets less inventory by current liabilities.

return equity (ROE)   Net income divided by book value; an indication of profitability.

return on assets (ROA)   Net income divided by total assets.

return on investment (ROI)   The amount you expect to earn from an investment over a given period of time. ROI is also called rate of return (ROR) and is expressed as a percentage of your original investment.

revenue bond   A bond issued by an agency of a city, county, or state for a specific purpose. Revenues from that agency pay the interest on bonds that are outstanding.

revolving line of credit   Credit that puts an upper limit on what you can borrow. You can borrow up to that amount, and you pay interest only on what you actually draw down.

rollover IRA   Used to shelter money that's in a 401(k) if you change jobs and can't put the money in your new job's retirement plan.

Roth IRA   A new type of IRA that is more flexible than the traditional IRA but is only available to families earning under $100,000 a year. As long as your Roth IRA has been open for at least five years, you can withdraw up to $10,000 to buy a first home.

round lot   One hundred shares of stock.

Savings Incentive Match Plan for Employees (SIMPLE) IRA   A new option for self-employed people and small businesses with few employees, growing in popularity because it's very easy to use.

Securities and Exchange Commission (SEC)   Regulatory agency started in 1933 by Congress to protect investors.

self-employment tax   A tax self-employed people have to pay into Social Security because they don't have an employer contributing on their behalf.

Simplified Employee Pension (SEP) IRA   Essentially an IRA for someone who is self-employed, and small businesses with few employees. A SEP is like a 401(k), but contributions are limited to 15 percent of pretax earnings or $49,000, whichever is less. A good retirement plan for a sole proprietor who doesn't have employees.

Social Security   A system managed by the federal government, which provides money to people who are retired or are not able to work because of disability.

sole proprietor   Someone who owns a business alone, without partners.

spread   The difference between the ask and the bid price of a security or between interest rates.

stock market   The stock market doesn't exist as a physical place—stocks are traded at various stock exchanges, such as the New York Stock Exchange or The American Stock Exchange. All the exchanges together, along with the over-the-counter market, are considered the stock market.

stock option   The right, but not the obligation, to buy a stock at a fixed price after a fixed period of time (usually 12 months) for a fixed period of time (10 years).

stock split   A division of stock that increases the number of shares outstanding and decreases share price of the stock.

strike price   Also called the exercise price; the price at which the holder of an options contract can buy (call) or sell (put) the underlying security.

trade   To buy or sell securities on the financial markets.

Treasury bill securities   Securities issued by the U.S. Treasury that mature in one year or less. Treasury securities are fully guaranteed by the government and can be sold within 24 hours.

Treasury bonds   Long-term securities issued by the U.S. Treasury with maturities over 10 years. Historically, the Treasury has issued 20- or 30-year bonds.

Treasury notes   Securities issued by the U.S. Treasury that offer maturities from 2 years to 10 years.

Treasury strip   A piece of a Treasury security, such as a coupon or principal payment, that has been stripped from the original security.

Unit Investment Trusts (UITs)   Hybrid mutual funds that invest like mutual funds but, unlike them, have a fixed termination date.

variable annuity   An annuity that provides an undetermined amount that depends upon the return of the annuity's underlying mutual fund; basically a mutual fund wrapped around an insurance contract.

venture capital fund   Fund that invests in new businesses by providing start-up capital. The investors in a venture capital fund are limited partners in the businesses in which the fund invests and are entitled to a share of its profits.

vested   Eligible to receive a pension. An employee is typically considered vested after five years at a company.

will   A legal document, signed by you and witnessed, that gives explicit directions as to who or what is to get whatever specific assets of yours you choose to list.

yield   The return on an investment expressed as a percentage.

Useful Investing Information

Whether you need to contact the Federal Reserve, get a copy of your credit report, or open a brokerage account, this information can help you get in touch with the appropriate people.

Government and Regulatory Contacts

Federal Reserve Board's website:
www.federalreserve.gov

Federal Trade Commission, Consumer Response Center:
www.ftc.gov

Internal Revenue Service:
www.irs.gov

Securities and Exchange Commission (SEC):
www.sec.gov

The Office of Consumer Affairs:
www.consumeraffairs.com

Social Security Administration:
www.ssa.gov

U.S. Treasury:

You may purchase T-bills directly from the U.S. Government via the Treasury Direct Program or via banks or brokers, usually for a service fee. If you buy direct from the Treasury, you can do so in person, by mail, by phone (1-800-722-2678), or via the Internet at www.publicdebt.treas.gov. To utilize the latter two alternatives, you will need to provide a signature to open your account.

Financial Exchanges

Most exchanges will let you come in and check out their pits full of screaming traders. It's a sight (and sound) worth experiencing at least once in your life!

New York Stock Exchange (NYSE)
11 Wall Street
New York, NY 10005
212-656-3000
www.nyse.com

NYSE Euronext
86 Trinity Place
New York, NY 10006
212-306-1000
www.nyse.com/attachment/amex_landing.htm

Other exchanges include the Chicago Mercantile Exchange, Boston Stock Exchange, Montreal Stock Exchange, and the Philadelphia Stock Exchange.

Credit-Reporting Agencies

For personal credit histories, contact:

Equifax
PO Box 740241
Atlanta, GA 30374-0241
www.equifax.com
1-800-685-1111

Experian
National Consumer Assistance Center
PO Box 2002
Allen, TX 75013
www.experian.com
1-888-397-3742

Trans Union
2 Baldwin Place
PO Box 2000
Chester, PA 19022
www.transunion.com
1-800-888-4213

If you own a business, you'll want to run a credit check on it periodically, too. The three top credit-reporting agencies in this field are the following:

Dun & Bradstreet
103 JFK Parkway
Short Hills, NJ 07078
www.dnb.com
1-800-234-3867

Experian Business Credit Services
PO Box 2002
Allen, TX 75013
www.experian.com
1-888-243-6951

Consumer Information

Consumer Reports:
www.ConsumerReports.org

Edmund's Automobile Buyer's Guide:
www.edmund.com

Kelley Blue Book (indispensable when selling or trading cars):
www.kbb.com

Investment Research

Standard & Poor's Stock Guides:
Annual subscription prices are $275 for the Stock Guide and $375 for the Bond Guide (plus $25 shipping and handling). You can order by calling 1-800-221-5277 or visiting the S&P website at www.standardpoors.com.

Value Line:
www.valueline.com
1-800-634-3583

A one-year subscription costs $538. You can subscribe to a 13-week trial for $65.

The Wall Street Journal:
www.wsj.com
1-800-JOURNAL

Online Articles, Tutorials, and Research Sites

There are some research sites on the web that you can access yourself, such as the following:

- beginnersinvest.about.com (investing lessons and articles)
- www.briefing.com (analysts' upgrades and downgrades)
- www.hoovers.com (company profiles and financial data)
- www.zacks.com (consensus earnings estimates, broker recommendations, and insider trading)

Internet Brokers

E*TRADE	www.etrade.com	1-800-387-2331
Fidelity	www.fidelity.com	1-800-544-6666
Muriel Siebert & Co.	www.siebertnet.com	1-800-872-0711
Schwab	www.schwab.com	1-866-232-9890
Scottrade	www.scottrade.com	1-800-619-SAVE
TD Ameritrade	www.tdameritrade.com	1-00-669-3900

Mortgages

Want to get some online mortgage quotes?

- ◆ E-loan at www.eloan.com; 1-888-533-5333

- ◆ Lending Tree at www.lendingtree.com; 1-800-555-TREE

Quick Reference Points

11 Investment Rules of Thumb

1. **Automatically reinvest whatever your investment earns.** Compounding—earning interest on your interest—is a simple but very effective way to build wealth. This rule applies to dividends and capital gains, as well as to interest.

2. **The sooner you start saving for retirement, the less you'll need to save.** Assuming an 8 percent return, the following savings rates will grow to $100,000 by age 65:

   At age 25: $7.14/week

   At age 35: $16.32/week

   At age 45: $40.40/week

   At age 55: $127.61/week

3. **Commit 10 percent of your salary to savings and investment.** Apply the 10 percent rule as your salary increases, giving you a growing pool of assets benefiting from the magic of compounding each and every year. If you're in debt, commit an additional 5 percent to paying it down.

4. **Your emergency fund should be roughly 10 percent of your annual income or $10,000, whichever is greater.** An emergency fund is your umbrella for when life drenches you with unexpected expenses. Put your emergency stash in insured, highly liquid investments—savings accounts and Treasury bills are two excellent choices.

5. **The biggest financial-planning error new parents tend to make is to put saving for their children's education ahead of saving for their own retirement.** It's much wiser to put your own financial security first. Save 10 percent of your salary—invest 2 percent of it in college funds and 8 percent for retirement.

6. **If an investment seems too good to be true, it *is* too good to be true.** If someone is offering you a high return on your investment, it's because the investment is high-risk. There's no such thing as a low-risk investment that generates high return.

7. **If your employer contributes to your 401(k) plan, fund it to the max.** This is *free money.*

8. **It's a lot easier to spend $1 less than to earn $1 more.** To earn more, you either have to work longer hours or take greater risks with your investments. What's more, you pay taxes on each additional dollar you earn on your job, but saving is free!

9. **Get rid of all your credit cards except for one.** Use one credit card for as many of your purchases as possible, and pay it off every month. You'll get an itemized list each month of your purchases that'll make it easy to track your spending.

10. **Buy individual common stocks only if you are committed to holding them for at least 5 years, and more ideally, for at least 10 years.** Unless you have a lot of money to invest in a wide range of individual stocks, stick with stock mutual funds because they provide great diversification.

11. **To determine the appropriate amount of stock to have in your portfolio at any age, subtract your age from 100.**

    100 – your age = maximum percent of stock in your portfolio

    If you are 60, for example, keep 40 percent of your portfolio in stock (and the rest in cash and bonds).

Investment Math Made Easy

1. **The "Rule of 72":** To figure how long it will take an investment to double, take the interest rate, change it into a decimal, and divide it into 72. The result is the number of years it will take for the investment to double.

2. **Compound interest trick:** Here's an easy way to figure out how much an investment will grow. Take the interest rate and add it to 1. Then multiply the investment by that amount. If the interest is 10 percent, for example, add 1 to .10, which gives you 1.10. Now, multiply the investment by 1.10. If your investment is $50,000:

   $50,000 × 1.10 = $55,000

   The investment will grow to $55,000 after one year.

3. **Return on investment:** Here's how to calculate ROI. A simple way to think about ROI is: what you made over what you paid, times 100.

   A = end-of-period wealth

   B = beginning-of-period wealth

   $\frac{A-B}{B} \times 100$ = Return on Investment

4. **Annual Retirement Savings Worksheet.** This worksheet gives you two options. One assumes you'll own your home by retirement, so you'll only need 50 percent of your current annual income. The other assumes you may still be paying a mortgage and will need 70 percent of your current annual income.

1. Present Annual Salary	$_____	$_____
2. Times Percent at Age 65	× .50	× .70
3. Equals Gross amount required	$_____	$_____
4. Less Social Security	$_____	$_____
5. Less Pension (if any)	$_____	$_____
6. Less Existing Savings	$_____	$_____
7. Equals Add'tl Income Required	$_____	$_____

5. **Price/Earnings ratio.** P/E ratio is a stock's price divided by the company's earnings. This ratio makes it easy to compare the company's performance to that of other companies with stock outstanding. The P/E ratio tells you whether a stock is over- or under-valued. A stock that is undervalued will probably rise in price to its proper value, so it could be a good buy.

6. **Asset allocation made simple.** To figure out the minimum percentage of your portfolio that you should keep in stock, simply multiply the number of years until you retire by two.

Age	Years to Retirement × 2	Stock %
Up to 25	40 × 2	80%
30	35 × 2	70%
35	30 × 2	60%
40	25 × 2	40%
50	15 × 2	30%
55	10 × 2	20%

Index

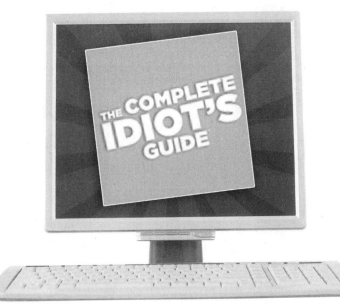